WHEN A GESTURE WAS EXPECTED

WHEN A GESTURE WAS EXPECTED

A SELECTION OF EXAMPLES FROM ARCHAIC AND CLASSICAL GREEK LITERATURE

Alan L. Boegehold

PRINCETON UNIVERSITY PRESS

PRINCETON, NEW JERSEY

PUBLISHED BY PRINCETON UNIVERSITY PRESS, 41 WILLIAM STREET,
PRINCETON, NEW JERSEY 08540
IN THE UNITED KINGDOM: PRINCETON UNIVERSITY PRESS,
CHICHESTER, WEST SUSSEX

LIBRARY OF CONGRESS CATALOGING-IN-PUBLICATION DATA

BOEGEHOLD, ALAN L. (ALAN LINDLEY)
WHEN A GESTURE WAS EXPECTED : A SELECTION OF EXAMPLES
FROM ARCHAIC AND CLASSICAL GREEK LITERATURE /
ALAN BOEGEHOLD.
P. CM.
INCLUDES BIBLIOGRAPHICAL REFERENCES AND INDEXES.
ISBN 0-691-00263-0 (ALK. PAPER)
1. GREEK LITERATURE—HISTORY AND CRITICISM. 2. GESTURE IN
LITERATURE. 3. NONVERBAL COMMUNICATION IN
LITERATURE. 4. BODY LANGUAGE IN LITERATURE.
5. GESTURE—GREECE—HISTORY. I. TITLE.
PA3014.G47B64 1999
880.9′001–DC21 99-14574

THIS BOOK HAS BEEN COMPOSED IN GALLIARD

THE PAPER USED IN THIS PUBLICATION MEETS THE MINIMUM
REQUIREMENTS OF ANSI/NISO Z39.48-1992 (R1997)
(*PERMANENCE OF PAPER*)

http://pup.princeton.edu

PRINTED IN THE UNITED STATES OF AMERICA

1 3 5 7 9 10 8 6 4 2

IN MEMORIAM

Sterling Dow

A GOOD TEACHER AND A GOOD FRIEND

CONTENTS

LIST OF ILLUSTRATIONS

ACKNOWLEDGMENTS

IT MAY HAVE BEEN my old mentor, Sterling Dow, who first gave me the image of Paul shaking his cloak as he cursed blasphemers at Corinth, but that would be thirty years ago, and I did not connect Paul's gesture with the sketchy simulacrum that a Greek performs in conversation today until one summer noon at Assos on Kephallenia in 1973: my wife, Julie, and I asked a local for a ride on his Messerschmidt (which was not an airplane but a three-wheeled, all-purpose farm vehicle). He would have liked to, he said, but he couldn't. He explained with a single word: police!! (ἀστυνομία) and as he pronounced the word he shook the front of his jacket vigorously with both hands. And I made a connection that has enriched my perception of ancient Greek representations of speech increasingly since then.

I did not, however, begin to arrange these connections in a formal way until 1985, when I presented a paper at the first joint AIA-APA panel in Washington, D.C. In succeeding years I have presented chapters or developing sequences to students and colleagues at Brown University, the University of Virginia, the Museum of Primitive Culture and Art in Rhode Island, Middlebury College, Yale University, the University of Minnesota, the American School of Classical Studies at Athens, the University of Glasgow, Boston University, New College in Oxford University, Royal Holloway College in the University of London, the University of Crete at Rethymnon, Eberhard-Karl University, Tübingen, Amherst College, and a session of the Greek National Humanistic Society in Athens. On every occasion I benefited from observations, criticism, and lore provided by my audiences, most of whose contributions have been absorbed one way or another into the text of this book.

Parts of various chapters have been published in other forms: Boegehold 1982, 1985, 1989, 1997, and 1999.

If I cannot name all those who have helped me in completing this book, I am especially conscious of what I owe to the following friends and colleagues for sympathetic, keen, helpful readings. Mortimer Chambers, Carolyn Dewald, Sir Hugh Lloyd-Jones, Donald Lateiner, Adele Scafuro, H. C. Stroud, and William F. Wyatt have commented on the whole in exacting and beneficial detail. Ronald Stroud, Douglas MacDowell, Charles Fornara, Dietrich von Bothmer, Philip Thibodeau, Ruth Caston, Frances Muecke, Angelos Matthaiou, Carolin Hahnemann, Ruth Elroi, George L. Huxley, Elizabeth Belfiore, Lucia Athanassaki, Shaye Cohen, Mark Davies, Daniel Tompkins, David Konstan, Jeffery Henderson, Alan Shapiro, John Oakley, Robert Parker, Nigel Wilson, James Kennelly, Richard Deppe,

Saul Olyan, Malcolm Hyman, and Amy Smith have all provided special learning at critical times. Leo Goldberger and Elizabeth Sidamon-Eristoff directed me to helpful books. Ruthann Whitten and Carol King helped with the preparation of the manuscript. Maud Chaplin, George and Anne d'Almeida, and Harry B. Marshall helped secure seemingly inaccessible images. I have been blessed with superior editors, Brigitta van Rheinberg and Marta Steele. The Salomon Foundation of Brown University provided a grant toward the final stages of the book. Brown University and The American School of Classical Studies at Athens have throughout my career provided numerous opportunities to learn about Greece in all its ages.

NOTE TO THE READER

ANGLE BRACKETS in Greek texts and in translations from the Greek signal additional text or directions inserted by an editor or by me to help comprehension.

In transliterating Greek into English, I relinquish all pretensions to consistency. When words and names look as though they have made their way into English, I generally use their Latinized/Anglicized form, e.g., Pericles and Aeschylus. Less familiar words have *k* where Greek has a kappa and *ch* where Greek has a chi, endings in *-os* instead of *-us*, and *y* for upsilon.

Translations that are not my own are attributed to their authors. Generalizing pronouns tend to be masculine because the groups and characters under discussion are mostly male. Representations in painting of goddesses and women yield some insights into nonverbal communication in the world of women, and I hope to pursue that line of inquiry further.

In the documentation of commentaries and translations, listed in separate sections of the Bibliography, commentary references are preceded by (**A**) and translations by (**B**). Where a source reference receives neither of these markings, assume it appears in the third section of the Bibliography, which comprises the secondary sources consulted in my research on this book.

ABBREVIATIONS

ABV	Beazley, J. D. *Attic Black Figure Vase Painters.* Oxford, 1956.
ARV^2	Beazley, J. D. *Attic Red Figure Vases.* 2nd ed. Oxford, 1963.
BM	British Museum.
comm. ad loc.	Commentary to the line just cited.
CVA	*Corpus Vasorum Antiquorum.*
D-K	Diels, H., and W. Kranz. *Fragmente der Vorsokratiker.* 9th ed. 3 vols. Rpt. Berlin, 1960.
FGrHist	Jacoby, F. *Fragmente der griechischen Historiker.* Berlin, 1923–30; Leiden, 1940–64.
IC	Halbherr, H., and M. Guarducci. *Inscriptiones Creticae.* Rome, 1935–50.
IG I^3	*Inscriptiones Graecae*, I, i. 3rd ed. D. M. Lewis, *Inscriptiones Atticae Euclidis anno anteriores.*
LSJ	Liddell, H. G., Robert Scott, and Sir H. S. Jones. *A Greek-English Lexicon.* 9th ed. Oxford, 1968.
Paralipomena	Beazley, J. D. *Paralipomena: Additions to Attic Black-Figure Vase-Painters and to Red-Figure Vase-Painters.* 2nd ed. Oxford, 1971.
PCG	Kassell, R., and C. Austin. *Poetae Comici Graeci.* Berlin, 1986–91.
RAC	*Reallexiikon für Antike und Christentum.* Stuttgart, 1985–.
RE	*Paulys Realencyclopädie der classischen Altertumswissenschaft.* Rev. ed., G. Wissowa. Stuttgart, later Munich, 1894–1972.
TLS	*Times Literary Supplement.*
[NAME]	signals doubt concerning identity.

WHEN A GESTURE WAS EXPECTED

INTRODUCTION

I AM A TEACHER of Latin and Greek—mostly Greek, ancient Greek. I accordingly spend an important part of my working day thinking about how to read ancient texts and how to explain them. First, of course, there are the words. What do they mean? How do they change meaning in varying positions, constructions, and contexts? To take a modern example, when a given word is first in a sentence, might it mean something different from what it means when it is third or last in a sentence? In Modern Greek, a word for "how," viz. πώς, when used by itself and in response to a question such as, "Are you hungry?" means "Yes." It is a shorthand representation of a full answer, which would be, "How am I not hungry?" (In Classical Greek, this would be πῶς γὰρ οὔ; the explanatory particle γάρ perhaps signaling a forward nod of the head.) If you do not know the shorthand, you might easily take πώς to mean "no" or "Please explain what you mean by that."

A modern example of another kind of obstacle in the way of understanding is the regional American usage, "I could care less," which native speakers know means "I could not care less." A contemporary novelist, however, with a sense of idiom could include such an expression in her characters' speech, and readers two millennia hence would find it a puzzle. They are required by instinct or inference to construct an additional, explanatory clause, one that completes the sense: "but I cannot imagine how I could care less."

Again, today when a train conductor announces, "At the next station, all the doors will not be opened," passengers understand him to say "some doors but not all the doors," and so they do not feel uneasy at the prospect of not being allowed to get off the train, although the conductor, strictly speaking, has promised that the doors will all be shut. In cases like these, a native speaker can quickly explain what is really meant, but where ancient, written texts are concerned and there is no native speaker at hand, many of the questions and the hypothetical answers we modern readers contrive fall into the domain of abstraction. No practical display confirms our conjectures. There are, to be sure, written accounts from later antiquity that may tell us in particular instances something like "No, you don't say that with a rising intonation," or "If you put that word first in the sentence, it means the opposite of what you intended." But often such accounts are efforts of later antiquity to understand earlier writers. These scholars are trying to answer questions that puzzled people of their time, and so they anticipate our own later needs only inadvertently. A result is that we present-day students of Greek strain without help from any such informants to imagine a sympathetic resonance, catching at sounds we will never hear. The frustrations and occasional apparent successes that attend this exercise provide some of the tensions, challenges, and satisfactions that come with the study of ancient languages.

To read these distant texts properly, we compose whole libraries of lexica, grammars, and commentaries, all of which a teacher tries to use, or at least to assess, if only to recommend—both to oneself and to students—the most helpful efforts. These efforts in turn lead to comparisons and rankings and surveys of the various routes one can travel in hope of understanding more of the whole. But now a question presents itself: what limits of their own do those routes impose? It transpires—not surprisingly—that certain well-traveled roads are so safe and sure that recourse to alternate routes may look willful or eccentric. A busy teacher accordingly walks on by the entrances to alternate routes and misses some of the landscape.

One alternate route is the use of studies concerned with nonverbal communication, and that of body language in particular. It is a way for all the world, including ancient Greeks, to communicate, and thoughtful readers of Greek have remarked its manifestations now and then in the course of over two millennia, but a general appreciation of its range and uses is still lacking. I asked a distinguished philologist once, "Do you think we can invoke a reader's or a performer's gestures sometimes to explain ellipses of meaning in an ancient Greek literary text?" He (who had been trained and finished in an old, universally admired, and largely emulated tradition) answered, "Well, we were taught to deal pretty much with what we had." In other words, this able traveler of well-tended roads was saying, "We do not have 'gesture here' written out on the manuscript page. Since the direction is not there, we do not use gestures in the interpretation of texts."

The matter of this book could be described in summary form as an extended demonstration that "gesture here" is often implied on the manuscript page. We only need to be alert for the signs by which those gestures are indicated. To be sure, not everyone needs to be told: some readers do enlist—more or less sporadically, however—a sense of body language to explain one or another seeming anomaly in syntax or sequence. But even these perspicacious few do not systematically try to explain how a putative gesture was conceived and executed. An underlying reason for that omission is a tendency to treat a text as transcript, or as historical account, and not as a work of the imagination, one whose composer visualized his characters as they spoke and at the same time had in mind a reader, who read aloud and by means of gesture and stance performed the text. A second reason may be a widespread and understandable modern assumption that modal particles in varying combinations provide all the direction, nuance, and emphasis required.

If we learn our grammars and lexica by heart and apply ourselves to the richest commentaries, we learn some things that are not explicit in the manuscripts: they are in a way deviations from normal usage and yet at the same time amplifications. For instance, a given dialect can come to be canonical in certain regions of endeavor and as a result have special authority. At least that is a phenomenon that the comic poet Alexis appears to reflect in a play. One of his characters says that Athenians, when ill, will ignore what a doctor tells them to do, unless he says it in Doric. If the doctor does say it in Doric, they are content to follow doctor's orders.[1] A hint of dialect can evoke a race or nation of people[2] or draw attention to particular qualities associated with them. A lisped consonant or flattened vowel may in one context or another evoke a single identifiable person. Conversely, Alcibiades' name at Aristophanes *Wasps* 44 prepares the audience for a play on words where from "crow" (κόραξ) a "toady" (κόλαξ) is lisped into existence.

We are trying to understand the complex, artistically, hence artificially, fashioned myths, legends, and tales of men and women who lived in a different world from ours. That difference can skew our lines of sight so that we miss potentially helpful directions. But if we pay attention to words, phrases, and sentences in Greek texts where a supplementary or independently meaningful gesture could fill out a speaker's expression, we discover hints and clues to the timing and placement of such directions. Although we cannot recover the gestures themselves in all their actuality, we may become better readers if we try to intuit their effect.

To turn to the clues and hints by which a reader can detect the author's intended performer reading aloud and gesticulating, what are they? They are absences or gaps. What the words seem to say is incomplete or contrary, unless something else is supplied to fill out or correct the sense; or the syntax is irregular, and at the same time, there is no evidence that words are missing because of physical damage or copyist's error. In such cases, a reader can very often make better sense by adding in thought the import of a nod or a wave of the hand.

But why specify gesticulation and posture as the modes of nonverbal communication to be applied? Why not instead postulate modulations of voice and tone, or facial expression? To answer the second question first, commentators do posit such modifications, sometimes indeed when it is inappropriate to do so, as when they invoke the expression on an actor's face, despite the masks that covered actors' faces. But even when it is appropriate to speak of tone and facial expression, it is also equally appropriate to speak of gesture and stance. For a variety of sources, written and graphic, show that in antiquity Greeks gestured when they spoke, and

[1] Alexis Μανδραγοριζομένη, *PCG* F 146; cf. Menander *Shield* 574.
[2] Aristophanes *Acharnians* 905 *inter alia.*

most of the Archaic and Classical Greek texts we have were composed to be spoken aloud. If accordingly we try to act out the texts ourselves, we discover that an imagined gesture can often complete the sense where canonical philology falls short.

A notice from Jonathan Swift's *Compleat Collection of Genteel and Ingenious Conversation* (1738) is apposite here: "There is hardly a polite sentence in the following dialogues which doth not absolutely require some peculiar graceful motion in the eyes, or nose, or mouth, or forehead, or chin, or suitable toss of the head, with certain offices assigned to each hand." Swift's prescription, quoted in the preface to the *Oxford Book of Conversation*, concerns a society whose day-to-day intercourse is not generally perceived as informed by modes of nonverbal communication. And yet that whole system was and is firmly in place there. How much more intently, then, should we study all the techniques of communication in an ancient society whose posterity use the language of head, hands, and torso everywhere.

Homer's *Iliad* and *Odyssey* were composed to be sung or recited. Archilochus, Sappho, Alcaeus, Stesichorus, Alcman, all the poets of Archaic Greece: no one doubts that their songs were meant to be heard. The forms they used—lyric, dithyrambic, epinician, iambic—all presuppose an audience. Athenian tragedy and comedy put the actors on stage in masks that covered their whole faces. Since they could not express themselves by means of grins and winks and sneers, they used their heads, hands, and bodies instead.

Speakers in the ekklesia and lawcourts, to continue using Athens as an example, did not wear masks, to be sure, but they were addressing audiences that could number anywhere from two hundred to well over six thousand citizens. The shadows and nuances of facial expression, effective as they are in close quarters, are lost when much of the audience sits too far away to see the expression on the orator's face. Speakers accordingly had to move their heads and hands and bodies to be fully effective.[3]

In the composition of histories, medical treatises, and philosophical pamphlets, oral performance may not seem to be a factor, especially not in today's world of silent readers. A historian's prose, which often takes the form of speeches, dialogue, or implied discourse, presents for the most part narrative and analysis in extended sections, not obvious matter for animated recitation. But to the ancients it was self-evident that Herodotus

[3] Aeschines 1. 25 implies that orators addressing the assembly should keep their hands to themselves. Unfortunately he invokes a phantom to illustrate his point. He describes a statue of Solon standing in the Agora on Salamis as having been fashioned after the living Solon. This misstep opens him up to ridicule from Demosthenes in due course (19.251), and a lesson to be drawn from the exchange is that by the fourth century, orators were not constrained to keep their right hand under their cloak. See, e.g., Zanker 1995: 45–50.

read his histories aloud,[4] and Thucydides makes it clear from the start that he wrote his history expecting it to be read aloud. When Herodotus and Thucydides allude to posterity as consulting their work, whether that posterity be near or far, they are thinking of an audience, that is to say, of listeners, not people reading silently to themselves. As for philosophy, a rhapsode, Cleomenes, recited the *Purifications* of Empedocles at Olympia.[5] And generally, Hippias of Elis, also at Olympia, would recite *inter alia* prose treatises on science and ethics.[6] We can accordingly read an Archaic or Classical Greek text as one that both author and readers read aloud. As a natural consequence of doing so, because they acted out their speech in daily life, they acted out the texts they read as well.

Silent reading can be assumed in areas of casual or informal correspondence, or in administrative and legal communications. Public notices, such as posted laws and marching orders, or private documents, such as letters, contracts, and wills, could be read in silence and their contents absorbed by single readers who wanted information and did not need to read aloud or perform. The sight of written letters surely did not at a glance prompt a Greek to start reciting the text out loud.[7]

A few ancient authorities treated rhetorical delivery (ὑπόκρισις) as a phenomenon worthy of study in itself, but not before Demosthenes had given to delivery first, second, and third place of importance in oratory.[8] Theophrastus, it can be supposed, included performance in his περὶ ὑποκρίσεως.[9] Cicero notes the effectiveness of delivery in his *de Oratore* (213–30) and his *Orator* (54–60). A Latin author sometimes identified in modern scholarship as Cornificius, writing in the second decade of the first century B.C.E., wrote briefly on delivery, the Latin word for which, *pronuntiatio,* includes quality of voice and movement of the body (*corporis motum*, a translation of κίνησις τοῦ σώματος). He says, "Therefore because no one has written carefully on this subject—all have thought it scarcely possible for voice, mien, and gesture to be lucidly described as appertaining to our sense experience—and because the mastery of delivery is a very important requisite for speaking, the whole subject, as I believe, deserves serious consideration." He is using earlier Greek writers, possibly Theophrastus's περὶ ὑποκρίσεως.[10] Quintilian, who in *Institutiones Oratoriae* 11.3.1-123 describes gesture and stance in oratory, includes a closely detailed survey of meaningful positions of the fingers. And Gaius Iulius

[4] Jacoby 1913: 242; cf. (**B**) Pritchett 1975: xxviii–xxix, note 4.

[5] Diogenes Laertius 8.63.

[6] Hippias, D-K 86 A1–11.

[7] Cf. Knox 1968: 421–35, and Thomas 1989: 16–31.

[8] Quintilian 11.3.5–6. Note Aristotle *Rhetoric* 2.8.

[9] Fortenbaugh 1985: 269–88.

[10] See (**A**) Caplan 1954: 190–91.

Victor, who wrote an *Ars Rhetorica* in the fourth century C.E., lists in detail some of the things hands can say by themselves (442), e.g., demands, promises, dismissals, threats, fears, questions, etc. etc. None of the ancients, however, contemplated in detail the whole variegated range of nonverbal expressions current in their own lifetimes and observable in official, ceremonial, and everyday private life.

As rules concerning effective delivery in rhetoric evolved, they included proprieties, with the result that some gestures and motions were approved and others discouraged. Aristotle (*Ath. Pol.* 28.3) regarded Cleon's behavior on the bema as abusive, for he had shouted and used insult and belted up his himation while addressing the assembly. Cleophon likewise merited censure for appearing before the assembly in armour (*Ath. Pol.* 34). Later, Hermippus described Theophrastus as not eschewing any motion or gesture while discoursing at the School. Once, in order to imitate a glutton, he stuck out his tongue and licked his lips (Athenaios 1.21a). The point of that detail may be that Theophrastus was acting boldly. The author of *ad Herennium* (3.15.26) cautions: "The facial expression should show modesty and animation, and the gestures should not be conspicuous for either elegance or grossness, lest we give the impression that we are either actors or day-laborers."[11]

John Bulwer's detailed studies of 1644 merit notice here (See Figure 20). His two studies, *Cheirologia* and *Cheironomia*, include contemporary drawings of hands in communicating displays. The drawings are meant to illustrate contemporary rhetorical practice, but Bulwer draws on Greek and Roman literature throughout his studies, and some of the displays coincide nicely with ancient descriptions of Greek and Roman usages. Austin 1806 likewise cites a number of relevant Greek and Latin texts in his attempt to develop a notation of rhetorical gestures.

It has now been a little over one hundred years since the compendious study of Carl Sittl (1890) appeared, his *Die Gebärden der Griechen und Römer*. The thoroughness and range of his documentation maintain that work as a rich source of information still today, for nothing of comparable scope has been attempted since. All subsequent studies of gesture in antiquity treat particular aspects of nonverbal communication. The monograph of Gerhard Neumann (1965), for instance, *Gesten und Gebärden in der griechischen Kunst*, focuses on a limited repertoire of gestures found mostly in Attic black- and red-figure vase paintings. Andreas Katsouris's monograph (1990), Ῥητορικὴ Ὑπόκρισις, addresses questions of rhetorical delivery, and the studies of Barasch (1976), Bérard (1918), Eitrem (1983), Jucker (1956), Lesky (1969), and others listed in the Bibliography reveal in their titles the aims of their studies. McNiven 1982 catalogues

[11] (**A**) Caplan 1954.

gestures pictured on Attic black- and red-figure vases. Donald Lateiner (1995) now presents a full and varied range of nonverbal modes of communication as Homer refers to them in the *Iliad* and the *Odyssey*.

Jones and Morey 1931 discuss gestures repeatedly throughout their two-volume publication of illuminated manuscripts of Terence. They do not, however, consider any of the pictured gestures as relevant to a time earlier than Quintilian, although one at least, Figure 19, seems to be as old as the late sixth century B.C.E. bilingual amphora depicted in Figure 17.

To persuade students to keep in their mind's eye a reader or performer who is reading aloud, the present study begins with a summary chapter reviewing sources of information about gestures in antiquity. One source comprises circumstantial references to gesture and posture in literature, that is to say, descriptions of what a character is doing with his or her body while speaking. A second important source is sculpture and painting, especially when—as all too rarely happens—a label or a bit of dialogue is included in the painting. A third source comprises certain gestures used by people in Greece and around the Mediterranean today. This last may at first glance seem to lack authority, but as I hope to show, some such gestures resemble those noted in ancient literature and art closely enough to serve as heuristic devices, i.e., templates by whose application missing elements of antiquity's body language can be inferred.

In Chapter 2, interpretation of gestures in a few well-known scenes on Attic red-figure vases introduces a few attendant problems. The scenes themselves should at the same time give readers a sense of how men and women expressed themselves with their hands and bodies while speaking.

In Chapter 3, the literary examples begin with Homer. The role of the rhapsode is considered, and in particular his responsibility for filling in the poet's deliberate ellipses. Among such ellipses, there are the "incomplete" conditional sentence and the rhetorical tactic, aposiopesis. With these examples, I include selections from philological commentaries, impressive in volume and density, and for the eminence of their composers; they show how hard it is to explain certain ellipses on the basis of grammar alone.

In Chapter 4, some fragments of Archilochus's poems preserve evocative words or phrases whose articulation seems to need an attendant gesture. Two "incomplete" conditional sentences in Pindar's epinician odes conclude this brief chapter. I do not attempt an appreciation of the language of dance because the topic is beyond my competence. I leave it to others to study the sorts of things that dancing can say when combined with the words of various Archaic songs.

In Chapter 5, on tragic drama, there is no question about the end for which the plays were written: they were to be spoken, sung, danced, and acted out. Even so, for many years the study of tragedy has lacked systematic considerations of physical action. More recently, leading Hellenists have shown increasing consciousness of the action on the stage,[12] but commentators are still slow to use gesture as a way of undoing certain knots grammar does not untie.

Chapter 6 is concerned with Aristophanes. The nonverbal communication of comedy could not have been exactly the same as that of tragedy, but no matter how exuberant and wild, it was always within the boundaries of intelligible communication. In Aristophanes, quotations used as parody, demonstratives, and the ramifications of a synergistic curse are considered in connection with the presentation of comedy.

Chapter 7 on orators follows. In oratory, as in epic and drama, the words were written to be spoken and acted out, and so it is not surprising to meet ellipses in the written text where an author has anticipated a gesture. He may have been gesticulating in imagination as he composed, whether the speech was to be delivered by himself or by another, whether or not it had already been delivered.

The examples from orators that precede Chapter 8, on historians, suggest that Herodotus, Thucydides, and Xenophon likewise saw the figures of their histories moving heads and hands and bodies as they spoke. It is principally but not exclusively where these historians are representing or implying speech that such examples present themselves. Instances from each of these authors are included.

Next, in Chapter 9, I examine some passages from Platonic dialogues. Socrates' demonstration in the *Meno* requires him to illustrate his demonstrative adjectives. Once this picture is established, it is easier to picture nods and other expressive body movements in, e.g., *Apology, Crito, Symposium*, and *Republic*, where deliberate ellipses in syntax may emulate the speech patterns of an actual person, one who was in Plato's mind as he composed. A final chapter offers some summaries and conclusions.

For the present study, I present examples collected over the space of a decade or so, but I have not made a systematic survey of all Archaic and Classical Greek literature, nor can I promise that examples of a given phenomenon represent an exhaustive search of any single author. The selection may, as a result, have a haphazard look in some areas, but the cumulative effect could nevertheless prompt readers and editors of the great ancient Greek texts to try while they read to imagine living, breathing presences whose words their authors saw being delivered with expressive movements of heads, eyes, hands, and torsoes. It can be an illuminating exercise.

I approach these texts as a student of Greek and so I do not represent myself as controlling the anthropological literature. While I have cited a few

[12] For example, Bieber, Taplin, Kaimio, Mastronarde. Cf. Kaimio 1988: 6.

authorities in the bibliography, namely Argyle, Birdwhistell, and Morris, in whose studies I have browsed, I do not adopt their vocabulary. What I call *gestures* are often what advanced students of nonverbal communication would call "emblems" or "regulators," but for the modest aims of this study, the general term *gestures* seems to suffice. Among Hellenists, Bieber, Dover, Taplin, Kaimio, and Mastronarde direct modern readers effectively to action on the stage. They try to see what was actually happening as the actors pronounced the words we have in our texts.

It is my hope that students of literature generally, and of oral tradition and performance, and of course in the case of Plato, of philosophy, will find matter for reflection in this old but often neglected way of reading texts. I have addressed myself to particular passages but I have by no means identified all the possible places where a heightened consciousness of nonverbal communication can enrich our understanding of the written words.

ONE

NONVERBAL COMMUNICATION

WHEN PEOPLE of any quarter talk, they often strengthen, refine, qualify, or even reverse the sense of the words that are coming out of their mouths. They modulate tone, rhythm, spacing, emphasis, pitch, and timbre. The way a mouth shapes vowels and consonants conveys meaning. Inarticulate noises also serve: think of grunts and groans, and sighs and tears, laughter, noises of digestive processes, sniffs, coughs, and throat-clearings, clucks, and whistles. Another kind of nonverbal expression, while not present in all speech, can nevertheless be a necessary element in the transmission of a given message. This group includes gesture, facial expression, mien, posture, stance, ease or tension in disposition of limbs, placement in a room or gathering, orientation to that gathering, and degree of awareness of situational context. Other ways still, although not always consciously employed, sometimes to the contrary despite oneself, convey messages. They are the rapid heartbeat, pale face, flushed face, enlarged or contracted eye-openings, trembling chin, chattering teeth, irregular breathing, clammy skin, trembling hands, signs of heightened adrenal activity, smells like those of fear and love. Any and all tell of inner feelings.

Circumstantial Notices in Literature

The preceding enumeration is not intended to be an exhaustive survey.[1] But it should be enough to remind us that in the ancient Greek world as in our own, numerous ranges of expression were in use, and that they can attend speech or stand for speech. These ranges with all their nuances are for us today so much taken for granted that we do not always use or find them in our own fictions and expositions. Ancient Greek authors—some of them—may have used such resources even less, but we latecomers who want to hear exactly what they were saying must try to sense the whole of an ancient recitation.

[1] Portch 1985, in a study of three American short-story writers, supplies nine categories, excluding that of conscious gesture (cited by Lateiner 1988). Cf. Lateiner 1992: 133–34.

What, then, were some of the invisible presences that influenced the initial composition of an Archaic or Classical Greek literary text? They were in the first place the poets, singers, orators, or philosophers who read aloud the songs, histories, orations, and dialogues they composed. For us, when we do not recognize those presences in our own reading, the written exemplars may lack important elements or qualifiers of meaning. Greeks used their heads, hands, and bodies to express mood and meaning in all their talk, and in Greek literature allusions to such forms of expression abound. To take just a few early instances: in Homer when Zeus says yes, he nods his head down and forward in affirmation (Homer *Iliad* 1.527–28). Odysseus, telling his men not to weep, tilts his head up and back to signify no to each one (Homer *Odyssey* 9.468). When Odysseus says good-bye to Penelope, he lays his hand on her wrist (Homer *Odyssey* 18.257–58).[2]

The ancient Greek vocabulary did not allow extensive and subtle distinctions between the ways head, arms, hands, fingers, and torso speak. In English we use terms like stance, posture, mien, and attitude, while in Greek the single word σχῆμα expressed any and all of these. In contrast, χειρονομία served for the range of gestures that were made with head and fingers. Another general term, *movement* (κίνησις), could include both the larger and the particular conceptions. Plato, *Laws* 816 provides an instructive example where the Athenian stranger is talking about dancing: "And in general, when a man uses his voice to talk or sing, he finds it very difficult to keep his body still. This is the origin of the whole art of dancing: the gestures that express what one is saying. Some of us make gestures that are invariably in harmony with our words, but some of us fail."[3]

Diodorus Siculus (18.67) has a memorable instance of κίνησις when he describes Phocion attempting to speak in his own defense at a meeting of the ekklesia: "Those who were near him could hear the justice of his case, but those standing further off heard nothing because of the noise made by the people who were interrupting with shouts: they could only see the motions he was making with his body, motions that became passionate and varied because of the greatness of his danger."[4] Diodorus does not provide any details that would help us to particularize his picture, nor do Greek authors generally. They tend to say that there was movement of some kind or that a posture was assumed, and then to tell in words what it was that the person in question had to say.

[2] See Lateiner 1995 throughout for body language in Homer.

[3] Translation by (**B**) Saunders 1984: ὅλως δὲ φθεγγόμενος, εἴτ' ἐν ᾠδαῖς εἴτ' ἐν λόγοις, ἡσυχίαν οὐ πάνυ δυνατὸς τῶι σώματι παρέχεσθαι πᾶς. διὸ μίμησις τῶν λεγομένων σχήμασι γενομένη τὴν ὀρχηστικὴν ἐξηργάσατο τέχνην σύμπασαν. ὁ μὲν οὖν ἐμμελῶς ἡμῶν, ὁ δὲ πλημμελῶς ἐν τούτοις πᾶσι κινεῖται.

[4] τὴν τοῦ σώματος κίνησιν γινομένην ἐναγώνιον καὶ ποικίλην. . .

Sometimes, however, authors do describe motions and postures as particular acts in particular circumstances. Thucydides, for instance, in describing Themistocles as suppliant before the wife of the King of the Molossoi (1.136.3), first without other specification says that he became her suppliant (ἱκέτης γενόμενος). Thucydides knew that his readers would know without needing to be told that Themistocles went down on his knees and took hold of her knees and her chin: that was the known, synergistic, nonverbal expression. It is how Thetis, for example, prayed to Zeus to give honor to her son (Homer *Iliad* 1.500–502). But then a little further on in the same story, Thucydides tells of a special form of supplication, one that might evoke the popular story of Telephos, and there he gives details: Themistocles sits in the hearth, holding the king's son (1.137.1). Sophocles *Aias* 1171–75 is comparable, when Teucer instructs Eurysaces in what attitude he must make his supplication. He must kneel and touch his father's corpse. He must have three locks of hair in his hand, one of his own, one of Tecmessa's and one of Teucer's. Again, when Jocasta describes a supplication, she notes that the suppliant had his hand on hers.[5]

Plato confirms this picture of an intimate association of voice and gesture when he has Socrates ask, while speaking of imitation: "When the poet speaks in the person of another, may we not say that he assimilates his style to that of the person who, as he informs you, is going to speak? . . . And this assimilation of himself to another, either in the way he uses his voice or in the attitude he strikes, is the imitation of the person whose character he assumes?"[6] And again, later in the same dialogue, he remarks a poor sort of speaker who can do little more than imitate odd sounds, who depends wholly on voices and postures.[7] Plato is telling us (in the course of saying something else) that poets did not use their voices alone when they performed. They used their whole bodies to amplify or perfect the particular imitation they were essaying at a given point in the poem.[8]

Aristotle *Poetics* 1455a22–31 says: "A poet ought to imagine his material to the fullest possible extent while composing his plot-structures and elaborating them in language. By seeing them as vividly as possible in this way—as if present at the very occurrence of the events—he is likely to discover

[5] Sophocles, *Oedipus the King* 760–61; Gould 1973: 74–103

[6] Plato *Republic* 393c: οὐκοῦν τό γε ὁμοιοῦν ἑαυτὸν ἄλλωι ἢ κατὰ φωνὴν ἢ κατὰ σχῆμα μιμεῖσθαί ἐστιν ἐκεῖνον ὧι ἄν τις ὁμοιοῖ;

[7] Plato *Republic* 397a: φωναῖς τε καὶ σχήμασιν.

[8] The pairing ἢ κατὰ φωνὴν ἢ κατὰ σχῆμα is found often enough to attest a generally recognized association. Cf. Aristotle *Rhetoric* 2.8, where the speaker is advised to combine σχήμασι καὶ φωναῖς καὶ ἐσθῆτι καὶ ὅλως τῆι ὑποκρίσει. Quintilian 11.3.109, half a millennium after Plato, lists among faults in young orators a tendency to shape the composition of an argument to conform with the gestures they imagine themselves making as they compose.

what is appropriate, and least likely to miss contradictions. . . . So far as possible, the poet should even include gestures in the process of composition: for, assuming the same natural talent, the most convincing effect comes from those who actually enter into the emotional states."[9]

At the same time, while a self-conscious, formal rhetoric was being developed, a canon of proprieties began to be recognized, one by which certain homely usages were discouraged. In a world where a man would not express himself much differently on the battlefield, on the bema, or in the agora, speakers would naturally use basically the same gestures and postures, whether addressing a judging or deliberative body of fellow citizens, or whether engaged in private conversations. Sometimes, if the audience was numerous—take for example a meeting of the ekklesia at Athens, where more than six thousand citizens would be listening and watching—bigger gestures would be needed.

Think of Nicias speaking at a meeting of the ekklesia (Thucydides 6.9.2). The expedition to Sicily is imminent. He says, "And yet I get honor from such an enterprise and have less fear for my own body than others—believing, however, that the man who takes forethought for his own person and his property is just as good a citizen <as I am>."[10] Nicias possibly put his hand to his chest, fingers just touching his cloak, as he spoke of his own person and property,[11] stretching out his arm to encompass all of his compatriots when he wanted to include them in his assessments. Pericles, at Thucydides 2.35, calls up another good picture: he is delivering his great Epitaphios Logos in the Kerameikos, and he gestures (we can imagine) to show the expansiveness of the city's concern for her first-fallen. A slow, outward sweep of the right arm, directing attention to the pleasant surroundings, might suffice. In neither of these two instances is there a break in sense or syntax to alert modern readers to the presence of a speaker who complements his speech with motions of head, hand, or body. A sense of Pericles and Nicius is, however, there, each as living, breathing, speaking, gesticulating whole, and not as a concatenation of phrases.

Gestures on the comic and tragic stage had to be exaggerated, for actors wore masks, and body motions had to be distinct and largely defined,

[9] δεῖ δὲ τοὺς μύθους συνιστάναι καὶ τῆι λέξει συναπεργάζεσθαι ὅτι μάλιστα πρὸ ὀμμάτων τιθέμενον· οὕτω γὰρ ἂν ἐναργέστατα [ὁ] ὁρῶν ὥσπερ παρ' αὐτοῖς γιγνόμενος τοῖς πραττομένοις εὑρίσκοι τὸ πρέπον καὶ ἥκιστα ἂν λανθάνοι [τὸ] τὰ ὑπενάντια. . . . ὅσα δὲ δύνατον καὶ τοῖς σχήμασιν συναπεργαζόμενον. πιθανώτατοι γὰρ ἀπὸ τῆς αὐτῆς φύσεως οἱ ἐν τοῖς πάθεσίν εἰσιν. (**A**) Lucas 1968: 175 presents reason to translate σχήμασιν as "gestures." The translation is that of (**B**) Halliwell 1987: 50 (modified).

[10] (**A**) Dover 1970: 231, who also urges readers to envision Nicias's gestures and to imagine his tone of voice, as Thucydides obviously would have done.

[11] Sittl 1890: 53–54 notes a general tendency among Greeks and Romans to touch themselves when referring to themselves.

when a good portion of the audience was a long way off.[12] The gestures were there, and some benefits that accrue from picturing them in our minds have been introduced. But what sort of gesture are we to imagine? Some allusions in literature have been noted (pp. 12–16 above). Some illustrations are discussed below as examples.

Illustrations

In ancient Greece, human figures as they were represented in sculpture, figurines, and paintings show a world in which gesture and posture were essential elements of communication. As early as the thirteenth century B.C.E., when funeral and burial scenes, battles, and ships appear in wall-paintings and on sarcophagi, human figures gesticulate. The same themes reappear on Geometric vases about five hundred years later, and in the Geometric funeral scenes one continuity of gesture merits notice: mourners at biers or in funerals painted on thirteenth century B.C.E. sarcophagi from Tanagra put their hands to their heads, presumably to tear out their hair. Mourners on Geometric amphoras also put their hands to their heads, as do mourners of the sixth and fifth centuries B.C.E.[13]

By the end of the eighth century, painters in the proto-Attic style began to include in their paintings recognizable figures from legend and myth. Toward the end of the seventh century B.C.E., Attic black-figure painting introduced a wider range of representations, including many scenes from private, daily life, with a correspondingly greater variety of gesticulating figures. Vase paintings in the red-figure style, which begins ca. 525 B.C.E. and supersedes black figure (except for Panathenaic amphoras), show still more examples of action and discourse in daily and heroic life and death. Actors in these scenes, regardless of whether they are gods, heroes, or mortals, are very rarely given words to speak. They must express themselves with their bodies. If they are represented as speaking, they are gesticulating.

Usually we must interpret these pictured gestures by inference, hoping to tell from context what is being said. Interpretation in such cases is approved by sympathetic imagination rather than by labels or sure parallels. Still, some interpretations are probable, and they serve as plausible guides. Neumann 1965: 10–36 cites a number of paintings in which inferences

[12] Cf. Taplin 1978: 15. Dover 1978: 139, note 6 says in connection with a line of Aristophanes *Clouds*: "We never have independent evidence for stage action, but it is legitimate to point out ways in which figurative language can be completely clarified by action."

[13] Neumann, 1965: 85–89 notes the continuity from the eighth to the fifth century B.C.E. but did not have access to the painted sarcophagi from Tanagra. He quotes Homer *Iliad* 24.710–12 where women are tearing out their hair in grief. Cf. Vermeule 1979: 63–65. Cf. Euripides *Helen* 371–72.

he has drawn from gesture and scene combined are especially informative. One gesture, that of an extended index finger, with the other fingers loosely closed, and arm in various positions, can signify invitation, exhortation, or imperious summons. Hand up, palm out, means refusal or denial. Hand up, palm turned sideways or slightly inward is a greeting.

Almost any single gesture can be ambiguous, even in the course of a conversation that is being conducted in spoken words. A hand flung up in a show of indignation could from a distance appear to convey great anger or surprise, or even to threaten physical injury. Close up, a partner to the conversation in turn colors the gesture in shades of his or her own mood. A gesture depicted in a painting, where there are no words, is frozen at one single point and for that reason cannot be unambiguous. Something more must be there to establish exact meaning, i.e., labels or emblems or a known story that gives the picture a context. Some postures continue to be of uncertain interpretation, even when they appear to coincide with gestures described in literature.

CONTROL: HAND ON WRIST

One person touches, holds, or grasps the wrist of another variously in both art and literature. The circumstances of this contact show in their variety that no single, tightly focused paraphrase serves each and every case. Obviously a kind of connection is being made, possibly it is always an intimate connection, but beyond that, we need context to say more. When Odysseus is described as putting his hand on Penelope's wrist in farewell, he shows affection and says goodbye (Homer *Odyssey* 18.257–58). A hasty student of gestures might accordingly be tempted to say: "Hand on wrist = Good-bye." But maybe Odysseus is reassuring her, telling her with this gesture that he will come safely home. It is the gesture Achilles used to reassure Priam (Homer *Iliad* 24.671–72). Dancers described on Achilles' shield (Homer *Iliad* 18.590–94) have hands on wrists, as do those in the Homeric *Hymn to Apollo* 182ff.

On an Attic Geometric bowl (Figure 1),[14] a warrior has his hand on the wrist of a woman as he prepares to board a ship. Is he taking her with him? Or is he saying good-bye? As Neumann 1965: 18 observes, the physical connection between woman, man, and ship may tell us that the scene is an abduction. Coldstream 1977: 354–55 writes, "Perhaps he is bidding her farewell; more probably he is hauling her aboard, to judge from his energetic forward gestures." Again in a painting by the Brygos Painter (Figure 2), when Menelaos puts his hand on Helen's wrist, is it a

[14] Brit. Mus. 1899. 2–19.1, Pfuhl 1923: #15.

wedding, or is he going to lead her home again?[15] Or is he merely asserting his authority? When Paris puts his hand on Helen's wrist in a painting by Makron (Figure 3), it is to elope.[16] And, when Zeus puts his hand on Hera's wrist on a metope from Selinos (Figure 4),[17] he is drawing her into a connubial embrace. But on a lekythos by Euphronios (Figure 5), Peleus holds Thetis's wrist as they are carried by chariot to their wedding.[18] And on the great Orpheus relief in Naples, Hermes has his hand on Eurydice's wrist to lead her back to Hades.[19] And then there are the scenes of dancers, women in a line each with her hand on the wrist of a companion in the dance (Figure 6).[20]

This brief list shows that clarity of representation does not guarantee clarity of meaning, and that the differing implications of a single, clear gesture are not mutually exclusive. Basically hand on wrist seems to show who will lead in the activity, whatever it may be, that is being proposed. Additional interpretation requires other data.[21]

CONNECTING: HAND ON CHIN

An Ionic frieze from the Siphnian Treasury at Delphi has seated gods in two groups.[22] Each of the seated gods has one hand outstretched, apparently to hold the chin of the god ahead. The arms can be imagined to have made a more or less continuous line within each group, knitting the divine figures together. Arms form a connecting, continuing line between otherwise separate figures likewise on the shoulder of a lekythos by the Amasis Painter (see note 20), where the dancers are connected each one by hand on wrist. There are comparable scenes on a Geometric skyphos from Athens (Figure 7) and on a Laconian pyxis (Figure 8).[23] In both the sculpture and the painting, an effect beyond that of mere design is intended, an appearance perhaps of some essential unity of purpose or identity.

In paintings, hand on chin seems often to show affection or a sense of union between two people.[24] When two Greek friends today conclude a

[15] Brygos Painter, Berlin F 2205, *ARV*² 383.202.

[16] Makron, Boston 13.186, *ARV*² 458.1.

[17] Palermo Museo Nazionale 3921. Neumann 1965: 66 with note 57 and plate 31E. Langlotz 1965; fig. 105.

[18] Athens, National Museum 15214. See Jenkins 1983: 140; cf. Oakley and Sinos 1995: 32 with figures 82–87, 94, 97.

[19] These examples are all discussed by Neumann 1965: 59–66.

[20] Dancers on the shoulder of a black-figure lekythos of the Amasis Painter (MMA 56.11.1) von Bothmer 1985: no. 47.

[21] Cf. Neumann 1965: 59–66, Lateiner 1995: 261. Cf. also McNiven 1982: 94.

[22] De La Coste Messelière 1943: plate 76.

[23] A Geometric skyphos from Athens (Athens, National Museum 874, *CVA* Athens 2, 1954, pls. 10–11); a tall pyxis from Amyclae (Athens, National Museum 234, Coldstream 1977: 158–59); note also a proto-Attic hydria, Athens, National Museum 18 435.

[24] I have seen just this gesture, hand on chin, used between middle-aged gentlemen today in Greece, as they take leave from each other after a conversation in a public square. Sittl

visit, one may put his hand to the other's chin briefly, cupping it in a gesture of affection, but also saying good-bye. A Hellenistic grave relief from Thera shows a woman, Alexibola, holding out her hand to cup the chin of a seated and stooped old man. She is saying good-bye just as one sees couples parting today.[25]

CONNECTING: SUPPLICATION

The suppliant's posture effected a bond or a sense of unity between two people. It is one particular use made of a more widely employed posture or gesture. It is presumably what Athena is doing as she leads Heracles by the wrist and extends her left hand toward Zeus's chin. She will ask a favor in Heracles' behalf. (Figure 9) On the other hand, Nessos, the famous centaur, pictured on one of the earliest black-figure amphoras (Figure 10) has his hand on Heracles' chin.[26] Obviously this is not an affectionate gesture: its full implications are present in abundance for those who can read. Both figures are named by labels, and the story is well known from other sources: Heracles killed Nessos, who was putting his hands on Heracles' wife. Furthermore, Heracles has his sword ready to strike. There is no confusion of meaning here: Nessos's hand on Heracles' chin means that Nessos is pleading for his life. The same is true in a painting of Theseus and the Minotaur[27] (Figure 11), where the Minotaur, with one hand on Theseus's knee, reaches with the other for Theseus's chin. As in the story of Heracles and Nessos, the conclusion of the episode is well known: Theseus kills the Minotaur. In a black-figure representation of the sack of Troy,[28] a figure immediately identifiable as Neoptolemos (he holds by the ankle a young boy, Astyanax, who hangs at his side) faces an old man on a throne, clearly Priam, who has extended his hand to touch Neoptolemos's chin. Priam's intent is unmistakable, because the artist has put his gesture in a context where it can have only one broad meaning: spare me/the child/my people. From literature we know that his appeal was in vain.

AN ARCHAIC BRIDE AND GROOM?

On an Archaic jug from Arkades (Afrati) in Crete,[29] (Figure 12) a young man, beardless, and a young woman stand facing each other. With his left

1890: 32–33 notes hand on chin as gesture of affectionate greeting in Greece and Italy. Neumann 1965: 66 cites a Hieros Gamos on a terracotta plaque from Samos. Cf. Dover 1978: 94 on the "up and down" position (Beazley's phrase); cf. also McNiven 1982: 90.

[25] Neumann 1965: pl. 33.

[26] British Museum B424; Athens, National Museum 1002; *ABV* 4; *Paralipomena* 2.

[27] Kleophrades Painter, British Museum E441, *ARV*² 187 number 57.

[28] Lydos, Berlin 1685. *ABV* 109.24.

[29] Herakleion 7961.

hand he holds her chin, while his right hand is at the level of her groin, where his fingers appear to be passing through incised lines that delineate her peplos. Her right hand holds his left at the wrist; her left hand holds his right likewise at the wrist. The two are sometimes identified in modern literature as bride and groom. But what really is the message here? On the basis of the brief summary of possibilities offered above (pp. 17–18), one might see the youth as wanting to make love and her as saying no. Is she restraining him? Is he imploring? Or are they brother and sister, and he is saying good-bye? We cannot know. The crossed arms that symbolically bind them together suggest an intimate family relationship. Although the artist has not labeled the pair, names from old stories of seduction and abduction persist in hopeful modern studies, Theseus and Ariadne, for instance. For the moment, let the two figures serve as emblem of a persistent difficulty, that of the inscrutability of one act frozen in time. A hand pictured holding a wrist, or touching a chin, or stopped in midair does not tell enough. How can we apprehend the direction, velocity, context, and complexities of an expressive physical motion? We need to know beginning, direction, trajectory, speed, and termination to say what the hand signifies. The question mark after "Bride and Groom" seems destined to stay.[30]

Continuities

A gesture described in a circumstantial way in a poem or play is hard to visualize in detail.[31] In the absence of slow-motion film images of ancient conversations, where can supplementary data be found? In the cases of yes and no—and in some other cases as well—these data are accessible in Greek-speaking communities of today, for in such communities, a yes can be expressed by a nod forward and slightly to one side, while a no is an upward or backward movement of the head, sometimes barely more than the raising of an eyebrow. Both gestures may be shorthand enactments of an impulse: the forward nod is a drawing near to what is being asked or offered. The motion up and back is a withdrawal or disassociation. Now with as much information as the verbs alone supply, a reader today can act out "nod up" (ἀνανεύω) and "nod down" (κατανεύω) and feel that an approximation at least has been effected. But the two gestures allow

[30] See Neumann 1965: 68–69, note 252 for bibliography and an account of some interpretations. Cf. Dover (above, note 24).

[31] Murray 1991: 3 in his review of Jean-Claud Schmitt, *La Raison des gestes* (*TLS* April 26), observes: "Even modern psychologists have to study 'body-language' by resorting to slowed film strip. The innumerable, intimate, ephemeral gestures of our mediaeval ancestors are thus irrecoverable."

many refinements and nuances, more than the Greek verbal vocabulary includes. To get a sense of that variety and complexity, one needs to see a wide assortment of people expressing themselves naturally and easily by means of these motions.

Continuities in the general area of modern Greek, nonverbal expression can be a result of direct transmission over the course of millennia. Think of the very beginnings of percipient life. Parents speak to their children with their whole bodies from the instant of birth, and infants begin to absorb that kinetic vocabulary, which is to say the totality of stance, gesticulation, and movement, with their first gulp of air.[32] In due course the grown-up children pass that totality on to their own children, no matter what other languages and cultures have passed around and through the land.[33]

Where the modern Greek world is concerned, some apparent continuities turn out to be self-conscious revivals. This is often the case in the naming of towns and rivers, and in modes of speech that are examples of "purifying" Greek, an impulse of the nineteenth century, whose effects one observes still today.[34]

But consider also the fact that "no Greek speaker was or is ever in doubt whether another man's speech is Greek or not."[35] If a continuity of the density, length, and complexity of the Greek spoken and written language can be confirmed simply by opening one's eyes and ears, why not suppose that certain widely employed gestures have had a comparable lifetime? The Greek word that means "sun" (ἥλιος) has an attested lifetime of close to three thousand years; the tilt of the head that means no has also been in use over the same span of time. In other words, both the word and the gesture are and have been working elements of the Greek vocabulary for thousands of years. It is accordingly a reasonable hypothesis to take as heuristic device any gesture current in Greece today and comparable to one pictured, described, or intimated in ancient literature or art. To proceed with such a hypothesis could recover the whole range of movement that constituted a modern gesture's distant antecedent.[36]

[32] Cf. Augustine *Confessions* 1.8, describing how he learned what the names of objects were: "When older folk would name a thing and would accordingly move toward something, I looked and caught on that the thing was named by the sound they made when they wanted to point it out. That this is what they wanted was revealed by body motion (*motu corporis*), the natural vocabulary, you might say, of all humankind, namely facial expression, play of eyes, movement of other body parts, and tone of voice showing state of mind in asking for, in having, in rejecting, and in avoiding things."

[33] See Mackridge 1985: 3–4.

[34] Browning 1969: 112–13.

[35] Ibid.: 12.

[36] On continuities of language, see "The Continuity of Greek Culture," in Knox 1993. He notes Shipp 1979 and Andriotis 1974.

I SHALL OFFER. . . : METROPOLITAN MUSEUM 24.97.104

An Apulian calyx crater (Figure 13) lends itself nicely to illustration of how this hypothesis may be applied. A puzzling scene, surely from a comedy, has recently been discussed by Taplin 1993: 30–32. From left to right we see four characters: first, a youth standing at a distance and labeled "Tragoidos"; next an arrogant young man with a stick, then an old man whose hands are bound above his head, and finally an old woman who stands on a balcony and extends her right arm toward the other figures. These last three have painted words to say: the arrogant young man, a word or words of uncertain meaning, the old man, "he (or she) has bound my hands above me," and the old woman, "I shall produce."[37] To leave aside questions of general interpretation, we appeal to modern Mediterranean practice and restore the old woman's gesture from start to finish. That is, when she says, "I," she touches the fingers of her right hand to her breast and as she says, "shall produce," she extends her arm with fingers apart in the position one sees on the crater.

Generally Understandable

Some nonverbal communication today is as clear as it was in antiquity. The reason is that the particular movement of hand, head, or torso either was already a sort of universal gesture by ancient times, or it has become so since. Six examples may serve to illustrate these long and widely dispersed usages: pointing with one finger to a distant object, clasping another's hand, biting one's lip, resting one's chin on one's knuckles, raising the right hand to vote, and holding out one's hand with first two fingers extended and spread.

POINTING

Pointing with arm and index finger outstretched is an almost universal gesture today. An obvious example is on a red-figure pelike by Euphronios (Figure 14),[38] where a bearded man, a younger man, and a boy point to a swallow. The young man's arm is outstretched. He points his index finger and says, "Look, a swallow." The bearded man also uses his index finger to point.

[37] Metropolitan Museum 24.97.104, on which appear the inscriptions NOPAPPETBΛO; κατέδησ' ἄνω τὼ χεῖρε; ἐγὼ παρέξω.

[38] Leningrad, Hermitage 615; *ARV*^{2} 1594.48, *Paralipomena* 507, 509; cf. the Laconian Arkesilaus kylix 189, *Bibliotheque National des Medailles, CVA* Plate 21.

In a different instance of pointing, where the immediate sense is not obvious today, a defeated boxer acknowledges defeat and wants the fight to stop. He raises his hand and points his index finger to the sky. What he says is painted out beside him: [ἀπ]αγορεύω, "I give up."[39] The combination of picture and inscription gives enough information for an accurate interpretation not only of the scene on this Panathenaic amphora but also of scenes on other pots where an inscription is lacking, and in references to the practice in literature, references that otherwise might have been obscure. Antiphanes *PCG* F189.13–15, for instance, says that when dramatists cannot say anything anymore, when they just get tired in their plays, they raise the machine the way an athlete does his finger. If the gesture is not current today, it did nevertheless survive for a thousand years and more, for it figures in a Greek medieval epic as a sign of defeat.[40]

HANDCLASP

In Attic red-figure vase paintings, departing warriors and fathers clasp hands as they say long good-byes. And a handclasp continues to be used in Greece rather more for that purpose than for conventional greetings. Δεξίωσις (a clasping of the right hand) can also be a last farewell signed by the living to the dead. On the marble stelai bearing relief sculptures and designed to mark graves, a living member of the family is often shown clasping the hand of the dead. The same is true of Attic white-ground lekythoi, which are terra-cotta vessels specially designed to commemorate the dead.[41] But the handclasp was and is also a way of certifying and affirming an agreement or treaty or reconciliation.[42] And Socrates recommends that a Guardian who has been preeminent in battle have his right hand shaken in congratulation by one and all (Plato *Republic* 468b7). Phaedra and her nurse signal an important connection with a handclasp.[43]

[39] Neumann 1965: 40 lists examples of ἀπαγορεύω as a sign made by a defeated boxer. Cf. Philostratos *Imagines* 2.6.5, τὸ ἀπαγορεῦον ἐπισημαίνων τῆι χειρί and Theocritus 22.130, where Amycus holds up both his hands declining further contest, since he was almost close to death" (ἀνέσχεθε νεῖκος ἀπαυδῶν ἀμφοτέρας ἅμα χεῖρας). Sittl 1890: 219 provides literary testimonia for ἀπαγορεύω. Beazley 1986: plate 98.6 shows a boxer signaling that he gives up. Cf. also McNiven 1982: 47.

[40] See Stephanopoulos 1983: 58–60, who cites τὸν δάκτυλον ἔδειξεν, line 391 from the medieval epic poem *Digenis Akritas* (ed. P. P. Kalonarou, Athens 1941) and identifies it as the Classical gesture of admitting defeat.

[41] See Shapiro 1991: 654.

[42] See Herman 1987: 49–53; Oakley and Sinos 1995: fig. 1 ("The bride's father accepts his future son-in-law with a handshake to seal their agreement.")

[43] Euripides *Hippolytos* 325–35; cf. δεξιώματα at Sophocles *Oedipus at Colonus* 619. (**A**) Jebb 1893 *ad loc.* notes only one other like usage, viz. Athenaios 159B. Gould 1973: 86 connects this handclasp with the necessity of physical contact in an act of supplication.

Heracles has his son shake hands to certify that son will do what Heracles will ask.[44] A handshake, therefore, like the act of cupping another's chin with one's hand, must have a context before its particular application is clear.[45]

BITING THE LIP

Members of today's community of the western world, many of whom have bitten their lip in frustration or chagrin or have seen or heard of such a response, do not need a list here. In Homer the applications are particular, but the meaning is familiar.[46]

KNUCKLES UNDER THE CHIN

Another widely recognized posture is that made most famous today by Rodin's bronze statue, *The Thinker.* An Athenian vase painter of the fifth century B.C.E., in the tondo of a cup, represented Oedipus in a similar pose, that is, with the knuckles of his left hand under his chin (Figure 15). He is pondering the riddle that the sphinx, sitting on a column a little above him, has just propounded.[47] The story of Oedipus's arrival at Thebes is well known, but even if viewers did not know the story, they would understand the posture, which is one of paying attention and thinking. To return to present-day body language, a row of listeners at a lecture given in New England in 1984 shows exactly the same posture (Figure 16).

RAISING THE RIGHT HAND TO VOTE

Another significant gesture made with the right hand is raising that hand to vote. The citizens of Argos make the air bristle with their raised right hands in Aeschylus's *Suppliants* 607–8, a play produced in 463 B.C.E.

[44] Sophocles *The Trachinian Women* 1181–89; likewise Philoctetes and Neoptolemos in Sophocles *Philoctetes* 813 and 942. Burkert 1983: 34 observes, "An agreement can be expressed quickly and clearly in words, but it is only made effective by a ritual gesture: open, weaponless hands stretched out toward one another, grasping each other in a mutual handshake—a mutual display of aggression sealing what had previously merely been spoken." When you are asking a favor, you grasp a person's hand (Old Oligarch 1.18, Aristophanes *Wasps* 553; Sittl 1890: 28). Flory 1978: 69–74 notes that Medea speaks of taking Aegeus's right hand (Euripides *Medea* 368ff.). Heracles wants Admetos's right hand in Alkestis's hand (Euripides *Alkestis* 1115–17).

[45] Cf. Morris 1986: 470–71: "The δεξίωσις motif (68) still perplexes, despite repeated analysis. Rather than a greeting, it probably expresses an oath or contractual relationship between living and dead (as implied in Euripides, *Alkestis* 375–76, 1115). Hence the gesture appears on Attic decree reliefs." Cf. also McNiven 1982: 95.

[46] See Lateiner 1989: 18–23.

[47] The Oedipus Painter, Vatican Museum, ARV^2 451.1; Neumann 1965: 124, plate 62.

Aeschylus seems to have invented a special word, viz. δεξιώνυμος, to emphasize the fact that it is the right hand that was used.[48]

ALERTING THE AUDIENCE

A gesture whose geographical and chronological spread is notable appears in a red-figure painting by the Andokides Painter (Figure 17) on an Attic bilingual amphora of the late sixth century B.C.E.: two warriors, Achilles and Aias, are seated opposite each other at a low table, playing dice, and Aias, on the right (to use Beazley's names), extends his right hand with index and middle fingers extended and spread. The other two fingers are folded into the palm.[49] The same display of hand and fingers can be seen in a variety of contexts. I note (summarily) fifth-century Athenian paintings of dramas,[50] a fourth-century Panathenaic amphora,[51] a fourth-century Apulian painting of a play,[52] another of an underworld scene (Figure 18),[53] manuscripts of Terence where actors playing roles in his comedies are drawn in miniature (Figure 19),[54] a seventeenth-century English manual of speakers' gestures (Figure 20),[55] and a photograph of Ronald Reagan and Andre Gromyko talking in 1984.[56]

To turn to circumstantial accounts in literature, Quintilian 11.3.96–100 describes several different gestures that properly attend modest speech. (Interestingly enough he claims to know what gesture Demosthenes more

[48] See LSJ *s.v.* χείρ, where the right hand is stipulated. Cf. (**A**) Johansen-Whittle 1980: II.494–95. In comparison, a Delphic oracle, quoted at Demosthenes 43.66, prescribes lifting the right hand and the left in thanksgiving (δεξιὰς καὶ ἀριστερὰς ἀνίσχοντας).

[49] Boston MFA 01.8037. Caskey-Beazley 1963: plates LXV. 114, LXVI. Beazley (ibid.: 5) says that Aias shows with his two fingers what he has scored with the dice. Cohen 1978: 8 concurs. McNiven 1982: 191 sees the gesture as a sign of good luck, or the averting of evil, or as a counting sign. But the display appears mutatis mutandis to be essentially that which McNiven ibid.: 10 cites as an example of a gesture whose sense changes over time. The comparanda offered below point to another interpretation.

[50] Webster 1961: TV4, TV5.

[51] Beazley 1986: plate 101.4, *ABV* 414.2, *Paralipomena* 178.2: an official advising two boxers.

[52] London British Museum F271. Hermes in the upper register, a youth in the lower register. Trendall and Webster 1971: 52 describe the youth as raising "one hand in a gesture of despair. . . ." Bieber 1961: 142, fig. 519 sees the gesture as "horns" on a vase from Bari. But those two fingers may show merely who is speaking.

[53] Toledo Museum of Art 1994.19; Johnston and McNiven 1996: plate 1.

[54] Jones-Morey 1931: text, figs. 29, 30, 44, 58, 59 (Jesus Christ's right hand); plates, figs. 70, 72–73, 77–80 (Figure 19), 304, 306–7, 404, 426, 428, 432, 628–31. A scene from *Phormio* 4.1 shows two actors both using the gesture at the same time! (738–40). Katsouris 1990: 136, 194–95 lists abundant illustrations and prints three pictures of modern instances (numbers 60–62 but not 64, which is quite another thing. Cf. Morris et al. 1979: 226–40).

[55] Bulwer 1644: 196–97, 213 A and G.

[56] See Katsouris 1990: plate 60.

than three hundred years earlier used at one point in his defense of Ctesiphon) One such gesture he describes as follows: "Sometimes we separate the first two fingers—not with the thumb between them—and with the other two fingers pointing inward, and the first fingers not fully extended. And sometimes the last two fingers press the palm at the base of the thumb, which is joined to the middle joints of the first two fingers."[57] Either one of these two displays would suit the gesture pictured on vases, manuscripts, drawings, and photographs cited here.

Compare now Apuleius (*Metamorphoses* 2.21), who has Thelyphron use this gesture as he embarks on his weird and ghastly tale. "He leaned on his elbow at the table and sitting up on his couch stretched out his right hand, and in the way of orators shaped it with the two smaller fingers closed and stretching out the others with the opposed thumb sticking up. Then he began to speak."[58]

Where a painted scene shows actors in costume, and where one of the actors is making that gesture, it is easy to infer that the actor was signaling, telling the audience which character is speaking. Picture two or three actors on an ancient Greek stage. One stops speaking, and another starts. In an interchange where big body movements would not be appropriate to the speech being uttered just then, a modest movement of the right arm, drawing attention to the hand whose index and third fingers are flexed, will localize the new speaker. On the Athenian stage, where actors wore masks and spectators were at a distance, the slight movement of the hand with those fingers extended and spread was instantly recognizable. The same would be true on the Roman stage, where actors were very often Greek. As for Ronald Reagan, he had been trained as an actor; his gesture could have been a result of that training.

Mostly Greek

Some body language used today needs to be translated. One such gesture is the *moutza*, known from Byzantine times, designed to be a gross insult. You open your hand and extend your palm with fingers spread, aiming at your object's face, not to touch it, but to show that you are symbolically smearing it with excrement.[59]

[57] "Binos interim digitos distinguimus, sed non inserto pollice, paulum tamen inferioribus intra spectantibus, sed ne illis quidem tensis, qui supra sunt. Interim extremi palmam circa ima pollicis premunt, ipse prioribus ad medios articulos iungitur" (Quintilian 11.3.98–99).

[58] Apuleius *Metamorphoses* 2.21.1: subrectusque in torum porrigit dexteram, et ad instar oratorum conformat articulum duobusque infimis conclusis digitis ceteros eminus porrigens et infesto pollice subrigens infit Thelyphron.

[59] See Sittl 1890: 45–46, 102; Eitrem 1953 cites A. Keramopoullos 1923, ὁ ἀποτυμπανισμός, Athens, where Keramopoullos associates the *moutza* with *faskelo* or *sfakelos*, i.e., terms for the evil eye and now more or less synonymous with *moutza*.

Among gestures that were full of meaning in antiquity but had to be studied and explained by modern students before their sense was made clear are three that can serve as examples. They are not in use today so far as I know, and their pristine import had been forgotten. One is that of covering one's head with a cloak, now plausibly explained as an expression of αἰδώς, a modesty about revealing strong emotions by one's facial expression.[60] Another is that of the woman who holds out a veil from her face. This gesture as it appears on black- and red-figure Attic vases is often clearly that of a bride opening herself to her husband, but wider extensions of meaning are possible.[61] The third is the spying gesture, i.e., hand held up to shade the eyes. On black-figure vases, satyrs might use it when looking toward or for a god.[62]

Other gestures—these not universal—were used by Greeks in antiquity in the same sense as they are used now. By their particularity they serve as heuristic devices, giving us a sense of how a Greek in Classical times would have expressed himself/herself in conversation and in formal argument inside and outside the house. The downward and sideways nod for yes, with the upward and backward motion for no, already mentioned, are obvious examples. But there is also that of spitting into one's bosom three times to avoid the evil eye. Another is that of shaking out the front of one's garment in obsecration. And in another gesture that means "Come here," the summoner points to the ground immediately in front of him/her, using a single finger or all of them loosely bunched.

The head motions for yes and no have been discussed above (pp. 20–21) and the shaking of the front of the clothes is discussed below (pp. 73–77). Here a word can be said about spitting to ward off the evil eye, and the summoning gesture.

SPITTING THREE TIMES INTO THE BOSOM

Theophrastus describes superstition as a cowardice about divinity, and in sketching characteristic responses of a superstitious man, ends by saying: "If he sees a madman or an epileptic, he shudders and spits down at his chest."[63] The Cyclops in Damoetas's song (Theocritus 6.39) admires his reflection in the sea and then recalls, "I spat three times into my bosom to avoid the evil eye." Sittl 1890: 118–20 cites these attempts to avoid the evil eye as well as others from later literary sources in Latin and Greek. He also notes modern spitting practices in Italy, Germany, and Greece.

[60] Ferrari 1990 studies Aias as he covers his face with his cloak for shame.

[61] See, e.g., Oakley and Sinos 1993: Index s.v. *anakalypsis.*

[62] According to Neumann 1965: 170, note 15, Jucker 1956: 111ff. shows continuation of the spying gesture into modern times.

[63] Theophrastus *Characters* 16.14 (translation of [**A**] Rusten 1993 *ad loc.*).

Today a Greek will do exactly the same thing that Theocritus's Cyclops did in the second century B.C.E. to avoid the evil eye, and he or she will use the same word (να μήν βασκανθώ).[64]

SUMMONING

The modern summoning gesture can be seen on a red-figure pelike that shows Athena face-to-face with a man (Figure 21).[65] She extends her right arm and points to the ground right in front of her with her index finger. She is saying, "Come here." It is true that the man who is being summoned is as close as one might want, but in the conventions of vase-painting narrative, it is possible to compact spatial and temporal elements in a single scene.[66]

Summary

Greeks used their heads, hands, and bodies when they spoke. Plato, Aristotle, and other authors say that body movement and gesture are integral components of communication. If we ask exactly what these gestures were, we may turn to references in Classical and Archaic literature where there are allusions to signifying motions of head, hand, and body. These references provide clues but cannot be complete in themselves. A second rich pool of data is that of nonverbal communication illustrated in vase paintings and sculpture. Such illustrations may show context and (instantaneous) aspect, but again, as in the case of verbal narrative, the medium cannot provide all the details one wants. A third source of information is that of the continuous tradition. The same motions of head, hand, and body current in Greece today can be used sometimes to fill out single, frozen poses of art, or nonpictorial descriptions in words.

[64] ὣς μὴ βασκανθῶ δὲ τρὶς εἰς ἐμὸν ἔπτυσα κόλπον. (**A**) Gow 1950 *ad loc.* provides ancient comparanda, all later in date. I asked a contemporary of mine, a physicist, brought up on Crete in the Orthodox church but fully Americanized, how he would go about avoiding the evil eye. He spit three times in the direction of his right breast pocket.

[65] Berlin F 2354; *ARV*^{2} 857.4; Neumann 1965: 28, fig. 13.

[66] For the gesture, compare the discussion below (pp. 33–34) of the Meidias Painter's representation of Eukleia and Eunomia.

TWO

SOME ATTIC RED-FIGURE SCENES

IN THE PRECEDING CHAPTER some representative gestures were identified, and our principal sources of information were assessed. In succeeding chapters a number of literary passages are examined, not for circumstantial references to physical motions, but for ellipses in sense or grammar that could easily have been filled with a nod of the head or a motion of hand or body. In the present chapter three scenes drawn from the corpus of Attic red-figure vase-painting are discussed to show how pictured gestures invite certain interpretations, and create some ambiguities, and in one case deliver what may be a political message.

The Vote on the Arms of Achilles

A series of red-figure vase paintings, all Late Archaic, i.e., 520–500 B.C.E., whose theme is the vote on Achilles' arms, exemplify varying interpretations and the application of sympathetic imagination as control. Douris, Makron, the Brygos Painter, and others show versions in which Odysseus, Achaean heroes, Athena, and Aias may appear. In Douris's version (Figure 22),[1] Athena stands behind an altar. She extends her right hand, open with fingers spread but not stiff, toward Odysseus, who is at her right at the end of the altar. On top of the altar at right and left ends, small deposits of pebbles show that a balloting is in progress. Warriors approach the altar from right and left, those nearest in the act of depositing a ballot, those following, about to. At one extremity of this scene, Odysseus throws his hands up in joy. He has won, and the painter has duly shown on his side of the altar a pile of pebbles that is larger than the one on the opposite side. At the other extremity, Aias pulls his mantle over his face. Now the observation has been recorded above (pp. 16–17, 20) that a gesture caught and frozen in a painting becomes thereby a posture, since there is no movement or direction. But the voting scene just described gives a good sense of what motions preceded and followed the postures in which Athena, Odysseus, and Aias are caught. The story is known, the chief characters can be named, and their responses divined.

[1] Vienna 3695, *ARV*[2] 429.26.

First consider Athena. What does that outstretched arm mean? One scholar says that she is guaranteeing divine help to her favorite: the balloting shows what she wanted and what she helped to happen.[2] Another says that she is cautioning Odysseus, telling him to moderate his feelings of exultation.[3] Méautis 1932: 74 says (correctly, I think) that Athena is indicating Odysseus's victory.

The lack of unanimity in the explanations just quoted (which are only a sampling) attests to the opacity of posture as solitary guide to meaning. But here as sometimes elsewhere another source of information can help, namely Euripides *Iphigeneia among the Taurians* 965–66. Orestes is explaining to Iphigeneia how he came to be acquitted when he was tried on the Areopagos at Athens for having killed his mother. As his audience knew, Athena's vote was the deciding factor in the judgment. The judging panel, convened on the Areopagos, sitting for the first time as homicide court, cast an equal number of ballots to condemn and to acquit. Athena tipped the verdict to acquittal with her single added vote. In Euripides' play Orestes says, "Pallas with <a gesture of> her arm certified the counting of the ballots as equal <and therefore> for me."[4]

Now Makron and Douris are usually thought to have painted their versions of the Vote on the Arms late in the sixth/early in the fifth century B.C.E. The postures and gestures they give their gods and heroes, it is natural to assume, are those the artists saw around them in real life. Haspels 1936: 158–59, note 2 commemorates a nice instance of that sort of adaptation when discussing sirens painted on a Melian vase: "The Bari sirens are playing the flute and the lyre . . . and therefore have arms; the Marburg siren is not playing, and so has none. This is the general rule: sirens have arms only when they need them. . . . Two sirens on a Melian neck-amphora . . . seem at first sight to be another exception. But Professor Beazley points out to me that they are not really so: they are talking to each other, and being Greek, need hands for the purpose."

One point of this story is that Greek artists gave supernatural beings not only human features (as in the case of gods) but also human use of

[2] Eitrem 1983: 601: ". . . streckt Athena ihre offene rechte Hand über die Stimmsteine aus, die sich auf dem Altare zu Gunsten ihres Schützlings Odysseus häufen. Die "freudige Anteilnahme" der Göttin, die Pfuhl Meisterstücke . . . feststellt, ist doch wohl hier ein zu schwacher Ausdruck. Sie gewährt mit ihrer rechten Hand göttlichen Beistand, die Abstimmung gibt das Resultat das sie eben wünscht und bewirkt."

[3] Neumann 1965: 99 writes: "Hinter dem Abstimmungstisch fast in der Mitte des Bildes steht Athena, welche auf die für Odysseus niedergelegten Steine herunterblickt, zugleich aber ihren rechten Arm mit der wie verwehrend emporragenden Hand gegen ihrer Schützling ausstreckt, als wolle sie sein freudiges Staunen dämpfen oder zu massvollen Äusserung auffordern."

[4] ἴσας δέ μοι ψήφους διηρίθμησε Πάλλας ὠλένηι. For this interpretation of the line, see Boegehold 1989: 81–83.

hands (as in the case of the sirens). They did not invent a special different divine body language. When accordingly Athena in paintings of the Vote on the Arms stretches her arm out toward Odysseus—or in the one case, Aias—the burden of her announcement is comprehensible to Athenians of the early fifth century, most of whom had known practically forever that Odysseus won and Aias lost. When therefore she points to Odysseus, she is saying, "He wins," and when she points at Aias, she is saying, "He loses." No more, no less. The gesture is in itself neutral and only transmits a specific message in context.

Athena's gesture in Douris's painting could have been used in athletic contests, court trials, and elsewhere in the early fifth century. And ninety years or so later, when Euripides wrote lines 965–66 in his *Iphigeneia among the Taurians*, what he saw in his mind's eye was an actor playing Orestes who made a gesture. The gesture itself may have resembled that of an umpire at a game, possibly larger, more dramatic, to insure that all the theater audience apprehended what was being revealed ("possibly," because at many athletic contests the same need for clarity of signal at a distance obtained). In any case, both could have been the same, an outstretched arm, hand up and fingers loosely extended, signaling by its direction who was being judged winner, and who loser. The fingers do not point.

Neumann 1965: 99 thinks of a warning or muting gesture, which the posture by itself might seem to convey. But in the case of a public announcement, where long-range visibility was the aim, the sweep and direction of the arm motion carried the message. When Orestes remembered the outcome of the trial, his most vivid impression was of that arm, as it was raised in his direction, signifying "You are free." The audience to be sure was not required to believe that Orestes actually saw the goddess (although he certainly does so in another tragedy, Aeschylus's *Eumenides*), but if she did attend the trial and if she did pronounce him free, she would have used a signal like the one judges and umpires use in real life.

Odysseus's expressive posture hardly needs analysis. He has thrown up his hands in surprise and joy. Aias too, it may be thought, can be regarded as expressing anger or frustration, as indeed commentators have observed. But in this particular case, we are aided by adequate literary testimony in our attempts to understand. The emotion Aias feels and expresses is shame, and the act of covering his face is a symbolic expression of that αἰδώς. Odysseus at the court of the Phaeacians hides his face in his cloak for shame. He does not want them to see that Demodokos has made him cry (Homer *Odyssey* 8.83–92). Phaedo covers his face to hide his tears at the finality of Socrates' act, that of drinking down the dose of poison (Plato *Phaedo* 117c). Phaedra asks her nurse to cover her head, again for shame (Euripides *Hippolytos* 243–45), and Heracles covers his head for the same reason (Euripides *Hercules Furens* 1198–1200).[5] Whatever expression, therefore, Aias has on his face—chagrin, tears, anger—he cannot permit himself to show it, and so he covers himself.

In a painting by the Brygos Painter of almost the same scene, Athena points to her left, in the direction of Aias. Hopfkes-Brukker 1935: 32 says that Athena is invisible but that the man nearest her left suddenly sees her, "die ihm mit gebietender Gebärde zuwinkt." Is Athena, however, doing more than beckoning to him in an imperious way? Is she telling him not to do it? Neumann 1965: 37–40 with plates 3, 16, 17, sees this gesture as a defensive or protesting motion. Méautis 1932: 75 says, "Au centre Athéna se tourne vers les deux personnages qui sont à sa gauche et semble vouloir les persuader de voter pour Ulysse, ce qu' ils vont faire du reste, car le geste de leur main montre très nettement que leur suffrage va augmenter le tas, déjà très imposant, des votes en faveur du subtil fils de Laérte." The artist could, however, have meant to say no more than that Athena has directed her attention at this moment to Aias. A Greek viewer knows what she is saying, namely, "The arms go to Odysseus."

Sociabilities

One class of scene, namely a composition on a number of red-figure vases which shows men and women in animated conversation, is tantalizing in that the gestures with which they express themselves are precisely rendered, even to finger positions. One ought to be able to sense something of what they are saying. On an Attic red-figure cup (Figure 23),[6] five standing adults, all fully clad, make up a single scene with two parts. On the left, a man with a staff in his left hand offers a small bag to a woman who holds a bag three times as big in her left hand and raises her right with thumb and forefinger almost touching, other fingers folded in. To the right of this couple, a trio makes up the second part of the whole scene: two men and one woman. One of these men, hand on hip under cloak, gesticulates with his other hand as he speaks to the woman who faces him. He holds up his left hand, thumb and forefingers almost touching, other fingers straight up.[7] The woman with her right hand makes an unmistakable gesture of refusal or denial, her palm, fingers pointing upward and spread,

[5] These examples are taken from Ferrari 1990.

[6] Manner of Douris, British Museum E51, *ARV*² 449.4. Cf. Makron, Munich 2656, *ARV*² 471.186 youths and boys.

[7] Neumann 1965: 13 and note 36 wants to explain the gesture in terms of Quintilian 11.3.92. Quintilian, however, describes the touching of thumb and middle finger ("medius digitus in pollicem contrahitur), not "Zeigefinger" (Neumann's word), which correctly names the finger with which the bearded man in the painting touches his thumb.

opening toward him. A second man stands behind her with a bag or sack or leather flask in one hand, a staff in the other. It is a vivid and detailed scene, but what does it represent? How are we to know whether the men are bargaining or remonstrating, being rude, persuasive, or familiar?

Quintilian 11.3.101–3 may help to interpret the first woman's response. He writes that one does not when asking questions make a hand gesture in just one way, although mostly one does so by turning the hand, no matter what position the fingers are in. When you touch the middle of the right-hand edge of the thumbnail with the tip of your first finger, and the other fingers are loose, it is a nice way to express approval and relate episodes and make distinctions. The Greeks these days especially use a similar gesture, except that the three fingers are folded in, whenever they round off their syllogisms with their gesture as though chopping."[8]

The woman, therefore, if we can use Quintilian as guide, is signaling approval. The terms offered are acceptable. What the gesticulating man in the second part is saying is less clear. If his gesture is a variation of the one just described, he could be asking if his proposed terms are satisfactory. The woman is saying, No, they are not. The man behind her is biding his time.

If we ask what is at issue, we find varying explanations. Keuls 1983: 209–30 discusses a comparable scene on the side of a red-figure kylix by Makron (Figure 24).[9] She sees the scene (and others like it) as a hetaira negotiating with a patron for money. While several of the women in the scene may seem in a photograph to be gesticulating, they are holding flowers. Ferrari 1990: 218 explores the history of interpretation of such scenes and proposes another. The bags held by the men, she suggests, contain *astragaloi,* proper gifts for proper matrons. There are therefore, she concludes, no hetairai involved. In an accompanying scene on the same vase, a man holding a bag converses with a woman who holds up her hand, thumb, and forefinger almost touching, other fingers closed. No money is in evidence. Compare, however, von Bothmer 1982: 42 and the lively scenes on a cup in the Villa Giulia (Figures 25 and 26).[10]

Come Here

A gesture that Greeks use today to say "Come here" was noted above in an introductory section on continuities (p. 28). It is made with the

[8] Pollici proximus digitus mediumque qua dexter est, unguem pollicis summo suo iungens, remissis ceteris, est et approbantibus et narrantibus et distinguentibus decorus. Cui non dissimilis, sed complicitis tribus digitis, quo nunc Graeci plurimum utuntur, etiam utraque manu quotiens enthymemata sua gestu corrotundant velut caesim."

[9] Toledo, Ohio 1972.55, her figs. 14.34a, 14.34b.

[10] Villa Giulia 916.

palm down, arm partially extended, fingers together, thumb touching index and third fingers, or one can merely point to the ground where one wants the person summoned to stand. Quintilian 11.3.94 describes a similar position of the hand as showing insistence on occasion. The gesture can be seen on a pyxis by the Meidias Painter (Figure 27).[11] Aphrodite is pictured as attended by Peitho, Hygeia, Eudaimonia, Paidia, Eukleia, and Eunomia, all represented as female figures, five of whom can be seen in Figures 27 and 28. Eunomia looks to Eukleia who stands next to her and points to the ground. She is saying, "Come here and stand by me." The two figures are linked by their gaze and by their stance. They are turned slightly toward one another to form a duet within the series of personified qualities. For an Athenian contemporary of the painter, Eunomia's gesture could have been as easy to understand as a cartouche in a cartoon is for a modern newspaper reader. But what was there to understand? Why should "Law and Order" be directing "Good Fame" to come and stand by her side?

A roughly contemporary pot may provide a clue. Schefold 1937: 63, 71–72 describes a pot in private possession in Budapest which he dates ca. 400 B.C.E. For comparison of style he cites the Meidias Painter, without, however, comparing the pyxis described above, whose Eunomia he could not have known.[12] The painter of the Budapest pot has a seated Apollo, who looks back and to his right at a female figure labeled EYNOMIA. A second female figure labeled EYKΛEA approaches him from his left. Both females hold myrtle branches (plates 20–23).

Two different artists whose style of ornamentation may link them in time and place have put Eunomia and Eukleia together in the context of a single scene. Is political resonance a possibility? "Eunomia" was a politically charged term at Athens, one that oligarchs tended to make their own, although it is true that the radical democracy at Athens was sustained throughout its life by strong conservative beliefs concerning the law. In the last years of the fifth century, there were two short-lived oligarchic regimes, those of 411 and 404/3. If their moments were brief, their proponents were powerful and articulate men. The personifications of Law and Order coupled with Good Fame may accordingly have had a particular meaning for Athenians of the time. And the beckoning or commanding gesture of Eunomia was full of purpose. Or, to take a more general view, the personifications are in accordance with an aspect of the politics of the time even if they were not deliberately composed to remind an owner and his friends of a specific agenda.

[11] MMA 09.221.40. Shapiro 1993: fig. I, 32–33 with the correction of Ferrari 1995: 17–18. On Eukleia, Shapiro 1993: 70–79; on Eunomia, ibid.: 79–85.

[12] Burn 1987 lists the oinochoe as MM67, i.e., in the manner of the Meidias Painter.

Summary

The Vote on the Arms, a legendary event that in its original telling could not have included such later implements as ballots, inspired a number of early Attic Red Figure painters to compose a version in which Achaian heroes act as judges. Although the heroes in the paintings are not labeled as such, the identification seems sure. In these scenes, Athena, Odysseus, and Aias express themselves vividly by means of gestures that the artists saw around them every day. Some postures, even when widely represented in varying contexts in painting and sculpture, continue to be ambiguous: lively genre scenes in which men and women gesticulate as they converse still do not reveal all of their secrets. In one popular scene, men and woman engage in spirited conversation, using their hands as they speak, either in the midst of some sort of mercantile situation or just concluding. In a third example, labels identify female figures on a pyxis by the Meidias Painter, where (among other personifications) Eukleia and Eunomia are set together by position and by gesture. The labels are consonant with certain political currents of the time.

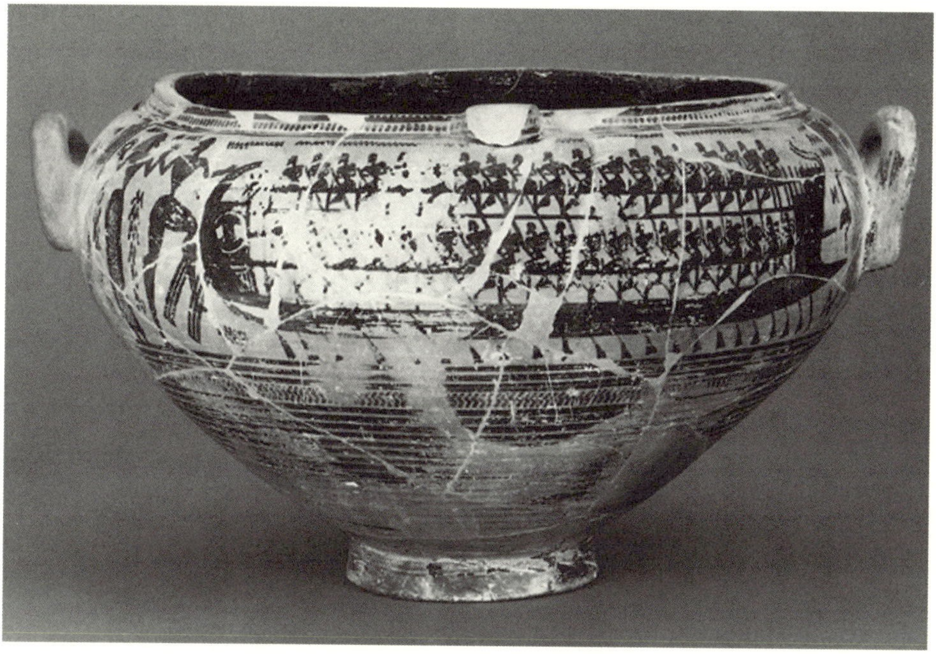

1. A bearded male on an Attic Geometric bowl says farewell (?), leads aboard (?) a woman who holds a wreath. © the British Museum 1899. 2-19.1.

2. Menelaos on an Attic red-figure lekythos with his hand on Helen's wrist. Berlin F 2205. Staatliche Museen zu Berlin–Preussischer Kulturbesitz Antikensammlung.

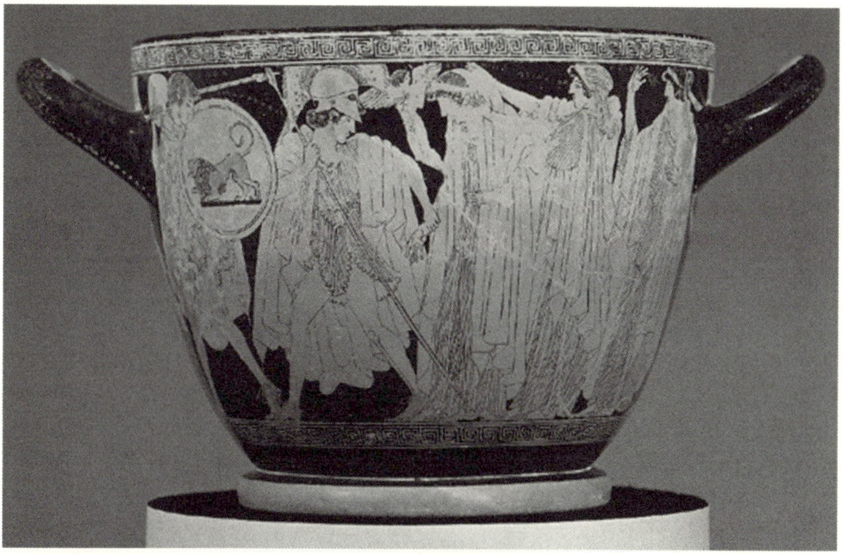

Above 3. Paris, labeled Alexandros here, on an Attic red-figure skyphos leads Helen off to Troy. Museum of Fine Arts. Boston 13.186. Francis Bartlett donation of 1912. Courtesy, Museum of Fine Arts, Boston.

Left 4. Zeus draws Hera to him, hand on wrist. Relief sculpture on a metope, Selinos. Palermo. Museo Nazionale #3921.

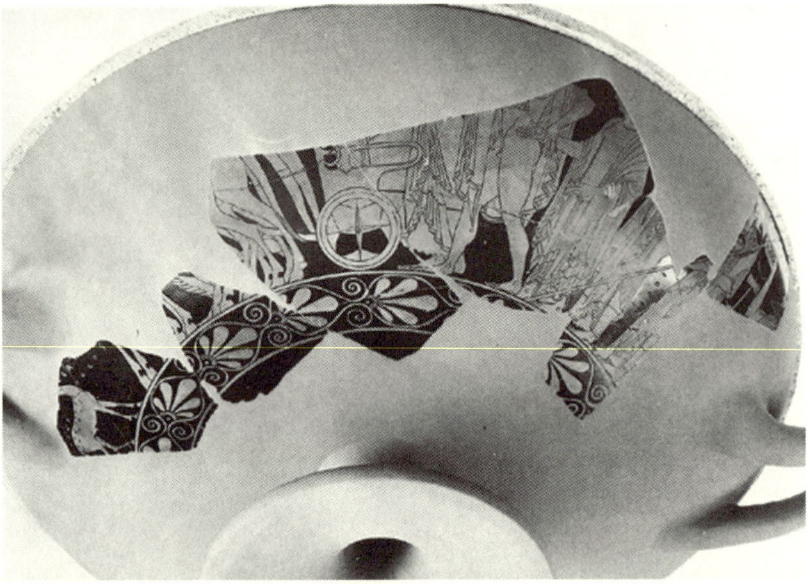

Above 5. Peleus on an Attic lekythos leads Thetis with his hand on her wrist. Athens, National Museum 15214.

Left 6. Women dancing on an Attic black-figure lekythos. Hand on wrist. All rights reserved, The Metropolitan Museum of Art, purchased 1956. Gift of Walter C. Baker (56.11.1).

7. Men and women dancing on a Geometric skyphos from Athens. National Museum 874.

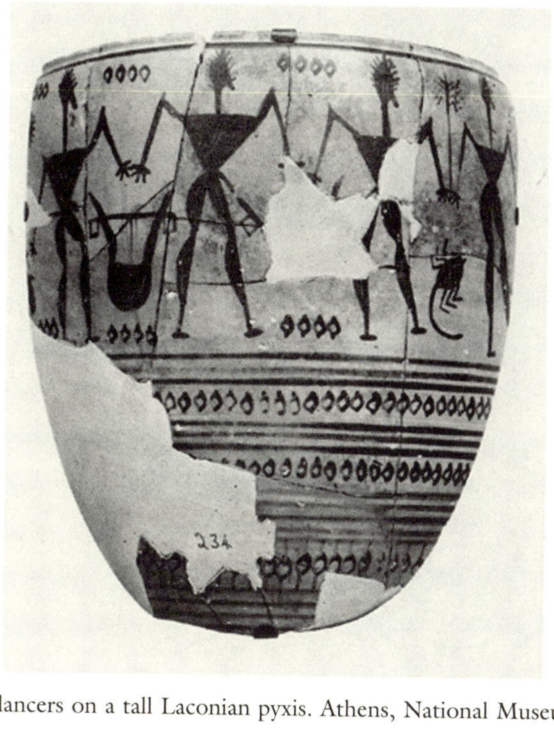

8. Male dancers on a tall Laconian pyxis. Athens, National Museum 234.

Above 9. Athena on an Attic black-figure cup leads Heracles, her right hand on his wrist, and extends her left toward Zeus's chin. © The British Museum B424.

Left 10. The centaur Nessos on the neck of an Attic black-figure amphora pleads in vain for his life. He has managed to touch Heracles' chin with his right hand. Athens, National Museum 1002.

Above 11. The Minotaur in Theseus's fatal grip on a red-figure stamnos attempts to touch Theseus's knee and chin. © The British Museum E441.

Left 12. An enigmatic scene, possibly erotic, on an Archaic Cretan oinochoe. Herakleion 7961.

13. An actor portraying an old woman extends his right hand from his chest while saying, "I shall provide. . . ." Apulian calyx crater. All rights reserved, The Metropolitan Museum of Art, Fletcher Fund, 1924 (24.97.104).

14. Pointing, on an Attic red-figure pelike, with arm, hand, and finger. Surely a universal gesture. Hermitage Museum 615.

15. Oedipus on an Attic red-figure kylix listens attentively as the Sphinx proposes her riddle. Vatican Museum, Archivi Alinari.

16. An inaugural message being delivered at La Maison Française at Wellesley College. Note the attentive postures. Photographed by Gustav Freedman.

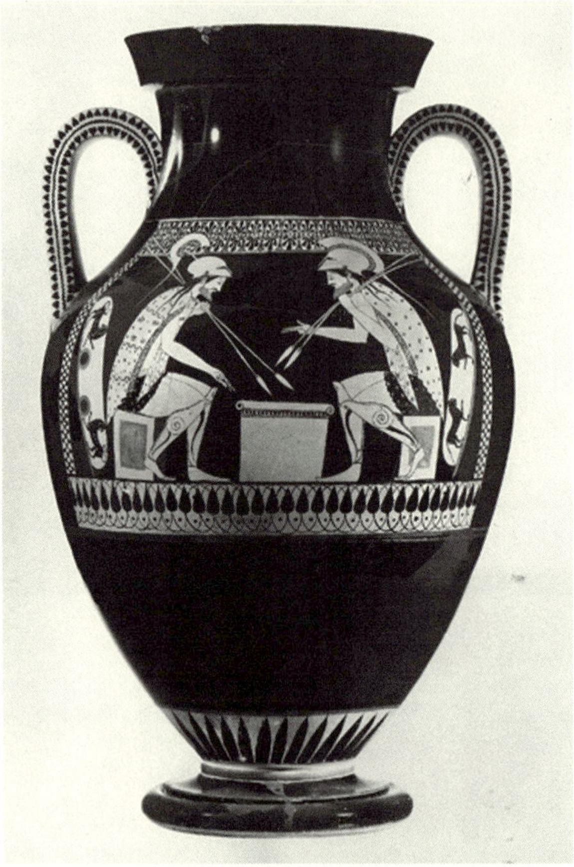

17. Aias, gaming with Achilles on an Attic bilingual amphora, is about to speak. He holds his right hand out with first two fingers extended as a signal. Henry Lille Pierce Fund. Courtesy, Museum of Fine Arts, Boston 01.8037.

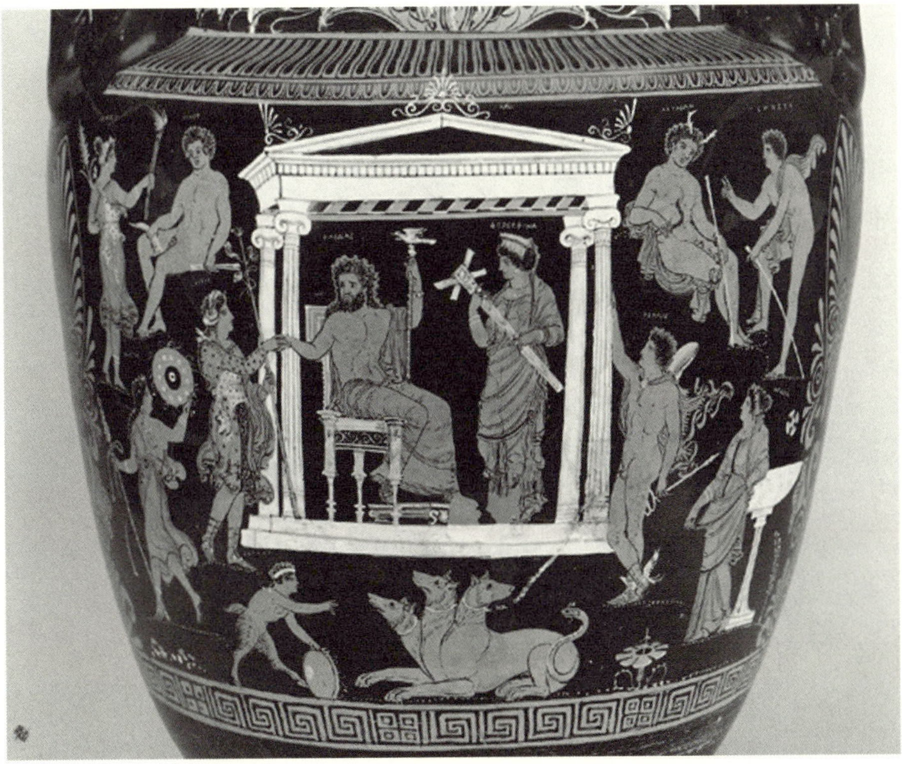

18. Pentheus addresses Actaeon on the upper right of this underworld scene on an Apulian volute crater. The Toledo Museum of Art 1994.19. Gift of Edward Drummond Libbey, Florence Scott Libbey, and the Egypt Exploration Society. By exchange.

77. – P: fol. 16v

78. – C: fol. 10

79. – O: fol. 17

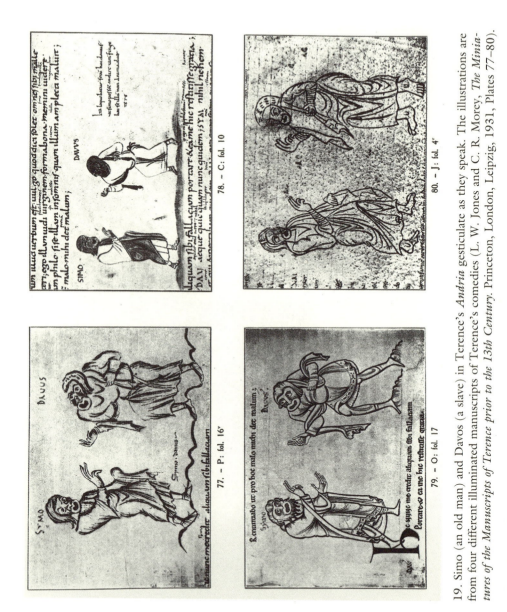

80. – J: fol. 4v

19. Simo (an old man) and Davos (a slave) in Terence's *Andria* gesticulate as they speak. The illustrations are from four different illuminated manuscripts of Terence's comedies (L. W. Jones and C. R. Morey, *The Miniatures of the Manuscripts of Terence prior to the 13th Century*. Princeton, London, Leipzig, 1931, Plates 77–80).

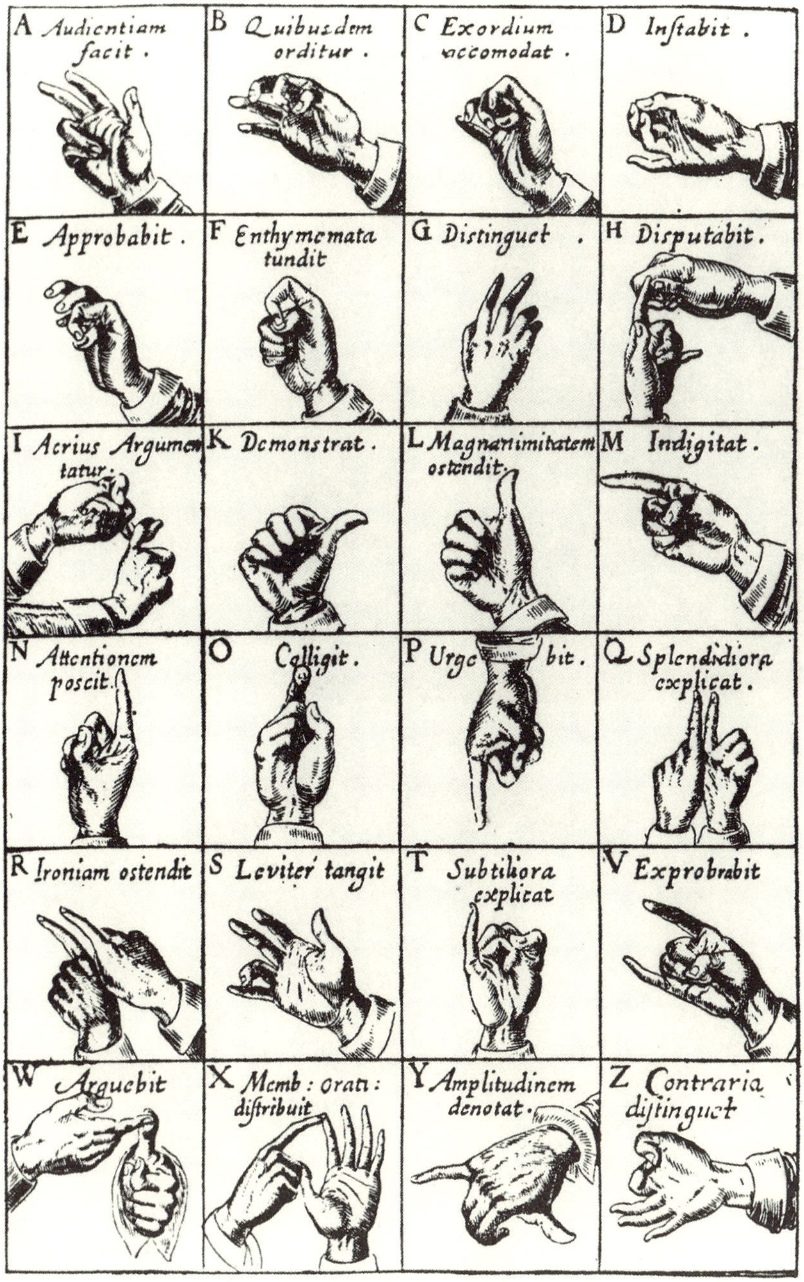

20. In this "Table of Rhetorical Indigitations" (Bulwer 1644), the first gesture (A) alerts hearers. It is not so very different from (G).

Left 21. The goddess Athena on an Attic red-figure pelike says, "Come here." Berlin F 2354. Antikensammlung. Staatliche Museen zu Berlin-Preussischer Kulturbesitz.

Below 22. Athena on an Attic red-figure cup signals Odysseus as winner of Achilles' arms. Odysseus holds up his hands in joy. Aias hides his face. Kunsthistorisches Museum. Vienna 3695.

23. On one side of an Attic red-figure cup, three bearded men and two women converse. © The British Museum E 51.

24. A young man on an Attic red-figure cup offers the contents of a receptacle to a seated woman. An older man does likewise with a standing woman. Toledo Museum of Art. 1972.55. Libbey Endowment. Gift of Edward Drummond Libbey.

25. Mature Athenians on an Attic red-figure cup paying court to adolescents. Villa Giulia 916. *ARV*^{2} 471.197.

26. An erotic scene: men and boys on an Attic red-figure cup paying court to adolescents. Villa Giulia 916. *ARV*^{2} 471.197.

27. A personified Eunomia on an Attic red-figure pyxis summons Eukleia to her side. Paidia sports to the left. All rights reserved, The Metropolitan Museum of Art. Rogers Fund 1909 (09.221.40).

28. A personified Eudaimonia on an Attic red-figure pyxis faces Paidia who balances a stick. At the left, Peitho; at the right, Eukleia. All rights reserved, The Metropolitan Museum of Art. Rogers Fund 1909 (09.221.40).

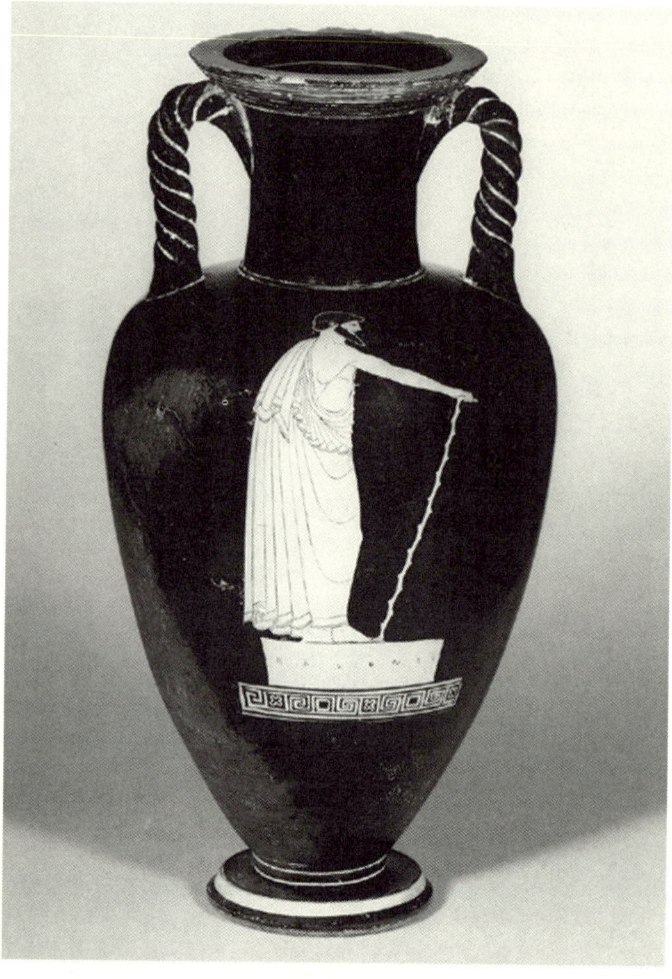

29. A rhapsode on an Attic red-figure neck-amphora as he might have looked performing in the late sixth century. Movement seems implicit in the angle of arm and stick. © The British Museum E 270 A.

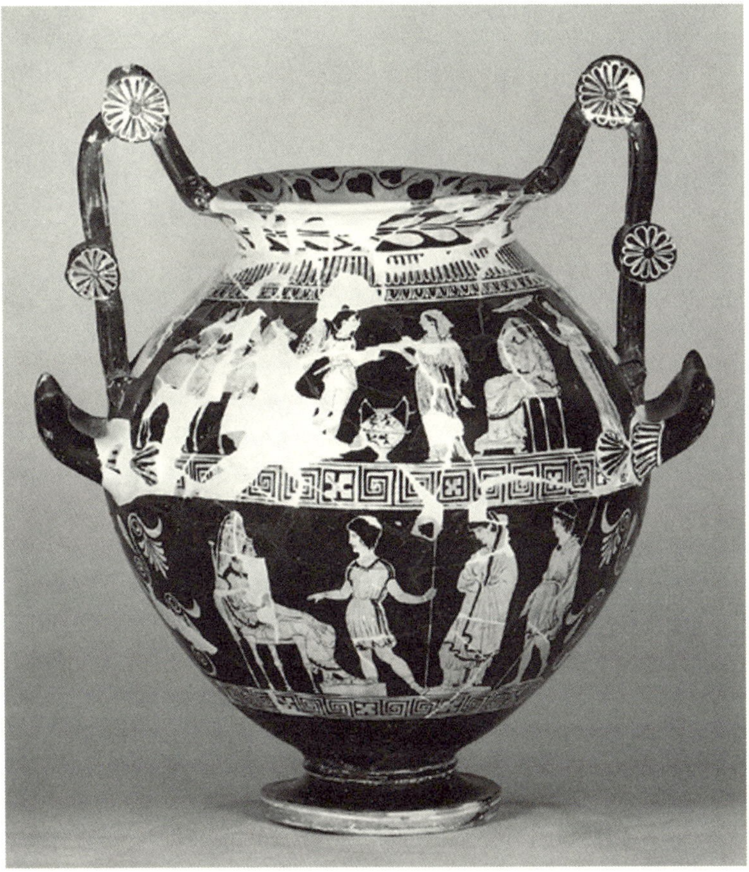

30. The lower register of this Lucanian Nestoris shows Kreon seated listening to the guard's account. Antigone stands behind him, her head (momentarily?) bowed. © The British Museum F 175.

THREE

HOMER

FOR THE PURPOSES of the present discussion, it will be convenient to speak of the author of the *Iliad* and the *Odyssey* as a single poet, named Homer. It will also be assumed without argumentation that the poems were in something like their present form in the eighth century B.C.E. and that they were recited in whole or in parts by succeeding generations of rhapsodes (Figure 29). Plato in the fourth century B.C.E. immortalizes Homeric rhapsodes with his characterization of Ion from Ephesos. Ion feels what he sings and tells how he acts out his songs: he weeps when he recites something piteous from Homer, but his hair stands on end and his heart pounds when he reads something frightening (Plato *Ion* 535c5–8). His head, his hands, and his shoulders, we can imagine, might each and all be put to use in the course of an epic tale. When Socrates addresses him as rhapsode and actor,[1] he certifies with the title "actor" Ion's use of head and hands, posture and gesture.

Demonstrative: Homer *Iliad* 16.844

Consider now such a rhapsode who not only recites but also tells his story with motions of head and hand—indeed, acts out his song. He has come to a strong scene such as that in which Patroclus, dying, addresses Hector, who has just wounded him mortally. "Boast loud now, Hector. For Zeus and Apollo gave you victory, they who conquered me easily. For they themselves took the armor from my shoulders. But such <mortals as you> if twenty had faced me, all would have died, laid low by my spear."[2] The demonstrative pronoun τοιοῦτοι, if only spoken aloud (or, as happens in the case of a modern, printed book, absorbed in the sweep of a solitary perusal) does not have direction. The adversative particle δέ can introduce some masculine plural subject other than Zeus and Apollo, but that is not enough in itself to supply the needed referent. The singer needs to make a gesture here, one that could embrace the mortals who are listening to him, or one that conjures up an imaginary Hector, standing over him.

[1] Rhapsode: British Museum [E 270 A]; Socrates addressing Ion: ῥαψωιδὸς καὶ ὑποκριτής, Plato *Ion* 536a1.

[2] . . .αὐτοὶ γὰρ ἀπ' ὤμων τεύχε' ἕλοντο/ τοιοῦτοι δ' εἴ πέρ μοι ἐείκοσιν ἀντεβόλησαν.

That way, he gives τοιοῦτοι its direction, and his hearers understand that Patroclus is saying "mortals such as you."[3]

What would that gesture be? How can a bard tell an audience that by his demonstrative pronoun he means "such as you"? Perhaps, since he has already established that Patroclus is addressing Hector, he could use a gesture by which one would emphasize a point while in conversation with another person. The merest nod or outward flutter of the hand would in that case situate Hector.

"Incomplete" Conditional Sentence

It is appropriate to introduce here a formulation that will appear in almost every succeeding chapter of this study. Grammarians of late antiquity applied the descriptive term ἀνανταπόδοσις (anantapodosis) to conditional sentences that seemed to lack the expected balancing clause, an apodosis (Anonymus *de Figuris*, (**A**) Spengel 1856: 157). But that lack is only apparent in most cases. For such sentences did not actually lack an apodosis in the author's original or final conception nor did they in a performer's execution. Consider to begin with what a conditional sentence is. It consists of an independent clause (apodosis) and a subordinate clause (protasis). The independent clause can be a plain statement of fact, a wish, a speculation, a question, an order—in short, any imaginable declaration that does not require another clause to complete its full sense.

Now suppose the apodosis to be supplied is as simple as yes or no or "It will be all right." These three messages almost everywhere and certainly in Greece are likely when spoken to be accompanied by a motion of hand or head. But they are each of them simple enough to be expressed by means of the motions alone, or indeed by a mere change of facial expression. Consequently, when an author wants to represent his characters talking as they might in actual life, and when he knows his text is going to be read aloud, he can use ellipsis to prompt a reader to improvise, i.e., to fill in blanks with gestures. The early grammarians, however, did not envision the gestures that Archaic and Classical authors knew would supply an apodosis, and so they called the sentences incomplete.

A few quotations from eminent authorities will attest the long and uninterrupted life of a presumption that derives from the scheme and the nomenclature. Goodwin 1900: 179, no. 482 says: "The apodosis is sometimes omitted when some such expression as 'it is well' or 'it will be well' can be supplied, or when some other apodosis is suggested by con-

[3] Bérard 1918 presents and discusses numerous other instances in Homer *Iliad* and *Odyssey* where a demonstrative pronoun requires a complementary gesture.

text." Kühner-Gerth 1904: II.2.484–85 ascribe to Attic writers especially a practice of leaving out the first apodosis when it is easy to supply, and going on to the following, more important one: "Oft wird, besonders bei den Attikern, wenn zwei Bedingungssätze durch εἰ (ἐὰν) μέν . . . εἰ (ἐὰν) δὲ μή entgegengesetzt werden, bei dem ersteren die Apodosis weggelassen, indem dieselbe einen leicht zu ergänzenden Gedanken enthält, und die Rede zum folgenden wichtigeren Gedanken eilt." Chantraine 1953: 274–75 similarly makes a general rule concerning such conditions, saying that when two protases are presented as alternates, the apodosis is only expressed after the protasis considered the most important. In other cases an apodosis can be omitted when it comes of itself (". . . lorsque la consequence va de soi").

But note the internal contradiction in Goodwin's counsel as it stands: "the apodosis is sometimes omitted" is contradicted by " 'it is well' . . . can be supplied." What Goodwin meant but did not say, we suppose, is "can be supplied in the reader's imagination." Kühner-Gerth cite a number of examples that are discussed below, e.g., Homer *Iliad* 1.135 (pp. 40–41), Herodotus 8.62 (p. 98), Thucydides 3.3 (p. 99), Xenophon *Anabasis* 7.7.15 (p. 106), *Memorabilia* 3.1.9 (pp. 106–7), *Cyropaideia* 4.10.5, 7.5.54, 8.7.24 (pp. 107–8 below), Plato *Republic* 575d (p. 124 below), *Protagoras* 325d (pp. 123–24).

For the present, let it suffice to say that in each of these instances a simple gesture can provide an apodosis. A nod of the head can say yes as clearly as a spoken or written word. A wave of the hand can say "It is well" or "It would be well" so that no one would mistake the meaning. A modest note to the effect that a gesture can supply an apodosis would be helpful in our grammars. In the present study I use the phrase " 'incomplete' conditional sentence," in place of the unwieldy *anantapodosis.*

Aposiopesis

Kühner-Gerth 1904: II.2 note Homer *Iliad* 1.580–81, an "incomplete" conditional sentence, as an example of aposiopesis.[4] It is argued below, however (p. 42), that the lines constitute an early example of an apodosis provided by gesture. The word *aposiopesis* describes accurately enough a falling silent, but when it denotes a purposeful rhetorical technique, the sense is that the silence is the desired effect. It is a silence showing reluctance to pronounce a word or phrase that is either too awful or shocking or

[4] Cf. Schwyzer 1966: 687, who concurs.

shameful to utter, or that may require listeners to supply the word out of their own vocabulary and expectations (duly prepared by the speaker).

Kühner-Gerth, 1904: II.2, 571–72 give examples of both desired effects. An example of the first comes from Sophocles' *Oedipus the King*: "He shouts for someone to show to all the Cadmeans the father-killer, the mother, . . ."[5] that is, the audience must supply for themselves the violent word that means "corrupter" or "stainer." A scholiast explains, "He is silent here for shame."[6] An example of the second is presented in Demosthenes 18.3, where the orator does not tell exactly what the disadvantage is to which he alludes. By means of a tactical silence, he avoids saying what might be construed as a test of fate or as arrogance. He says: "Because for me now to lose your good will and for him to lose the case are not equally important for me. For me—I do not want to say anything at the beginning of my talk that might cause trouble—while he is accusing me from an advantageous position."[7] What the audience is to understand is that for Demosthenes to lose the general approbation of the Athenians would be a great catastrophe, while for Aeschines to lose his case would be no more than another in a series of losses in a grubby life.

A third kind of aposiopesis differs from these two in intention and effect. Where the first prompts listeners to supply an obvious but in some way awful word or phrase, one that a character/performer cannot bring himself to utter, and the second plants in hearers a notion that the speaker wants them to have but that would sound wrong coming from his own mouth, the third is a falling silent only in the strict sense of the word. For when in a conditional sentence the apodosis is supplied by a gesture, the lack of a written or spoken apodosis is not in its actual effect a falling silent, because the hearer does not have to complete the sentence in his mind. A sentence has been completed by hand or head movement rather than by tongue and vocal chords.

Gesture for Apodosis

Once we recognize that nonverbal communication by means of gesture was an integral function of discourse in ancient Greece, we see in a different light a long series of apparent ellipses in Archaic and Classical Greek

[5] βοᾶι . . . δηλοῦν τινα τοῖς πᾶσι Καδμείοισι τὸν πατροκτόνον, τὸν μητρὸς *sc.* μιάστορα, Sophocles *Oedipus the King* 1287–89.

[6] Schol. *Oedipus the King* 1289: σιγᾶι δὲ τοῦτο διὰ τὸ αἰσχρόν.

[7] οὐ γάρ ἐστιν ἴσον νῦν ἐμοὶ τῆς παρ' ὑμῶν εὐνοίας διαμαρτεῖν καὶ τούτωι μὴ ἑλεῖν τὴν γραφήν, ἀλλ' ἐμοὶ μὲν—οὐ βούλομαι δυσχερὲς εἰπεῖν οὐδὲν ἀρχόμενος τοῦ λόγου, οὗτος δ' ἐκ περιουσίας μου κατηγορεῖ.

literature. In this chapter, examples are presented of sentences in which an apodosis (mostly) or protasis (rarely) was expressed by gesture.

WELL AND GOOD: HOMER *ILIAD* 1.134–39

In the first book of Homer's *Iliad*, Agamemnon in anger addresses Achilles. "Are you telling me to give her back? Well, if the great-hearted Achaians will give me a prize, fitting it to my liking, so that it is of equal value—. But if they do not give <such a prize>, then I shall go and take your prize or Aias's, or I shall take Odysseus's and lead <her off>."[8]

This is a fairly literal translation of the Greek, with angle brackets showing nouns that can easily be supplied. It shows an incomplete sentence. Agamemnon does not say in these hexameters what the result will be if the Achaeans do give him an appropriate gift. Why does he not do so? Why did Homer leave that part of the sentence out?

The question was addressed early on by a scholiast: "The deliberate omission is Attic and characteristic of earlier writers, as for example Aristophanes. . . . For in every case, the phrase, 'It will be all right,' is missing, as here."[9]

Compare now Eustathios, Archbishop of Thessaloniki in the twelfth century. He writes of Agamemnon's threat as follows: "The syntax limps, and because it remains hanging, it is not complete. There is missing the phrase, 'I shall be content' or 'I shall stop' or some such thing, so that he says, 'if they will give, I will be still.' It has been left out in the manner of earlier writers (ἀρχαικῶς) by reason of its being obvious from where it is. Because who does not know that if the Achaeans will give him his prize, the king will be still? There are other such forms of ellipsis among the ancients [various examples here]. But the people who put the sentence in order with 'it will be' and remove thereby the ellipsis make the interpretation syntactical, but they damage the Homeric excellence, and erase the representation of an angry man, and they say nothing serious. For they claim that 'But if the Achaians will give me a prize, so that it is in that way of equal value, it will be,' i.e., the matter will be all right. And they do not know that they are healing the ellipsis by an ellipsis again, and that a cold one. For in the 'it will be' there is lacking the word 'good' or 'right' or some such, for him to say that it will be right or good. The Homeric ellipsis, I think, is better than an elliptical construction like that."[10]

[8] . . . κέλεαι δέ με τήνδ' ἀποδοῦναι, ἀλλ' εἰ μὲν δώσουσι γέρας μεγάθυμοι Ἀχαιοί, ἄρσαντες κατὰ θυμόν, ὅπως ἀντάξιον ἔσται. εἰ δέ κε μὴ δώωσιν, ἐγὼ δέ κεν αὐτὸς ἕλωμαι ἢ τεὸν ἢ Αἴαντος ἰὼν γέρας, ἢ Ὀδυσῆος ἄξω ἑλών) Homer *Iliad* 1.134-39.

[9] Ἀττικὴ τῶν προτέρων ἡ παράλειψις . . . here he gives examples from Aristophanes . . . ἐπὶ γὰρ πάντων τὸ καλῶς ἔχει ὡς καὶ ἐνταῦθα ἐλλείπει, Schol. Homer *Iliad* 1.135.

[10] Eustathios 66.26-40 (1.106.2–21).

In both of these early recognitions of an "incomplete" conditional sentence, the writer refers the practice back to earlier times: τῶν προτέρων in the commentary of the scholiast, ἀρχαικῶς in that of Eustathios. These commentators were writing at a time when people read silently to themselves and for that reason they did not assume that the texts on which they commented were written to be read aloud and performed. Greeks in Eustathios's day surely used their hands when they spoke, and they could read aloud whenever they wanted, but the composition of a written text no longer had as an abiding presence a person who performed while reciting or reading it aloud. The ellipse in question was, just as Eustathios said, from an older time and did indeed signify an older way of presenting a poem.

A poetic translation in the twentieth century like that of Robert Fitzgerald or Richmond Lattimore resolves such questions without comment,[11] but editors of scholarly editions must alert readers to the apparent lack of a clause. (**A**) Leaf 1895 *ad loc.* writes, "The apodosis of the clause εἰ δώσουσι has to be supplied." (**A**) Monro 1906 *ad loc.*: "The apodosis is left unexpressed because it is only on the second of the two alternatives (if they do not give) that anything is to follow." (**A**) Kirk 1985 *ad loc.*: "A difficult verse: ὅπως ἀντάξιον ἔσται cannot mean 'see to it that . . .', or at least this construction is not paralleled in Homer. Rather '(let them give it) fitting it to my wishes, in such a way that it will be a just equivalent.' " (**A**) Ameis-Hentze 1965 *ad loc.* complete the sentence by invoking a gesture: "Dass er dann zufrieden würde, deutet er durch eine Gebärde an." Goodwin 1900: 179, no. 482, writes, "The apodosis is sometimes omitted when some such expression as 'it is well' or 'it will be well' can be supplied, or when some other apodosis is at once suggested by context." Wakker 1994: 395, note 64 writes, "The omission of the apodosis suggests that Agamemnon is getting more and more angry while he speaks and hastily proceeds to the second alternative."

The explanation in Ameis-Hentze touches on the scenario proposed above in connection with Homer *Iliad* 16.844–47 (pp. 36–37 above). Leaf's comment is almost mysterious: he does not hint at how the apodosis is to be supplied, nor by whom. Monro likewise does not really face the question. Wakker's evocation of ethopoeia can be accepted without excluding further speculation concerning delivery. Ameis-Hentze intuit a gesture made by Agamemnon, and this is true insofar as the rhapsode has become for the moment Agamemnon. But one could helpfully add, "The poet himself (or in later generations, the rhapsode) acting as Agamemnon completes whatever sense is needed with a gesture."

[11] (**B**) Fitzgerald 1974: "The army will award a prize to me and make sure it measures up, or if they do not etc."; (**B**) Lattimore 1951: "Either the great-hearted Achaians shall

BEWARE! HOMER *ILIAD* 1.580–81

Ameis-Hentze in their commentary to another passage (Homer *Iliad* 1.580–81) may be saying just this. Hephaistos is speaking: "For if lightning-maker Zeus wants to hurl us from our seats—for he is far the strongest. . . ."[12]

So a literal translation runs. In a poetic translation into English one might justify a minor, yet virtual distortion, as the adroit version of (**B**) Robert Fagles 1990 illustrates: "The Olympian lord of lightning—what if he would like to blast us from our seats? He is far too strong." But Ameis-Hentze tell their student readers that Homer has left what follows for the reader to imagine: the speaker indicates it by a gesture. Here I only wish to emphasize that "the speaker" is at once Hephaistos and the singer who is in effect performing at that moment the role of Hephaistos.[13] The audience, all of whom reinforced their own day-to-day communications with a multiplicity of gesture, accepted the convention as naturally as breathing, just as the poet, when he originally composed the line, knew he could leave out the apodosis, because the sense would be adequately transmitted by gesture, his own or that of any successor he could imagine. The line, when the force of a gesture is registered, can be represented as follows: "For if lightning-maker Zeus wants to hurl us from our seats <GESTURE = Beware!> for he is far the strongest."

WELL AND GOOD: HOMER *ILIAD* 16.559–61

Homer *Iliad* 16.559–61 may present another sentence completed by a gesture that says "well and good." Patroclus in the heat of battle urges the two Aiases to gain control of Sarpedon's corpse. He shouts: "If we could get him and savage him, strip the armor from his shoulders, and cut down with pitiless bronze any comrade of his who tries to defend him . . ."[14] The protasis has been explained as a wish, but not to everyone's satisfaction.[15] Suppose instead we see a rhapsode complete that condition

give me a new prize, chosen according to my desire to atone for the girl lost, or else if they will not give me . . . etc."

[12] εἴ περ γάρ κ' ἐθέλησιν 'Ολύμπιος ἀστεροπητὴς/ ἐξ ἑδέων στυφαλίξαι· ὁ γὰρ πολὺ φέρτατός ἐστιν.

[13] (**A**) Ameis-Hentze 1965 *ad loc.*: "A condition without a conclusion, where it is left to the audience to imagine the consequences themselves: the speaker indicates them by means of a gesture."

[14] ἀλλ' εἴ μιν ἀεικισσαίμεθ' ἑλόντες/ τεύχεά τ' ὤμοιιν ἀφελοίμεθα, καί τιν' ἑταίρων/ αὐτοῦ ἀμυνομένων δαμασαίμεθα νηλέϊ χαλκῷ.

[15] A scholiast at Homer *Iliad* 16.559 ((**A**) Erbse 1975: 276–77) says that one must understand "it would be well" (καλῶς ἂν ἔχοι) here. Another says, "Read 'would that' (εἴθε γὰρ) for if (εἴ μιν). Monro 1891: 285, para. 312 comments, "The Conditional Protasis

with an emphatic version of the gesture that means "well and good." The sense then is complete, and removed from questions about Homer's use of εἰ without γάϱ to signify a wish.

I ASSURE YOU: HOMER *ODYSSEY* 1.187–89

To take another instance of a missing apodosis, in the first book of Homer's *Odyssey*, Athena is presenting herself to Telemachus as one Mentes. She says: "I claim that we are guest friends to each other from the beginning, if you just go to the old hero Laertes and ask."[16] Now what is missing is an assurance that Telemachus will find that it is so if he goes to Laertes. Ameis-Hentze here envision Athena as seeing doubt in Telemachus's face and for that reason offering assurance. What, however, would the singer have done at this point? Can it not be surmised that there was a widely recognized gesture, one by which you could say, "You will know for a certainty," a reassurance that comes up over and over again in civilized discourse everywhere? A mere emphatic nod yes of the head would be enough to convey the sense.

YES: HOMER *ILIAD* 6.150

A nod of the head for yes would complete another Homeric line that has provoked extensive editorial comment. Glaucus and Diomedes confront one another on the battlefield, and Diomedes asks Glaucus to identify himself. Glaucus adduces the justly famous simile, "lives of mortals and the generations of leaves" and then begins: "But if you want to know even this, so that you know well, our lineage—many men know it—there is a city . . .[17]

(**A**) Kirk 1990: 176 provides a neat summary of previous commentary on the seeming ellipsis: "There are several ways of construing these vv. . . .(i) with Aristarchus . . . to punctuate after εἰ ἐθέλεις and take the infinitive δαήμεναι as imperative; (ii) to make δαήμεναι depend on ἐθέλεις which is rhythmically smoother, in which case, either (a) ὄφϱ' ἐὺ εἰδῇς is parenthetical and the object of δαήμεναι is γενέην (Ameis-Hentze); or (b) πολλοὶ δέ is the apodosis (with δέ redundant, i.e., apodotic) leaving

when used without an apodosis becomes a wish. . . . More frequently a wish is introduced by εἰ γάϱ or αἲ γὰϱ."

[16] ξεῖνοι δ' ἀλλήλων πατϱώιοι εὐχόμεθα εἶναι ἐξ ἀϱχῆς, εἴ πέϱ τε γέϱοντ' εἴϱηαι ἐπελθὼν Λαέϱτην ἥϱωα. (**A**) Stanford 1967: 234, *ad loc.* comments, "The apodosis, which would be something like 'you will find this to be true' is omitted when the sentence rambles away into a description of the present condition of Laertes."

[17] εἰ δ' ἐθέλεις καὶ ταῦτα δαήμεναι, ὄφϱ εὖ εἰδῇς/ ἡμετέϱην γενέην, πολλοὶ δέ μιν ἄνδϱες ἴσασιν/ ἔστι πόλις 'Εφύϱη.

'and you shall know it too' *vel sim.* to be understood; or (c) with Leaf the apodosis is 152 ἔστι πόλις . . . , i.e. the beginning of the genealogy itself."

But if we imagine a nod for yes, the singer filling in with his own nonverbal communication what was in Homer's mind when he wrote the line, a literal translation <amplified> would run as follows: "But if you want to know even this, so that you know well <NOD = Yes, I assent, I will tell you>. There is a city . . ."

I'LL SHOW YOU: HOMER *ILIAD* 21.487–89

The Olympian gods have now joined the battle, and Artemis has incautiously (or with the marmoreal assurance of a god) rebuked Apollo for avoiding combat with Poseidon. Hera in response descends on her. She says: "If you want to learn about war—for you to learn how much stronger I am, because you are pitting your strength against mine . . . " And then Homer describes the physical action that completes Hera's conditional sentence. That is, she completes her thought with her hands: "She seized both her hands by the wrist." In that way his narrative description of Hera's violent physical action tells how Hera completed her sentence.[18] Would a bard limn that unspoken apodosis with a gesture? My feeling is that he would, that he would have said "I'll show you" with his hands or shoulders, as he switched into his narrative mode.

SO WHAT! HOMER *ODYSSEY* 21.259–62

Antinoös, chief of Penelope's doomed suitors, counsels Eurymachos, another suitor, to put aside for the day concerns for Odysseus's bow, and for the axes. "Be calm," he says, "If we just leave all the axes be <GESTURE = What could possibly come of it?> Because I do not think anyone will come into the megaron of Odysseus, Laertes' son, and take them."[19] Today, in the United States, the gesture would be a shrug of the shoulders transmitting the message "So what?" In Archaic Greece, if men and women did not shrug their shoulders, they surely had an equivalent way of saying the same thing with their hands or bodies.[20]

[18] εἰ δ' ἐθέλεις πολέμοιο δαήμεναι ὄφρ' εὖ εἰδῇς/ ὅσσον φερτέρη εἴμ', ὅτι μοι μένος ἀντιφερίζεις/ ἦ ῥα καὶ ἀμφοτέρας ἐπὶ καρπῶι χεῖρας ἔμαρπτε. Cf. Chantraine 1953: 275: "It is Hera's hand motion at line 489 that provides the apodosis."

[19] ἀλλὰ ἕκηλοι / κάτθετ' ἀτὰρ πελέκεάς γε καὶ εἴ κ' εἰῶμεν ἅπαντας/ ἑστάμεν· οὐ μὲν γάρ τιν' ἀναιρήσεσθαι οἴω/ ἐλθόντ' ἐς μέγαρον Λαερτιάδεω 'Οδυσῆος.

[20] A scholiast to Homer *Iliad* 16.569 says that καλῶς ἂν ἔχοι should be understood here. This tends to be the phrase that ancient commentators invoke to fill ellipses, but its universal applicability has not been established. On shrugging, see p. 115, note 9 below.

Gesture For Protasis

Kühner-Gerth 1904: II.485, note 1 say that lines such as Homer *Iliad* 1.524, 302; 7.376 et al. used to be considered partial ellipses, so that εἰ δὲ ἄγε (But if . . . come now) and once even εἰ δέ (But if . . .) were thought to be shortened ways of saying εἰ δὲ βούλει ἄγε (But if you wish, come now). But now, they affirm, εἰ (if) has its own independent force as an exhortation or wish. But here again a simple gesture could easily fill in the sense required, namely, "If you please." Two examples, both from the ninth book of the *Iliad*, are instructive.

IF YOU LIKE: HOMER *ILIAD* 9.46–47

An apodosis supplied by gesture has completed some sentences discussed above. We turn now to a sentence whose protasis may have been expressed by gesture. Diomedes is reproaching Agamemnon, who has just recommended that the Achaian host return home and not conquer Troy. Diomedes tells Agamemnon to go if he wants but that "the rest of the long-haired Achaians will stay until we take Troy. But—if you like—let them flee too in their ships to their homelands, and the two of us, Sthenelos and I, will fight until we reach Ilion, our goal."[21]

Modern authorities generally agree to abide by the interpretation of an ancient commentator who says that εἰ here has the force of an exhortation (δύναμιν παρακελευστικήν) that emphasizes the following imperative, viz., φευγόντων (let them flee). The sense of the line accordingly would be, "All right, let them flee too." It follows that if εἰ is an exhortation, then the sentence is not a conditional sentence and therefore no protasis is lacking.[22]

But consider the sentence now as one that will be performed. Suppose that εἰ δέ prompted a gesture in certain contexts that said in effect: "If you like," or "If you please." What that gesture would have been in Archaic Greece we do not know. In some societies today, a nod and an opening of the right arm would serve. If we assume that there was some such gesture, lines 46–47 could be construed—with amplification—as follows: "But if <GESTURE = you like> let them also flee in their ships to their homelands." The gesture would be one that accompanied a full formulation, namely, εἰ δὲ βούλει, in conversation.

[21] The critical Greek words are εἰ δὲ καὶ αὐτοί/ φευγόντων σὺν νηυσὶ ἐς πατρίδα γαῖαν.

[22] A representative selection of modern authorities who subscribe to this interpretation includes the following: (**A**) Leaf 1895 *ad loc.*, (**A**) Erbse 1971 *ad loc.*, Monro 1891: 291–92, para. 320, LSJ *s.v.* εἰ, Hainsworth *apud* (**A**) Kirk 1993 *ad loc.*

The scholiast who counsels that εἰ be read as exhortation records two other lines of interpretation current in his time: "Some say 'they want' is missing and place a comma after the word αὐτοί; others take ἐπέσσυται ὥστε νέεσθαι (<if you yourself> are eager to return) as a common construction from above" (i.e., line 47). This second version yields a sentence in which "if you yourself are eager to return" would be understood as the protasis of a sentence that began: "And if they <too are eager to return>, let them flee." He judges both efforts inferior.[23]

Although neither of these two other readings is in accord with the one I have proposed as performed, both assume what modern authorities deny, namely that there is an ellipsis. Now the scholiast and his authorities were native speakers of the language. If they perceive an ellipsis, we later readers should take that perception seriously. It is this ellipsis that a gesture could have filled.

IF YOU PLEASE: HOMER *ILIAD* 9.262

A second instance of εἰ δέ plus imperative is regularly cited to support the view that εἰ functions as exhortation. It is likewise found in Book 9. Odysseus, in trying to persuade Achilles to return to the fight, says, εἰ δὲ σὺ μέν μευ ἄκουσον, ἐγὼ δέ κέ τοι καταλέξω, which a canonical reading would turn into something like, "Come now, listen to me, and I will list for you." But if the gesture is imagined, one that invites the hearer to participate in the transaction, then the sense would be "If <GESTURE = you please> listen to me and I will list for you." The combination of conjunction plus particle need not have in itself much more force than "please," but with proper emphasis and placement it can also be strong.

Summary

To sum up this chapter, evidence is presented for a deduction that rhapsodes acted out to some degree the works they recited. Homer anticipated the rhapsodes' (or his own) performance and employed elements of that performance as he composed. It is therefore not quite enough to say that such and such a character in the story makes a suitable gesture, for that explanation does not include the author's creative manipulation of syntax (as its rules are conceived by later grammarians). Homer's syntax includes nonverbal communication as well as words. Accordingly, when we invoke gesture to explain an ambiguity or an anacolouthon in a text, let us note also that for the poet both forms of expression, the verbal and the corporal,

[23] (**A**) Erbse 1971 *ad loc.*

are so closely intertwined as to be indistinguishable at times. A poet or rhapsode provided the gestures that established clarity and consequence. A corollary follows naturally: it is that the word *aposiopesis* is not in itself without qualification appropriate in every case as a way of explaining ellipses, because physical movement, while it may be silent, does nevertheless transmit information. It is the writing that makes sentences appear to be elliptical. A speaker would have filled such silences with expressive body language.

Two lines from the Palatine Anthology, 9.505.17–18, can conclude this chapter. A Muse, not named, is speaking: "I am silent as my hand moves rhythmically in a way that enchants the spirit; with a nod I announce a speaking silence."[24]

[24] σιγῶ φθεγγομένης παλάμης θελξίφρονα παλμόν/ νεύματι φωνήεσσαν ἀπαγγελοῦσα σιωπήν.

FOUR

ARCHAIC POETS

TWO RENOWNED POETS, one, Archilochus, who lived in the early Archaic age of Greece, and the other, Pindar, who lived at its close and on into the time we call Classical, repay study at this point. Their audiences and their modes of performance may have differed, but the two poets spoke the same essential language, and that language included nonverbal communication.[1]

Archilochus

What we have of Archilochus's poetry may all be fragments. Mostly the fragments are preserved because a later writer quoted single words, a line or two, or even sometimes several stanzas of a poem, in the course of an explanation or demonstration; a few fragments were saved as poems copied onto papyrus. Thanks to the quotations, or to the author who introduces the quotation, we learn that a speaker in a poem who uses the first person singular is not necessarily Archilochus himself.

ARCHILOCHUS 19

Aristotle *Rhetoric* 1418b23 cites Archilochus's well-known poem on Gyges' wealth as an instance where the poet has a character speaking. In this case it is Charon the carpenter:

> I don't care what Gyges has with all his gold.
> Envy has not caught me yet and I don't
> admire gods' works and I don't love tyranny;
> they are far from my eyes.[2]
>
> frag. 19

Now when Archilochus recited these lines, he was acting a part, that of Charon, an ?independent? and ?threadbare? carpenter. How would

[1] Burnett 1983: 32 says of Archilochus's songs: "Some were meant for public ceremonies—funerals, military reviews, or festive rituals—and some perhaps were made for less regular occasions when roaming bands of men used the streets for serenades that might be appreciative or the opposite." On Pindar's audiences, see Lefkowitz 1995: 139–50.

[2] οὔ μοι τὰ Γύγεω τοῦ πολυχρύσου μέλει/ οὐδ' εἶλέ πώ με ζῆλος, οὐδ' ἀγαίομαι/ θεῶν ἔργα, μεγάλης δ' οὐκ ἐρέω τυραννίδος/ ἀπόπροθεν γάρ ἐστιν ὀφθαλμῶν ἐμῶν.

Archilochus have acted the part? At a bare minimum he would tilt his head back for "no" and touch his own chest for "me." And the last line seems to ask for a gesture of some kind if only a finger pointing to the eyes.

ARCHILOCHUS 5

Fragment 5 may be a complete poem. Is it therefore autobiographical? Who was it who left his shield in a bush?

> A Saian is happy with my shield—in a bush
> I left it, a blameless one, not wanting to,
> but I saved myself. Why does that shield bother me?
> Forget it. I'll own one another time no worse.[3]

Was it Archilochus, or was it a character in his poem? In either case Archilochus in reciting the poem could have touched his chest when he said, "I saved myself " (ψυχὴν δ' ἐξεσάωσα); and when he said "Forget it" (ἐρρέτω), he could make a chopping motion with his hand that said, "This shield has now been totally eliminated from my mind."

ARCHILOCHUS 43

Neither the identity nor the profession of the speaker in fragment 43 is attested. He or she says of some local valiant:

> His cock like that of an ass—Prienian . . .
> stallion . . . would ejaculate . . . a well-fed one.[4]

The reciter on conjuring up the size of the man's equipment could not fail—in a society where one spoke with one's hands—to hold up both hands to show how big.

ARCHILOCHUS 31

A gentler celebration of physical characteristics could also prompt gesticulation. "Her hair made a shade for her shoulders and back."[5] The poet may be praising a lover; he might have touched his own hair and shoulders as he spoke the lines.

[3] ἀσπίδι μὲν Σαίων τις ἀγάλλεται, ἣν παρὰ θάμνωι/ ἔντος ἀμώμητον, κάλλιπον οὐκ ἐθέλων/ αὐτὸν δ' ἐξεσάωσα. τί μοι μέλει ἀσπὶς ἐκείνη / ἐρρέτω· ἐξαῦτις κτήσομαι οὐ κακίω.

[4] ἡ δέ οἱ σάθη / ὥστ' ὄνου Πριηνέως/κήλωνος ἐπλήμυρεν ὀτρυγηφάγου.

[5] ἡ δὲ οἱ κώμη / ὤμους κατεσκίαζε καὶ μετάφρενα.

ARCHILOCHUS 89

"I wish I could get to touch Neoboule." Here Archilochus could touch his own breast.

ARCHILOCHUS 103

"Glaukos, look: waves are troubling the deep sea." Here the poet would point.

Pindar

Pindar, the great Theban poet of the early and mid fifth century B.C.E., is most fully represented by the victory odes he composed to honor winners at the Pan-Hellenic competitions held at Olympia, Isthmia, Delphi, and Nemea. From these epinician odes (as they are called) two instances of an "incomplete" conditional sentence offer an opportunity for a gesture.

NO: PINDAR *NEMEAN* 4.79–81

Pindar composed his *Fourth Nemean Ode* to honor Timasarchus, a noble Aeginetan lad, who had won a crown for wrestling at Nemea. Toward the end of the poem, he introduces a comparison with a protasis: "If you are bidding me still to set up a stele whiter than Parian stone for Kallikles, your mother's brother," but no apodosis follows, and there is no suggestion of physical danger to the documents that carried the poem. Instead, Pindar invokes gleaming gold (which he often does), but only to assess it as second in value to hymns of praise.

If a rhapsode could complete a sentence in Homer's epic poems with a gesture (see pp. 39–44 above), Pindar or a chorus could use the same complementary nonverbal communication here. An amplified translation, then, might go as follows:

> But if you are telling me still to erect a stele
> whiter than Parian stone for your mother's brother, Kallikles,
> <GESTURE = No, I will not do that>.
> Gold refined shows all its bright shine
> but a hymn to brave deeds makes a mortal
> equal in fortune to kings. Let Kallikles
> who dwells by Acheron find my sounding tongue
> where in the contest of loud-thundering Poseidon
> he bloomed with Corinthian parsley.[6]

[6] . . . εἰ δέ τοι / μάτρωι μ' ἔτι Καλλικλεῖ κελεύεις / στάλαν θέμεν Παρίου λίθου λευκοτέραν/ ὁ χρυσὸς ἑψόμενος / αὐγὰς ἔδειξεν ἁπάσας ὕμνος δὲ τῶν ἀγαθῶν/

How was that no expressed? If the poet himself sang the song, a signifying tilt of the chin would serve. A single member of the chorus could do the same, as indeed could chosen members of a chorus, singing and dancing together. Lucian reports of dancing in earlier times than his own that at Delos "choruses of boys assembled by flute and cithara would perform as chorus, and the best of them, judged ahead of time, would dance the roles of characters."[7]

WELL AND GOOD: *OLYMPIAN* 2.56–60

Pindar's *Second Olympian Ode* honors Theron of Akragas, who won a four-horse chariot race at Olympia in 476 B.C.E. Around the middle of the ode, Pindar embarks on a promise of justice in the afterlife, and the form and tenets of this promise have exercised students for generations. In the present study, only the "incomplete" state of the sentence is the object of inquiry.[8] I attempt here a fairly literal translation, adding in

---

ἐργμάτων βασιλεῦσιν ἰσοδαίμονα τεύχει/ φῶτα· κεῖνος ἀμφ' Ἀχέροντι ναιετάων ἐμάν/ γλῶσσαν εὑρέτω κελαδῆτιν, Ὀρσοτριαίνα/ ἵν' ἐν ἀγῶνι βαρυκτύπου/ θάλησε Κορινθίοις σελίνοις.

[7] Lucian *On Dancing* 16: παίδων χοροὶ συνελθόντες ὑπ' αὔλωι καὶ κιθάραι οἱ μὲν ἐχόρευον, ὑπωρχοῦντο δὲ οἱ ἄριστοι προκριθέντες ἐξ αὐτῶν. In a later time, Demetrios, a Cynic, called out in praise of a dancer/pantomimist: "I hear what you are doing. I don't just see: you seem to me to be talking by means of your hands." *id.* 63: ἀκούω ἄνθρωπε ἃ ποιεῖς, οὐχ ὁρῶ μόνον, ἀλλά μοι δοκεῖς ταῖς χερσὶν αὐταῖς λαλεῖν.

[8] (**A**) Gildersleeve 1885: 149: *comm. ad* 2.62: "The passage has an enormous literature to itself. In despair, I have kept the reading of the MSS, with the interpretation, 'If in truth, when one hath it (νιν = πλοῦτον) he knows (of) the future that,' etc. δέ in P. is often not far from δή. This would make the sentence an after-thought. Böckh's εἴ γε, which is simple, is not lyrical (Mommsen). εὖ δέ and ἓν δέ are not convincing conjectures. εὖτε has been suggested. Bergk considers οἶδεν to have been used once by brachylogy instead of twice, and punctuates εἰ δέ νιν ἔχων τις, οἶδεν τὸ μέλλον, 'if anyone that hath it knows, he (Theron) knows.' In that case Theron would have been mentioned. Metzger makes εἴ τις οἶδεν . . . ἀνάγκαι the protasis, and ἴσαις δέ . . . τύρσιν the apodosis, or rather the apparent apodosis, the real apodosis being some verb of ascertainment understood. . . . It would be better to leave the first sentence frankly without an apodosis." (**A**) Farnell 1932: 16, *comm. ad* 56 says: "MSS. εἰ δέ νιν ἔχων: if this reading is kept, there is no more to say than that Pindar is guilty here of bad syntax, and it does not help us to find other examples of bad syntax in Greek literature, or to say, like Wilamowitz, the suppressed apodosis is not uncommon in Attic prose." [Wilamowitz's actual words are, "Man soll sich nicht abquälen, die unterdrückte Apodosis in Worte zu kleiden. Schlimm genug dass ein Gebrauch lange verkannt werden konnte der in attischen Poesie und unverkünstelter Prosa keineswegs selten ist" (Wilamowitz 1922: 247.1). At Plato *Euthydemos* 286e6, if Wilamowitz intuits the relevant gesture, why here does he recommend to the reader that he "clothe in words" the missing apodosis? [Cf. p. 120 note 28 below] Schroeder also defends the text, on the view that the apodosis can be easily supplied and "quanto gravius silentium!" (**A**) Kirkwood 1982: 71 offers: "the εἰ clause is an added thought: wealth joined with excellence is a star, a light, (but only fully so) if one understands man's experience after death." (**A**) Willcock 1995: 154 *ad loc.* makes short work of the formulation that Gildersleeve despaired of. He says: "But we never come to an apodosis

angle brackets a GESTURE that I hope will recommend itself as a possible interpretation of an otherwise puzzling syntax.

> Wealth wrought with good qualities
> brings the right time for one thing and another,
> offering support against deep and fruitless care.
> A star highly visible, truest ray of light for a man.
> And if one has it and knows what is to come,
> namely that of those who die here reckless spirits
> pay a penalty immediately <GESTURE = well and good>.

Now Pindar adds a parenthesis in which he secures this promise with circumstantial detail.

> A judge beneath the earth judges sins
> committed in this realm of Zeus, and he
> presents his judgment in hateful necessity.[9]

Then in five following stanzas, Pindar enlarges on the happiness the good will enjoy (with a single and telling look at "the others" in line 67). He has, however, completed his conditional sentence with that gesture. The sense is that if a person has wealth and excellent qualities of spirit and knows that the reckless are immediately punished after they die, all will be well with that person. An implacable judge is waiting in Hades, but for the good, there are many comforts to come.

Summary

Archilochus, in creating a character who expressed himself vividly, can hardly have failed to use his head and hands to accentuate words or pictures as he recited his poems. If there is a question as to who exactly performed the odes that Pindar composed, whether it was the poet himself or a chorus-leader or selected members of a chorus, the sort of gesture that was needed to make sense of two "incomplete" conditional sentences was easy to do.

---

of this condition, but we are unlikely to notice, because the word ὅτι in 57 introduces a description which develops and continues all the way to line 83. There is no reason to treat this as a grammatical oddity." Cf. Hummel 1993: 387–88. See Lloyd-Jones 1990: 80–107 on Pindar's view of the afterlife.

[9] ὁ μὰν πλοῦτος ἀρεταῖς δεδαιλδαμένος φέρει τῶν τε καὶ τῶν/ καιρὸν βαθεῖαν ὑπέχων μέριμναν ἀγροτέραν/ ἀστὴρ ἀρίζηλος, ἐτυμώτατον ἀνδρὶ φέγγος· εἰ δέ νιν ἔχων τις οἶδεν τὸ μέλλον/ ὅτι μὲν ἐνθάδ' αὐτίκ' ἀπάλαμοι φρένες / ποίνας ἔτεισαν–τὰ δ' ἐν τᾶιδε Διὸς ἀρχᾶι/ ἀλιτρὰ κατὰ γᾶς δικάζει τις ἐχθρᾶι/ λόγον φράσαις ἀνάγκαι.

FIVE

TRAGEDY

ACTORS on the tragic and comic stage performed with their heads, hands, and bodies as well as their voices. Because they all wore masks, they could not convey added sense by means of facial expression. Effects had to be achieved by voice and by nonverbal communication, and a poet who like Sophocles acted in his own productions had this requirement as an informing principle of composition. Why then have editors of ancient Greek drama not taken into account systematically the implications of such activity?[1] A tentative answer to this question may be couched in the single word *particles.* The Classical Greek language is so rich in modal particles that impart tone, sense, and direction to most utterances that we latecomers, once we begin to apprehend the wonderful variety and flexibility of these small parts of speech, can easily tell ourselves that the particles express anything at all that needs to be said. No need consequently, if the particles are there, to look for other aids to communication. So the line of assumptions might go. But faith in any single approach is limiting. What follows is notice of some representative instances where a reader, by imagining the actors' nonverbal communications, can answer questions that have been raised in the past, and for which traditional philology has not provided fully satisfactory answers.

Take quotation of a single word. When we assume that a single word or phrase could be signaled on stage by gesture, we enlarge our range of information, and additional possibilities of interpretation become immediately apparent. In conversation (both then and now), it is true, one can stress a word or phrase by tone or intensity to label it as quotation, and the same sort of emphasis works on the stage as well. A minute pause, a trace of a stutter, almost any slight interruption will also be enough to emphasize a word or phrase. But what is enough and what is redundant are not relevant considerations in the present inquiry. An accompanying gesture was part of talking, regardless of whether in any single instance it

[1] Pickard-Cambridge 1953: 169–74 describes some gestures in tragedy but mostly he is concerned with weeping, laughing, and masks. He cites Aristotle *Poetics* 17 and 26, and *Rhetoric* 2.8, which are useful. Bieber 1961: 82–83 is fully aware of the necessity of nonverbal communication. Recently Oliver Taplin (see, e.g., Taplin 1978: 15–16, 60–61, 65 *et passim*; Arnott 1991). (**A**) Dover 1993, Mastronarde 1979, Kaimio 1988, and others have evoked the actual look of a Greek drama, but the full range and implications of nonverbal expression have still to be explored.

complemented, supplemented, supplied, or duplicated meaning or not. That is to say, in any vocal expression at all, a gesture is fully as much to be expected as a modulation of tone or timing in utterance. Consequently, when an actor wanted his audience to understand that he was about to pronounce a word or phrase that needed special attention—a quotation, for instance—he could use a sign of some sort.[2]

Aeschylus

In Aeschylus the characterizations stiff and stately, archaic and terrifying (and more to be sure) of the man and his work have found a venue. From his late trilogy, the *Oresteia*, and from his *Prometheus Bound*, a few lines show where nonverbal communication could clarify ambivalences and at the same time impart an almost conversational suppleness to their structure.

QUOTATION: AESCHYLUS *PROMETHEUS BOUND* 79–80

An exchange at the beginning of Aeschylus *Prometheus Bound* 79–80 may contain words that were meant to be understood as quotation. As Bios and Kratos nail the Titan, Prometheus, to a rock, Hephaistos, who is supervising, reproaches Kratos, saying, "You talk the way you look," and Kratos answers, "Be soft. But do not throw in my face my "willfulness" and "roughness of temper."[3] In modern conventions of editing, "willfulness" and "roughness of temper" could be printed with quotation marks to show that Kratos is not making those qualities his own: he pronounces words that Hephaistos and others use when speaking of him. He has heard them before. He does not want to hear them again now. In antiquity an actor or a reader of that written text could signal the distinction both by modulations of voice and by gesture. Kratos, for instance, to indicate the source of such abusive speech, might nod toward Hephaistos or even make some sweeping gesture with his hand as he enunciated the words *willfulness* and *roughness of temper*. The motion should be big enough for audience in the back rows to comprehend. This last is true also if an actor did not see exactly the sense recommended here: a different interpretation would prompt different body language.[4]

[2] Cf. (**A**) Dover 1993: 34.

[3] σὺ μαλθακίζου· τὴν δ' ἐμὴν αὐθαδίαν ὀργῆς τε τραχυτῆτα μὴ 'πίπλησσέ μοι.

[4] Cf. (**A**) Rose 1957–58 *comm. ad loc.*; *aliter* (**A**) Griffith 1983: 98 who sees Kratos appropriating the traits. In support of the interpretation offered here, see pp. 96–97, 99–100,

YES/ WHAT THEN?/ WELL AND GOOD: AESCHYLUS *CHOEPHOROI* 775

The leader of the chorus instructs the nurse Kilissa to deliver a message to Aigisthos directing him to come to the palace without his usual bodyguard. The leader cannot reveal that Orestes is alive and present: he must therefore be inscrutable, mantic in fact, in his prescription. Kilissa, fishing for enlightenment, proceeds by indirection: she asks if the Leader is pleased with a message he has just received. The Leader answers: "But if Zeus will someday cause a change of the wind in our ills—"[5] and Kilissa asks how there can be a change, now that Orestes, their hope, is gone. The Leader's unfinished conditional sentence gives an actor room to be creative in his interpretation. He could be asking a question, for one thing, so that the sense would be, "What if someday. . . ?" And with that question, he could nod Yes, signifying that such a change could someday happen. Or the Leader could pronounce the protasis and then complete the sentence with a gesture asking some question such as, "What then?" But if the line is not read as a question, a hand or head motion signifying that everything will be all right can be envisioned. "But if Zeus will someday cause a change of the wind in our ills, <GESTURE = then well and good>."[6]

SO BE IT: AESCHYLUS *AGAMEMNON* 1060–61

Clytaemnestra at Aeschylus *Agamemnon* 1060 grows impatient. She has been trying to tell Cassandra to descend from the carriage in which she has been conveyed as booty. But Cassandra does not answer. And so Clytaemnestra says: "But if, because you have no understanding of Greek, you are not receiving my words . . . / instead of speaking, make an indication with your barbaric hand."[7]

Commentators have denounced Clytaemnestra's words as nonsense: if Cassandra cannot understand instructions to speak, they protest, how can she be expected to understand an instruction to gesticulate? Commentators have also paused at the particle δέ which seems to appear in the apodosis of a conditional sentence. (**A**) Fraenkel 1950 *ad loc.*, in a succinct review of both questions, opens the way for settling the first by quoting with

---

and 88–90 below, where Herodotus, Thucydides, and Demosthenes are shown to use a similar mode of expression.

[5] ἀλλ' εἰ τροπαίαν Ζεὺς κακῶν θήσει ποτέ.

[6] Cf. (**A**) Garvie 1986: 254: "With Page's stop at the end of the line, the sense is, 'well (why not?), it is right to rejoice, if . . . ' . But Murray's question mark is preferable—'but what if . . . ?' "

[7] εἰ δ' ἀξύνημων οὖσα μὴ δέχηι λόγον, σὺ δ' ἀντὶ φωνῆς φράζε καρβάνωι χειρί.

qualified approval (**A**) C. G. Schütz, who had written in 1780: “In saying this the queen supplements her speech by nodding, by facial expression, and by gesture.” (“Ista dicens regina ipsa nutu vultu gestu sermonem adiuvabat.” Fraenkel’s qualification is to identify *vultu* as inappropriate). For once we picture Clytaemnestra nodding and gesticulating as she speaks, she is not nonsensical if she expects some kind of gesture or nod in answer, even if only, as Fraenkel surmises, to make “a slight sideways movement of the lower arm, with the hands open and the fingers apart.”

As for the second question, the δέ prompts some readers to have Clytaemnestra address line 1061 to someone other than Cassandra. Fraenkel justly says no. He does not, however, avail himself of the gestures he has attributed to Clytaemnestra attempting to have Cassandra descend from the carriage and enter the palace. And yet that same chain of speculation easily includes movements of head and hand that provide an apodosis for the protasis enunciated in line 1060. The resulting order can be presented schematically as follows: “But if, because you have no understanding of Greek, you are not receiving my words, <GESTURE = “So be it”>. Instead of speaking, make an indication with your barbaric hand.”[8]

WELL AND GOOD: AESCHYLUS *EUMENIDES* 885–88

(**A**) Fraenkel 1950 in his discussion of Aeschylus’s *Agamemnon* 1061 cites Aeschylus *Eumenides* 885–88 as a useful parallel. At this point in the play, Athena has cast the deciding vote that acquits Orestes. The prosecution, i.e., the Erinyes, are raging with frustration and dangerous. Athena offers them—and continues to offer—an honored place in Athens and a beneficial metamorphosis. “I do not, you see, tire of telling you good things, this so that you may never say that you, an elder god, were sent off without honor and without hospitality by me, a younger god, and by the mortals, who hold the city. But if you hold reverence for Persuasion holy, the sweetness and enchantment of my tongue, if you would then stay . . . But if you will not stay, it would not be fair for you. . . . ”[9] Athena says “if ” but then does not complete her sentence with words. A gesture, however, that says, “well and good” would easily provide an apodosis. The motion, whether of head or hand, was one a mortal might make. Hence: “But if you hold Persuasion holy, the sweetness and enchantment of my tongue,

[8] Cf. (**A**) Denniston-Page 1989 *ad loc.*: “δέ in the apodosis, without change of subject, is not uncommon.” Also Denniston 1966: 181.

[9] ἀλλ’ εἰ μὲν ἁγνόν ἐστί σοι Πειθοῦς σέβας, γλώσσης ἐμῆς μείλιγμα καὶ θελκτήριον, σὺ δ’ οὖν μένοις ἄν· εἰ δὲ μὴ θέλεις μένειν, οὔ τἂν δικαίως . . . . Cf. Denniston 1966: 467.

if you would after all stay <GESTURE = that would be well and good>. But if you will not stay . . . etc."

Sophocles

Poet, general, statesman, and actor, Sophocles in two of his Theban plays, *Oedipus the King* and *Antigone*, gives his characters lines that actors must present with appropriate gestures to be rightly understood.

NOT TO FEAR: SOPHOCLES *OEDIPUS THE KING* 227–29

Oedipus has heard from Kreon that the man who killed Laios is the cause of the pollution that infests Thebes. At line 227 he presents a way of identifying the culprit, but the articulation of his proposal has been a puzzle for readers for many years. The common text is as follows: κἐι μὲν φοβεῖται τοὐπίκλημ᾽ ὑπεξελὼν/ αὐτὸς καθ᾽ αὑτοῦ πείσεται γὰρ ἄλλο μὲν/ ἀστεργὲς οὐδέν γῆς δ᾽ ἄπεισιν ἀβλαβής/ εἰ δ᾽ αὖ τις ἄλλον οἶδεν ἢ ᾽ξ ἄλλης χθονός/ τὸν αὐτόχειρα μὴ σιωπάτω. A scholiast paraphrases: "If he should be the culprit and he is afraid to speak, himself against himself, he is to set his fear aside and speak. Because he will suffer nothing awful, except that he will leave this land."[10] (**A**) Jebb 1893: *ad loc.* offers from among numerous proposed interpretations seven besides his own that "claim notice." LSJ *s.v.* ὑπεξαιρέω notes Jebb's summary and presents yet another different one. (**A**) Lloyd-Jones and Wilson 1990a: 85 provide a secure starting point for the interpretation that is recommended here: "Supposing that we have here an instance of the not uncommon idiom by which the apodosis of the first of two alternate conditional sentences is suppressed . . . we could understand after the conditional clause and before πείσεται "he need have no fear"; for an example of the idiom in which the first conditional sentence is followed by the sentence whose second word is a γάρ giving a reason why the preceding conditional sentence should be true, see *Il.* 1.580–1."[11]

Suppose, however, that an apodosis is not suppressed but communicated by means of a single, easily comprehensible motion of head or hand. In a society where nonverbal communication is continual, a gesture that says

[10] καὶ εἰ μὲν αὐτὸς εἴη πράξας, καὶ φοβεῖται λέγειν αὐτὸς καθ᾽ αὑτοῦ, τὸν φόβον ὑπεξελὼν λεγέτω. οὐδὲν γὰρ δεινὸν πείσεται, εἰ μὴ ὅτι τῆσδε τῆς γῆς ἀπαλλάξεται.

[11] (**A**) Kamerbeek 1967: 72 notes the possibility in line 228 that an expressive gesture could take the place of the main verb.

essentially, "Not to fear!" has a place here. With some such gesture, the lines can be presented in English as follows: "And if he is afraid <and because he is afraid> he has done away with the charge, he <the perpetrator acting> against himself <GESTURE = he is not to fear>, for he will suffer nothing unseemly. He will leave the land unharmed. Again, if someone knows the killer as someone else or from another land, let him not be silent."

I AM LEAVING: SOPHOCLES *OEDIPUS THE KING* 324–27

A seeming anomaly in the *Oedipus the King* has been explained as an instance of aposiopesis. Nonverbal communication, however, and not silence, may convey the message. Teiresias at Sophocles *Oedipus the King* 324–25 says to Oedipus: "Because I see that your speech does not proceed seasonably. And so, for me not to have the same thing happen to me—" and here a dash signals a break in modern texts.[12] Now Teiresias has already said at line 320 that he wants to be allowed to go home, and with that wish he may have turned his body toward an exit and tried a step or two. Now at line 325 he makes a more determined move, one that Oedipus remarks: "If you do know, do not by the gods turn away. We are all here bowing down to you as suppliants."[13] Teiresias, therefore, in turning to leave at line 325, had expressed by means of nonverbal communication the clause that if spoken would balance μηδέ. The sense is: "And so for me not to have the same thing happen to me, <GESTURE = I am leaving>."[14]

[12] ὁρῶ γὰρ οὐδὲ σοὶ τὸ σὸν φώνημ' ἰὸν πρὸς καιρόν· ὡς οὖν μηδ' ἐγὼ ταὐτὸν πάθω —. (**A**) Jebb 1893 translates: "Nay, I see that thou on thy part openest not thy lips in season: therefore I speak not, that neither may I have thy mishap." In a footnote he clarifies: "(I do not speak) for I see that *neither* (μηδὲ) may I share your mishap (of speaking amiss). If he speaks not, *neither* will he speak wrongly. Cf. Thuc. 2.63: εἰκὸς . . . μὴ φεύγειν τοὺς πόνους, ἢ μηδὲ τὰς τιμὰς διώκειν. I now prefer this view to taking μηδ' ἐγὼ as irregular for μὴ καὶ ἐγὼ ('lest I too . . .')—resolving μηδέ into μή not, δὲ on the other hand; though the place of ἐγώ suggests this." (**A**) Lloyd-Jones and Wilson 1990 *comm. ad* line 325 say: "Aposiopesis rather than interruption; see Mastronarde, *Contact and Discontinuity*, 72–3." Mastronarde (1979) *loc. cit.* speaks of "stage actions collaborating with unusual conditions of dialogue . . . which he has previously observed . . . in instances of imperfect contact accompanied by the movements of turning or departure."

[13] Lines 326–27: μὴ πρὸς θεῶν φρονῶν γ' ἀποστραφῇς, ἐπεὶ πάντες σε προσκυνοῦμεν οἵδ' ἱκτήριοι.

[14] Argyle 1988: 294: "Gesture language has clear similarities with verbal languages. Nouns standing for objects or persons can be communicated by pointing or by illustrative gestures. Verbs standing for action can be communicated by the actions themselves, or reduced versions of them like intention movements."

Oedipus, to state the obvious, has asked Teiresias not to do what the audience has seen him doing: he said, "do not turn away" (μὴ ἀποστραφῇς) because Teiresias was turning away. This particular kind of underlining or focusing can be observed elsewhere in tragedy in exchanges where a character utters a cry of grief, such as οἴμοι or the like. A second character then in answer refers to the cry with a word that one might use in narrative to describe what has just been sounded. Sophocles *Oedipus at Colonus* 820 is one example: Oedipus cries "Alas," and Kreon answers, "The following may cause you to say 'Alas' the more."[15] Sophocles *Aias* 939–40 is another. Consequently, to turn from exchanges of this sort back to Teiresias and Oedipus, if we can think of Teiresias's physical action as a statement of what he is doing, that is, if he is saying with his body, "I am turning away," then Oedipus's response "Don't turn away" shows the same underlying pattern as "Alas!" and "say Alas" with all its variations.[16]

YES: SOPHOCLES *ANTIGONE* 441–43

In Sophocles' *Antigone* at line 441ff., an analogous exchange takes place between Kreon and Antigone. The exchange is analogous in that one character delivers a message by means of gesture, and the other describes that gesture in words, thereby reinforcing the message.

At this point in the play, a very relieved guard has brought Antigone before Kreon. He has caught the malefactor, the previously unknown rebel who defied Kreon's edict, and so he is himself exonerated. Antigone stands by as the guard explains to Kreon exactly what happened. When the guard stops talking, Kreon turns in anger and surprise to Antigone. What does he say? σὲ δή, σὲ τὴν νεύουσαν ἐς πέδον κάρα, φής, ἢ καταρνῇι μὴ δεδρακέναι τάδε; (line 441). Translators differ among themselves as to single words and phrases here, but the overall sense of their interpretations leads a reader to suppose that Antigone is downcast, frightened, or ashamed of what she has done. (**A**) Jebb 1906 translates: "Thou—thou whose face is bent to earth—dost thou avow or disavow this deed?" and then interprets in a note: "Antigone has her eyes bent on the ground: she is neither afraid nor sullen but feels that Creon and she can never come to terms." Mazon in (**A**) Dain and Mazon 1962: "Et toi, toi qui restes là, tête basse, avoues-tu ou nies-tu le fait?" (**B**) Watling 1947: "You, what do you say—you, hiding your head there?" (**B**) Wykoff 1954 implies a languid Antigone,

[15] Oedipus: οἴμοι.
Kreon: ταχ' ἕξεις μᾶλλον οἰμώζειν τάδε.

[16] Jackson 1955: 86–87 lists examples of exclamations followed by narrative reference from Aeschylus, Sophocles, and Euripides. Cf. Plato *Euthyphro* 15e3–6, discussed below, p. 113.

one faint perhaps with apprehension: "You there, whose head is drooping to the ground, do you say you did, or do you deny you did it?" Arnott 1991: 63 sees Antigone as grieving: "You there whose face is bent to the ground." (**B**) Lloyd-Jones 1994 translates accurately, "you there, you that are bowing down your head towards the ground, do you admit, or do you deny . . . " but does not convey the affirmation.

A paradoxical aspect of such translations is that they present an Antigone whose demeanor (even if only for the moment) is markedly different from that which characterizes her elsewhere in the play. From the very beginning, Antigone as she declares herself to Ismene (lines 1–99) is righteously angry: she could be described as "fierce" and "outraged," but not as "shamefaced," "guilty," or "pathetic." Why ever then should she stand with her eyes fixed on the ground[17] or worse, hiding her head, a way of showing sorrow or shame?[18] Furthermore, when Antigone answers Kreon's question, she says, "I say I did it, and I do not deny it."[19] This is not a frightened, guilty, or shamefaced response, but that of a bereaved sister, who does not regret what she has done. Consider her very next words, when Kreon asks her if she actually knew of the edict. She says, "Yes, of course, it was perfectly clear" (ἐμφανῆ γὰρ ἦν). Again, her forthright answer is consistent with the character and temper of Antigone as she appears in the opening lines of the play.

Sophocles' Greek returns the same unrepentant Antigone, once the implications of a literal translation are faced. Kreon says: "You there, you nodding your head toward the ground, are you saying Yes? Or do you deny that you did it?" That is, the Greek verb νεύω, "nod," tells of motion, and in its present, continuative aspect implies repeated noddings. Translations that have Antigone merely face to the ground render νεύω inert. The Greek verb ἀνανεύω means to move the head up and back, a gesture of the head that says no. The Greek verb κατανεύω, "to nod down," means "to affirm, to say yes." Kreon uses the uncompounded form νεύω but adds ἐς πέδον κάρα which turns νεύουσαν into κατανεύουσαν in sense. From Kreon's words, it is clear that Antigone is nodding down, toward the ground: she is confirming the guard's account; the guard is saying that she is the culprit. Kreon cannot believe his eyes. Here is a blood relation, who very much appears to be a lawfully apprehended lawbreaker. But how can that be? Still, she stands there and says with her posture and gesture, "Yes, I did it." Kreon accordingly must ask Antigone to say aloud that she

[17] Muecke 1984: 105–12 cites and discusses passages in Latin and in Greek where someone is indubitably looking down at the ground. None of these employs a form or compound of νεύω.

[18] Sorrow: Homer *Odyssey* 8.92 κατὰ κρᾶτα καλυψάμενος γοάασκεν. Shame: Ferrari 1990: 185–200.

[19] καὶ φημὶ δρᾶσαι κοὐκ ἀπαρνοῦμαι τὸ μή.

has done it, so that there cannot be any possibility of misunderstanding. This is to make her confession public and official. But then he offers her an escape: she could plead ignorance. But she does not. She asserts once again the passion of her belief.

OTHER NODS (*ANTIGONE* CONTINUED)

In Aristophanes' *Acharnians* at line 115, Dikaiopolis sees that the supposed visitors from Persia are actually Greeks: he has asked them questions that they have answered with uniquely Greek gestures, namely, head back to signify no, head forward and down to signify yes. "These men nodded Greek. No way they're not from here."[20] LSJ cite comparable gestures in Homer, Plato, and later authors under the headings νεύω, ἀνανεύω, διανεύω, ἐπινεύω, κατανεύω, and to this day, the same motions of head, neck, and eyebrows remain endemic.[21] A Greek may tilt the head back a little to say no, even when saying οὐχί aloud, or even almost imperceptibly (for a foreigner) lift the eyebrows, sometimes making a little click against the upper teeth. A spoken or unspoken yes can be signed or reinforced with a nod forward and down that goes slightly to one side.

Why have editors and translators not used these widely accessible data as an aid in interpreting Kreon's question at *Antigone* 441? It may be that they have been influenced by a similarity to the phraseology of lines 269–70. There the unhappy guard, in explaining how he was allotted to bring bad news to Kreon, tells of the fellow guard who caused the whole company to nod their heads toward the ground in fear.[22] LSJ *s.v.* νεύω cite Sophocles *Antigone* 270 as meaning "nod, bend forward," but without any implication of assent, and that sense, given context and the presence of a word for "fear," seems right. But then the editors add a reference to line 441 as comparable: "(cf. Sophocles *Antigone* 441)." A caution may be helpful here: the abbreviation *cf.* should be understood to say "compare and contrast," because the sense of νεύω in line 441 really is different.

A later usage may likewise be instructive. Chairemon of Alexandria (fl. 30–60 C.E., *FGrHist* 618 F2), in describing an Ethiopian sign language, has the sign for grief "a man holding his chin and nodding toward the ground."[23] Here it is the hand holding the chin that defines exactly how "nodding toward the ground" is to be taken. Again, compare Homer *Odyssey* 18.237, where the hope is that the suitors will incline their faces toward the ground after they have been overpowered (δεδμημένοι).

[20] Ἑλληνικόν γ' ἐπένευσαν ἄνδρες οὑτοιί κοὐκ ἔσθ' ὅπως οὐκ εἰσὶν ἐνθένδ' αὐτόθεν.
[21] At LSJ *s.v.* διανεύω, add Plato *Republic* 441c4.
[22] ὃς πάντας ἐς πέδον κάρα νεῦσαι φόβωι προὔτρεψεν.
[23] ἀντὶ λυπῆς τῆι χειρὶ τὸ γέννειον κρατοῦντα καὶ πρὸς γῆν νεύοντα.

Aristophanes *Wasps* 1110 presents a use of νεύω that is suggestive if not so clear: the old heliasts (i.e., jurors as chorus of wasps) describe themselves as "nodding toward the ground, barely moving, like larvae in their cells."[24] What can this simile be supposed to mean? Larvae do move in their cells, and a bee-keeper informs me that they do indeed appear to nod. But what is the relevance of that for old heliasts? In Plato *Republic* 405c5–6, Socrates evokes the "dozing juror" as if that might be a kind of standard description (νυστάζοντος δικαστοῦ), and a universally recognizable signal of drowsiness is nodding. But perhaps Aristophanes has seen aging jurors nod steadily in affirmation, giving an appearance of listening closely to the arguments.[25]

SOPHOCLES *ANTIGONE* 441–43 (CONT.)

To return to line 441 of the *Antigone*, once the sense of Antigone's nodding is clear, she can be seen standing before Kreon—not cowering, not fearful, not ashamed, but brave and sure of her place in an ordered universe. The actor who plays Antigone, masked and robed, will have nodded—we can imagine—slowly, majestically, unmistakably while the guard spoke. Kreon, in asking what this nodding means, directs the audience's attention to Antigone. They turn their eyes from him to her, prepared to see and understand the statement she is making with her head, a solemn and unflinching affirmation.

A Lucanian Nestoris from the early fourth century (Figure 30, British Museum F 175; Ghali-Kahil 1955: II, Plate 27) shows a scene painted by the Creusa Painter in which two guards bring Antigone before Kreon, just the scene apparently of Sophocles *Antigone* 441. Antigone inclines her head forward: she is nodding, saying yes. If she were showing shame or guilt or confusion, she would be covering her face with her *himation*. This should be clear enough, but a convention of the times was for a painter to represent honorable women as looking downward. She could as well be abashed, afraid, or uncertain, so far as the picture can tell. But these responses would be incongruous with her character as limned at the beginning of the play. And so the illustration is ambivalent.

NO: SOPHOCLES *ANTIGONE* 511

Kreon in examining Antigone disputes her assertion that the people of Thebes view her act with sympathy. He asks if she is not ashamed of herself

[24] νεύοντες εἰς τὴν γῆν, μόλις ὥσπερ οἱ σκώληκες ἐν τοῖς κυττάροις κινούμενοι.

[25] (**A**) MacDowell 1971: 275 in his commentary on the line sees the jurors (heliasts) as bent over somehow toward the ground. Hesiod *Works and Days* has corn nodding in its fullness (ἁβροσύνῃ) toward the ground. LSJ s.v. νεύω cite Homer *Iliad* 13.133, where the

for setting herself apart from her fellow citizens. She responds (line 511), "Because there is nothing shameful in showing piety to siblings."[26] (**A**) Jebb 1906 in his note *ad loc.* says, "She answers 'No, I am not ashamed, for I am doing nothing shameful.' " Jebb is right if elliptical, for the actor must have answered with a clearly defined backward nod signifying no.

WELL AND GOOD: SOPHOCLES *ODYSSEUS AKANTHOPLEGĒS* 458

To close examples from Sophocles and provide a transition to Euripides, consider a single Sophoclean fragment where an "incomplete" sentence may have had an apodosis expressed by gesture. A speaker says εἰ μέν τις οὖν ἔξεισιν· εἰ δὲ μή, λέγε.[27] And an amplified translation might look like this: "And so if a person goes out, <GESTURE = that's all right>, but otherwise, speak."

Euripides

Third in time of the three greatest Athenian tragic poets was Euripides, whose reliance on an actor's interpretive movements can be intuited in tragedy (*Antiope, Andromache, Hercules Furens, Hippolytos*) and in satyr drama (*Cyclops*).

WELL AND GOOD: EURIPIDES *ANTIOPE* 212

A brief presentation of some representative lines in which Euripides uses "incomplete" conditional sentences shows again what a gesture can effect. A gesture signifying "well and good" can be the apodosis in a fragment (*Antiope* 212): "If there is intelligence in her, <GESTURE = well and good>. Otherwise what need is there of a pretty wife if she lack good wits?"[28]

WHAT THEN? EURIPIDES *ANDROMACHE* 845

Hermione, mad with shame and remorse, wants to kill herself. Her Nurse wants her to stay alive. Hermione asks why her Nurse took away from her

---

bunched-up warriors are described variously by modern commentators as looking steadfastly ahead or peering around shields.

[26] οὐδὲν γὰρ αἰσχρὸν τοὺς ὁμοσπλάγχνους σέβειν.

[27] Sophocles *Odysseus Akanthoplegēs*, fr. 458; Schol. Homer *Iliad* A 135–37 ([**A**] Erbse 1971: 1, 48ff.) Cf. Aristophanes *Ploutos* 467–69, Plato Comicus *Hellas* 23, Menander fr. 779, (**A**) Eustathios 66.30 (1.106.30 (**A**) van der Valk [1971]) εἰσὶ δὲ καὶ ἄλλα τοιαῦτα σχήματα ἐλλείψεως παρὰ τοῖς παλαιοῖς ὡς παρὰ τῶι κωμικῶι.

[28] εἰ νοῦς ἔνεστιν· εἰ δὲ μή, τί δεῖ καλῆς γυναικός, εἰ μὴ τὰς φρένας χρηστὰς ἔχοι;

the means of self-destruction, and Nurse responds, "But if I should let you, when you are out of your mind, so that you died—."[29] (**A**) Stevens 1971: 196 comments as follows: "A conditional protasis, with an apodosis such as τί ἂν γένοιτο to be understood, is commonly used to express a supposition." But if we imagine actors on a stage, we ought to be able to see Nurse making a large gesture by means of which she expresses . . . what? Here again an actor had a range of creative opportunities. The gesture could have said, for instance, not "What would happen?" as Stevens conjectures, but "What would happen to *me*?"

WHAT THEN? EURIPIDES *HERCULES FURENS* 1198–1202

A second example of a scene in which an actor would have asked, "What then?" by gesture apppears in Euripides *Hercules Furens* 1198–1202. Heracles has come to his senses and knows now that he has butchered his own children. The stages by which line 1202 has reached the form one reads in (**A**) Diggle 1986 can be reviewed in Jackson 1955: 88–89 and (**A**) Bond 1988: 370. As the text now stands, Theseus approaches and sees Heracles with his head covered. He asks, "Why is he hiding his wretched head?" Amphitryon replies, "Ashamed to have you look at him, ashamed for family love, and for the blood of children slain." Theseus then says, "But if I share his pain—Uncover him."[30] If Theseus is asking a question, as Jackson recommends and Diggle and Bond approve, there is an ellipsis, for an apodosis is wanting. Suppose the sense to be supplied is "What then?" That question serving as an apodosis could easily be expressed by a gesture.

If, however, Theseus is not asking a question, the actor could use a different gesture. He could, for instance, touch Heracles, and an expanded translation would look like this: "But if I have come sharing his pain, <GESTURE = See! We are as one>. Uncover him." Shame is a feeling one must have in the presence of another. Theseus with a gesture—one as simple as laying an arm across Heracles' shoulders—identifies himself as one with Heracles and therefore not "another." Alternatively, a hand signal to "uncover him," made as the words are spoken, might likewise carry with it Theseus's command to disregard Heracles' feeling of shame.

SO BE IT: EURIPIDES *HIPPOLYTOS* 507

Phaedra has disclosed to her Nurse her terrible passion for Hippolytos. Nurse wants to help, and with her practical outlook, she sees getting the

[29] ἀλλ' εἴ σ' ἀφείην μὴ φρονοῦσαν, ὣς θανῇς;
[30] ἀλλ' εἰ συναλγῶν γ' ἦλθον; ἐκκάλυπτέ νιν.

man as a direct way to help. Phaedra protests but not convincingly. The Greek in question starts at line 505 and runs to line 508: Phaedra says, "And if you speak well for shame, I shall use myself up on that which I am now fleeing."[31] Nurse answers: εἴ τοι δοκεῖ σοι . . . χρῆν μὲν οὔ σ' ἁμαρτάνειν, εἰ δ' οὖν, πιθοῦ μοι· δευτέρα γὰρ ἡ χάρις. Now commentators do not all agree on the sense of this response, which is hardly surprising, since ambiguity is the intent here. (**A**) Barrett 1978: 253–54 is persuasive on Nurse's response, which begins with a protasis, εἴ τοι δοκεῖ σοι: he sees its apodosis as acquiescence in a contemplated action, variously expressed. (He does not, however, include the possibility of nonverbal communication in this last). His translation will serve for the present discussion. He submits: "Very well then, if you wish. . . . You ought not to be erring at all; but since you are, do as I say—that favor is the next best thing."

An actor could by means of gesticulation turn the words "if you wish" into acquiescence, i.e., Nurse accepts as fact what Phaedra has just said. The sense of her response here would be, "If you think so, <GESTURE = so be it>. You should not be doing wrong, but since you are, do as I say . . . etc." A scholiast and previous editors complete the conditional sentence within the line, producing a response like the following: "If you think that, you should not be making this mistake." But Barrett is persuasive when he says no to this effort.

I HOPE YOU DIE: EURIPIDES *CYCLOPS* 261

Odysseus has given Silenos wine to drink and Silenos has given Odysseus and his men lambs and milk that belong to his master, Polyphemos, who on returning to his cave wants to know who has been appropriating his things. Silenos accuses Odysseus and his men, saying that they beat and robbed him. Odysseus says Silenos is lying (line 259–60). Silenos is indignant: "I? Because I hope you die a horrible death." Odysseus turns Silenos's curse into a testamentary oath of sorts by capping it with the protasis, "if I am telling a lie."[32]

The word *because* (γάρ) may have explained a simultaneous gesture. That is, Silenos on saying "I" puts both hands to his chest but then shakes them to make a curse gesture, which he explains with the words, "Because I hope you die. . . . " In a satyric drama like *Cyclops*, the gesture could be the same as that used in comedy and discussed below (pp. 73–77).

[31] ταἰσχρὰ δ' ἢν λέγεις καλῶς εἰς τοῦθ' ὃ φεύγω νῦν ἀναλωθήσομαι.

[32] Silenos: ἐγώ; κακῶς γὰρ ἐξόλοι'

Odysseus: εἰ ψεύδομαι. (**A**) Biehl 1986 sees Silenos making a threatening gesture and fills in the sense as follows: "Me? (Me get caught?) (Die!) I'd like to have you made shorter

Summary

Actors' movements of hand and body could alert audiences to single words or phrases that were meant to be quotations. Kratos is an example near the beginning of Aeschylus's *Prometheus Bound.* In other scenes in Aeschylus's *Agamemnon*, *Choephoroi,* and *Eumenides*, conditional sentences are completed by gesture. Nonverbal communication likewise provides coherence in Sophocles' *Oedipus the King* when Oedipus begins his search for Laios's killer. His guarantee of safety needs to be supplemented by a gesture that tells the putative source of infection not to fear. Another example of nonverbal communication occurs where Teiresias completes a sentence by turning away and starting to leave, stating effectively with his whole body what he wants to say. Furthermore Sophocles' Antigone, when she acts out as well as speaks her assertion that she did indeed attempt to bury Polyneikes, shows continuing confidence in the rightness of her actions. Some illustrations from Euripides show where actors had choices when it came to interpreting an "incomplete" conditional sentence. The nurse's response to Hermione in *Andromache*, Theseus's to Amphitryon in *Heracles Furens*, and the Nurse's to Phaedra in *Hippolytos* are each of them ambiguous as written text, pellucid when acted out.

---

by a head." Denniston 1930: 213–15 reviews attempts to emend the line and concludes by assigning the part beginning with κακῶς to Odysseus (reaffirmed in Denniston 1966: 94). He translates as follows:"Yes, damn you if I am lying (γάϱ having its normal confirmatory force)" He goes on to say (justly), "This is at first sight nonsense." (**A**) Seaford 1984: 155 prefers to read γ' ἆϱ', which like (**A**) Diggle's (1986) γ' ἄϱ' is possible, but a gesture seems to be wanted here, and γὰϱ would explain the gesture.

SIX

ARISTOPHANES

ARISTOPHANES is represented by eleven complete comedies and more than a thousand fragments of other plays. From antiquity on, his earlier plays, i.e., those produced between 426 and 405 B.C.E., belong to a classification called Old Comedy in recognition of certain distinguishing characteristics such as bawdiness, attacks on public figures, and freewheeling inventions, as opposed to the milder situation comedies of Middle and New Comedy. One notable characteristic of Old Comedy is the profusion of quotations from earlier and contemporary poets, much of it intended as parody.

Quotation and Parody

To consider the opening of a comic play, how did an audience with no libretto in hand appreciate a parody of a line from a tragedy? How could an Athenian, the average man on the street, that is, be expected to recognize quotation and parody in comic and tragic plays, and for that matter in other sorts of oral presentation such as oratory? Did he carry about whole collections of texts of tragedy, comedy, and lyric in his head? Obviously writers, especially comic playwrights, felt they could make such demands on an audience.

Convention can be important in such matters, and that may be part of the answer. The audience knew at what time of day they were to be watching a tragedy, and when they were to be watching a comedy. Consequently, when they were expecting comedy and a play opened with a clearly tragic line they recognized that the effect was meant to be comic.[1]

Now an actor could pronounce a tragic line as parody using nothing more than his voice, but it was also in his nature and in his training—quite apart from its being his vocational responsibility—to speak with his body. A hand gesture (noted above, pp. 25–26), which has index and middle fingers of the right hand extended and spread, could have enabled an actor embarking on a speech to direct the audience's attention to himself. The audience, alerted by this gesture, were therefore watching his hand when he started speaking, and so any further movement of that

[1] McLeish 1980: 146

hand could signal approaching quotation or parody. But an actor could just as easily break off from whatever the plot required of him at that moment, and turn to the audience. He would then hold up a hand, or both hands, or do nothing more than stand motionless long enough to establish a break. Or he could express himself richly just by moving his cloak skillfully.[2] Different actors, it can be assumed, developed different styles.

An introduction by means of nonverbal communication would not be strictly necessary for a line such as Aristophanes *Birds* 808. There Peisetairos says, "We've been made the object of these comparisons as in Aeschylus: 'This not by others but by their own feathers.' "[3] (**A**) Dunbar 1995 *comm. ad loc.* says: "808 reproduces exactly, but for the omission of the verb ἁλισκόμεσθα <'we are being taken'> at the beginning of the next verse, part of the much quoted speech of Achilles from Aesch. *Myrmidons* (fr. 139.4–5) alluding to the Libyan tale of how an eagle, struck by an arrow which it sees to be fitted with eagle's feathers, exclaims that it has caused its own disaster—as Achilles has done, by lending his beloved Patroclus his armour and sending him out to his fatal fight with Hector."

This is a complex set of associations for an audience whose varying capacities did not equip each and every member to recognize the line instantly as a direct and unaltered quotation from Aeschylus's *Myrmidons* (fr. 139). But that recognition was vital if they were to appreciate the humor of the line in its dislocation. For that reason, Aristophanes made provision: he ended the previous line with the words "as in Aeschylus" (κατ' Αἰσχύλον). A gesture, however, could also and at the same time announce to the audience that a line from tragedy was about to be heard. In a line like this, therefore, more cues were offered than were necessary, if transmittal of information alone was the point of the exercise. But if the point of the humor was a discordant juxtaposition of comic and tragic diction, nothing would be lost by cuing the audience twice. The name Aeschylus may have had a special resonance that added to the humor, but the mention of his name did not by itself obviate the ever-present use of a gesture.[4]

In some other cases of parody, the audience was given less, if words alone were to convey the sense. At Aristophanes *Acharnians* 883, the Theban says, "Lady of fifty Copaic maids,"[5] and the line is a parodic distortion of Aeschylus Fragment 174, "Mistress of fifty Nereid maids."[6] But how were listeners to appreciate that modest subversion of the original

[2] Wiles 1991: 188–208

[3] τάδ' οὐχ ὑπ' ἄλλων ἀλλὰ τοῖς αὑτῶν πτεροῖς . . .

[4] Cf. (**A**) Dover 1993: 34: "An audience can be alerted to parody by language and rhythm and probably also by pose, stance, gesture, and style of declamation."

[5] πρέσβειρα πεντήκοντα Κωπάιδων κορᾶν.

[6] δέσποινα πεντήκοντα Νηρῄδων κορῶν.

text unless they were told it was coming? Modern readers know that the line is a parody thanks to the learning of an ancient commentator, a scholiast, who quotes the original line and identifies it as from Aeschylus's *Award of the Arms* (῞Οπλων Κρίσις).[7] These scholiasts had many more texts available to consult than we do—certainly more than audiences ancient or modern can reasonably be expected to have in their heads. The same is true in Aristophanes *Knights* 1240 where the Sausage-Seller cries out, "Oh, Phoebus Apollo Lycian, whatever will you do to me?"[8] and a scholiast notes that part of the line comes from Euripides *Telephos* (fr. 700).[9] Agreed, the *Telephos* was popular and widely quoted, and Aristophanes had used the play for parody before, but still a gesture or introductory stance would have amplified the effect. Again, Aristophanes *Frogs* 1471 starts out with a famous qualification, that of Hippolytos at Euripides' *Hippolytos* 612. Hippolytos had said, "My tongue is sworn, my heart is not,"[10] and it may well be that every Athenian in the audience knew the line as a chestnut. And so when Aristophanes had Dionysos say, "My tongue is sworn, but I shall choose Aeschylus,"[11] the audience was surprised. But an audience prepared to be surprised might have enjoyed it the more, and a cue given by body language would have given the audience just that anticipatory edge.

But now to some harder cases. At Aristophanes *Knights* 1249 the beaten Paphlagonian says, "Roll this poor person in."[12] A scholiast says the line is from Euripides' *Bellerophon* but with one word changed. Instead of κυλίνδετ' Euripides had written κομίζετ'. This slight difference would be easy to miss without special amplifying devices. Or consider Aristophanes *Knights* 836 where the Chorus in tragic style hails the Sausage-Seller, turning around Io's greeting to Prometheus in Aeschylus's *Prometheus Bound* 613. Io had said, "Oh you who have appeared as help in common to mortals,"[13] but now the Chorus says, "Oh you who have appeared as greatest aid to to all mankind."[14] In both of these parodies, an advertisement was wanted; otherwise the lines were throwaways. Surely an actor signaled with his hand or his whole body beforehand that something outside the action was about to transpire, so that those in the audience who had any chance of recognizing the reference were given their cue.

[7] Schol., Aristophanes *Acharnians* 883.

[8] ὦ Φοῖβ' Ἄπολλον Λύκιε, τί ποτέ μ' ἐργάσει; see (A) Austin 1968: 69, number 106 with apparatus, where only the first four words are assigned to *Telephos*.

[9] Schol., Aristophanes *Knights* 1240

[10] ἡ γλῶσσ' ὀμώμοχ', ἡ δὲ φρὴν ἀνώμοτος.

[11] ἡ γλῶττ' ὀμώμοκ', Αἰσχύλον δ' αἱρήσομαι.

[12] κυλίνδετ' εἴσω τόνδε τὸν δυσδαίμονα.

[13] ὦ κοινὸν ὠφέλημα θνητοῖσιν φανείς.

[14] ὦ πᾶσιν ἀνθρώποις φανεὶς μέγιστον ὠφέλημα.

Others in the audience could at least nudge their more knowledgeable neighbors and ask what was being revealed.

NO: ARISTOPHANES *KNIGHTS* 1278

A movement of the head signifying no could easily accompany the adversative phrase, "But as it is . . . ." The gesture seems clearly required in a configuration that Aristophanes, Antiphon, and Plato employ. Examples from Aristophanes and Antiphon are presented with minimal comment in anticipation of the more numerous examples in Plato.[15] The first example comes toward the end of the *Knights*. The chorus of Knights celebrates the victory of Sausage-Seller over Paphlagonian. They will now honor good men by abusing the vile. "Well then, if a fellow who ought to hear a lot bad about himself was himself famous, I wouldn't have cited a friend. But as it is, <GESTURE = No, that is not the case here>, because everyone knows Arignotus, who he is.[16] Now he has a brother, no relation in character, Ariphrades, the vile."

NO: ARISTOPHANES *ECCLESIAZUSAE* 610

Praxagora is describing a new way of life to Blepyros. Everything will be owned or used in common. But Blepyros is slow to understand. Don't people keep stealing now even when they have enough to eat? So Praxagora explains further: "Previously, yes, my friend, when we used the previous laws, but as it is now <GESTURE = No, those previous laws are not relevant anymore> because our sustenance will be from the community store. What is the gain of not contributing?"[17]

DEMONSTRATIVES: ARISTOPHANES *FROGS* 1503–8

The nonverbal communication of comedy, we can be sure, included a great many postures and gestures that would never be seen on the tragic stage. For examples of what would not be appropriate, one need go no further than the numerous ways a leather phallus could come into play. As for the use of demonstrative adjectives that have no meaning unless an actor is displaying or pointing, Aristophanes *Frogs* 1503–8 provides excellent examples. There, for instance, Plouton urging Aeschylus to arrange travel to Hades for four named Athenian public figures, indicates

[15] Antiphon, pp. 82–83 below; Plato, pp. 113–17 below. It is, however, worth noting here that (**A**) Dover 1993 on almost every page of his excellent commentary finds parallels in Plato's dialogues to illuminate Aristophanic idiom.

[16] νῦν δέ—'Αρίγνωτον γὰρ οὐδεὶς ὅστις οὐκ ἐπίσταται κτλ.

[17] πρότερόν γ' ὦταῖρ' ὅτε τοῖσι νόμοις διεχρώμεθα τοῖς προτέροισιν· νῦν δ'—ἔσται γὰρ βίος ἐκ κοινοῦ, τί τὸ κέρδος μὴ καταθεῖναι;

the means in our printed texts by demonstrative pronouns. He says, "Give this to Kleophon and these to the *poristai* Myrmex and Nikomachos alike and this to Archenomos."[18] What, then, were the objects that Plouton handed to Aeschylus? Four main ways to commit suicide were generally contemplated in antiquity: cutting or stabbing oneself, hanging oneself, jumping from a height, and taking poison. An editor therefore who wants to clarify these lines can choose two or three of the known ways, adjust the gender of the demonstrative pronouns to make them fit, and offer readers the particulars. Sword, noose, and hemlock are possibilities,[19] but in any case, there had to be in addition big, vivid gestures and significant objects that were recognizable at a distance. Compare the discussions of some demonstrative pronouns in Homer above (pp. 36–37) and in Plato below (112–13).

I HOPE TO DIE: ARISTOPHANES *KNIGHTS* 180–86

Aristophanes *Knights* 180–86 requires a different sort of gesture, one that should have a counterpart in tragedy but could at the same time be different in direction and sweep when used in one form of drama or the other. The sense required is that of calling down destruction on oneself if the oath being sworn is not true. When such oaths are fully verbalized, an imprecation like ὀλοίμην (I hope to die) or ἀπάγξομαι (I'll be hanged) or the like is pronounced. At the same time, a synergistic action is to accompany the words. Where exactly and how hands and arms and face were disposed, and the extent to which posture and gesture would differ in different contexts surely varied from person to person and place to place.

In the present example, a gesture provided such an apodosis. Household slaves A and B (who remind us of Nicias and Demosthenes) are persuading the Sausage-Seller that he has a great future before him. But he has to be personally rotten if he is going to have success as a leader of the people. Slave A says: "You'll be great, because you're trash from the marketplace and pushy." Sausage-Seller responds as a modest, well brought up young man might do: "I don't think I deserve to be great." Slave B becomes alarmed: "Oh oh! Why ever do you say you're not worthy? I think you are conscious of some good quality in yourself. You aren't from a high-class family, are you?" And here the Sausage-Seller swears he is not: "No, by the gods—if I am not the product of trash."[20] Here, as in the examples cited above, (pp. 37–38) a protasis is uttered, but no apodosis.[21]

[18] καὶ δὸς τουτὶ Κλεοφῶντι φέρων καὶ τουτουσὶ τοῖσι ποϱισταῖς Μύϱμηκί θ' ὁμοῦ καὶ Νικομάχωι τόδε τ' Ἀϱχενόμωι·

[19] See (**A**) Radermacher 1954: 350–51, (**A**) Dover 1993: 205–6, 382.

[20] μὰ τοὺς θεούς / εἰ μὴ 'κ πονηϱῶν γ'.

[21] Cf., e.g., (**A**) van Leeuwen 1909 *comm. ad Knights*, line 186, εἰ μὴ . . . γε = ἀλλά γε, (**A**) Neil 1901 *ad loc.*: "The answer εἰ μὴ . . . γε, which puzzled or baffled copyists of several

An actor on the stage spoke as much with his body as with his voice, and his movements were continuous. He did not stop moving for three lines of dialogue and then start again only when one special thing he had to say needed reinforcement by gesture. When therefore we meet an "incomplete" conditional sentence, we are not to imagine that this is a single instance of gesticulation. The ellipse is a clue, a pointer, an index to vigorous and continuous body movement. And so when the Sausage-Seller starts his oath with, "No, by the gods," a gesture can supply the punishment he asks for if he does not fulfill his oath. Essentially what the gesture says is, "I hope to die,"[22] and on the comic stage we can suppose that some extravagant ways to die could be evoked by hand and body signals. Along with or right after his gesture, he produces his surprising protasis, "If I am not from trash."

I HOPE TO DIE: ARISTOPHANES *THESMOPHORIAZOUSAE* 897–98

Aristophanes *Thesmophoriazousae* 897–98 is very like *Knights* 185–86, although the protasis, "If I am not Kritylla etc.,"[23] does not carry a comic surprise. An invocation of self-destruction is possibly implicit here also, as it was in the Sausage-Seller's oath, for an oath if not made truly or if not carried out to the letter could hurt the oath-taker, no matter whether one included an explicit invocation of self-destruction or not.

I HOPE TO DIE: ARISTOPHANES FR. 654

A fragment from an unknown play has Prometheus uttering a possibly similar affirmation. He says: ". . . if I am not Prometheus I am lying about the rest."[24] Kassel and Austin 1984 cite Koch, who fills out the line in Latin that can be translated as follows: "Prometheus is speaking: <I hope to die> if I am not Prometheus <which the other party had doubted>. I concede that the rest of what I said are lies."[25]

The phrase "I hope to die" could have been expressed by means of the synergistic action that normally accompanied such oaths. Cf. the discussion of Euripides *Cyclops* 261 above (p. 65).

MSS . . . as well as Porson, Elmsley, Dobree. . . . There is probably an ellipse of οὐδὲν ἄλλο, τί ἄλλο, τί δέ or the like, after which we find εἰ μὴ . . . γε often." (**A**) Fritzsche 1838:" εἰ μὴ . . . γε vim habet graviter minuendi estque tantummodo." Wakker 1994: 284, note 27: "The qualification offered by the εἰ μὴ constituent may be so radical that it wholly replaces the preceding (negative) assertion by its opposite."

[22] Watson 1991: 9–10 notes instances of "Selbstverwünschung" in tragedy and later poetry.

[23] μὰ τὼ θεὼ εἰ μὴ Κρίτυλλά γ'.

[24] εἰ μὴ Προμηθεύς εἰμι τἆλλα ψεύδομαι.

[25] Prometheus loquitur (*dispeream*) *ni Prometheus sum* (de quo aliter dubitaverat): *cetera quae dixi mendacia esse concedo.*

POINTING: ARISTOPHANES *BIRDS* 438–44

An amusing example of what might seem at first glance to be an instance of aposiopesis can be found at Aristophanes *Birds* 438–44. Peisetairos cites the monkey knife-maker who compacts with his wife that she will not "bite these or pull at my balls or excavate my—"[26] and here the Chorus interposes: "I don't suppose you mean the—no way."[27] And Peisetairos continues: "No, I mean my eyes."[28] But aposiopesis is not the issue here. A commentator explains that the hoopoe or the chorus leader is pointing to his bottom as he speaks.[29] The commentator, himself a native speaker although some centuries perhaps later than Aristophanes, understands that a hand gesture can complete a sentence.

Continuities: Curses!

Use of continuities as reliable guides to the look and sense of an entire signifying movement of head, hands, or body has been discussed above (pp. 20–21). One particular such gesture, observable among modern Greek speakers and detectable in ancient texts, has hardly been noticed. A Greek male today, if he finds something abhorrent, may hold both hands an inch or two away from his chest, palms in, thumbs out, and revolve both hands a quarter turn, vigorously back and forth. He may even actually touch or pluck at the cloth of his shirt or coat. A Greek woman may sketch the same gesture by making a plucking gesture in the area of her collarbone. What they are doing symbolically is shaking out their clothes. A popular jingle explains the gesture: "If ever I go by Naxos, I shall shake my jacket."[30]

In the following pages I display examples of this gesture from the New Testament, Acts, from the Septuagint, Esdras, and from Lysias's speech against Andocides in order to compose a long if spotty history of the gesture's use, and to illustrate some scenes in Aristophanes.

CURSES! NEW TESTAMENT, ACTS 18.6

With all the reservations one must apply in such extrapolations, the gesture one sees today appears to be a direct lineal descendant of Paul's gesture

[26] δάκνειν τούτους ἐμὲ μήτ' ὀρχίπεδ' ἕλκειν μήτ' ὀρύττειν—
[27] οὔτι που τὸν—; οὐδαμῶς.
[28] οὐκ ἀλλὰ τὠφθαλμὼ λέγω.
[29] δεικνὺς τὸν πρωκτόν (Schol. Aristophanes *Birds* 442).
[30] κι όταν περάσω απο τη Νάξο / το γιακά μου θα τινάξω.

once he was through remonstrating with the blaspheming Jews at Corinth: "He shook out his garment and said, 'Your blood be on your own head.' "[31]

Authoritative translations of the New Testament do not alert readers to the significance of this gesture, a reticence that is, given the exigencies of responsible translation, not only understandable but even desirable. The King James version has, "And when they opposed and blasphemed, he shook his raiment and said unto them . . ." The Holy Bible, Revised Standard Version, has, "And when they opposed and reviled him, he shook out his garments and said to them. . . . " Both of these versions give a bare and yet adequate summary of what the Greek conveys. In a third example, however, an attempt to provide lively detail by means of specificity turns out to be a misdirection. In The New English Bible, the translators import into their version more detail than the Greek warrants: "But when they opposed him and resorted to abuse, he shook out the skirts of his cloak and said to them . . . etc." By adding skirts, they depict Paul symbolically shaking the dust of the road from the bottom of his long cloak.

Now Paul is uttering what could be a curse as he leaves. He is doing so more or less in accordance with instructions Jesus Christ issued to his apostles when he sent them out into the world. For Jesus told his departing apostles what to do if the people of a house or city would not accept them and would not hear their message. The apostles in that case were to leave that household or city, and as they left they were to shake the dust from their feet.[32] To shake the dust from one's feet might seem no more than a symbolic way of saying: "I want no part of this place. I am leaving." Indeed the text of Mark adds that they are to do so "in witness" (εἰς μαρτύριον αὐτοῖς). But a later text suggests that the act of shaking off the dust from one's shoes in a particular context can be understood as a synergistic act that completes or reinforces a curse. "St. Quintilian shook the dust from his shoes and said cursed be the house and cursed its inhabitants for eternity" (Gregory of Tours, *Life of the Fathers* 4.3). If this provides the right interpretation of Jesus' instructions, then the phrase "in witness" introduces the promise that the unheeding will find the day of judgment less tolerable than will the people of Sodom and Gomorrah.

To return, however, to Paul at Corinth, he is shaking out his cloak, which is equally a synergistic act that capacitates or reinforces a curse. The difference is that he is shaking his cloak and not his shoes. He is therefore not shaking the dust off, as "skirts of his cloak" implies. He is shaking them out of his bosom, as the following passage from Esdras shows.

[31] ἀντιτασσομένων δὲ αὐτῶν καὶ βλασφημούντων ἐκτιναξάμενος τὰ ἱμάτια εἶπεν πρὸς αὐτοὺς τὸ αἷμα ὑμῶν ἐπὶ τὴν κεφαλὴν ὑμῶν.

[32] NT, Matthew 10.14, Mark 6.11, Luke 10.10–11; cf. Acts 13.50–51.

CURSES! SEPTUAGINT, ESDRAS 2.15.13

A passage in the Septuagint, Esdras 2.15.13, is comparable. Although the mise-en-scène is admittedly that of another society, there are nonetheless some cultural similarities throughout the Mediterranean area, and the language of the translation—for all its inelegancies—is Greek: "And I called the priests and swore them to act in accordance with this word. And I shook out my mantle and I said that God in that way has shaken out from his house and his work every man who would not set up this word, and he will be shaken out and empty. And all the church said Amen and praised God."[33]

CURSES! LYSIAS 6.51

An earlier, ceremonial form of the curse may be inferred from sketchy references in older literature. At Lysias 6.51 the speaker describes how Andocides was formally cursed: "And after this, priestesses and priests stood facing west and cursed him, and they shook out their scarlet cloaks in accordance with the old and venerable lawful custom."[34] In another comparable case, imagine the priests and priestesses as they cursed Alcibiades: all but Theano shook out their red cloaks as they uttered the words of the curse (Plutarch *Alcibiades* 22.4).

The combination of word and act has the look of a synergy, which is to say that in order to reinforce a curse, a known, prescribed body motion should accompany the words. The phrase σπόνδας τέμνειν shows action in terminology.[35] To go a little further: if by shaking out one's cloak in a

[33] καὶ ἐκάλεσα τοὺς ἱερεῖς καὶ ὥρκισα αὐτοὺς ποιῆσαι ὡς τὸ ῥῆμα τοῦτο. καὶ τὴν ἀναβολήν μου ἐξετίναξα καὶ εἶπα οὕτως ἐτίναξε ὁ θεὸς πάντα ἄνδρα ὃς οὐ στήσει τὸν λόγον τοῦτον, ἐκ τοῦ οἴκου αὐτοῦ καὶ ἐκ κόπου αὐτοῦ, καί ἐστι ἐκτετιναγμένος καὶ κενός. The word ἀναβολήν, which, following LSJ *s.v.* I translate "mantle," represents a Hebrew word *ḥṓṣen* that appears both here in the Hebrew text, i.e., Nehemiah 5.13, and at Psalms 128.7, where it is translated in the Septuagint as κόλπον, "the bosom of his cloak." Cf. the King James version (Nehemiah 5.13): "Also I shook out my lap and said . . . etc." Another expression is suggestive: Septuagint, Isaiah 33.15: καὶ τὰς χεῖρας ἀποσειόμενος ἀπὸ δώρων. LSJ does not offer parallels s.v. ἀποσείω for this expression.

[34] καὶ ἐπὶ τούτοις ἱερεῖαι καὶ ἱερεῖς στάντες κατηράσαντο πρὸς ἑσπέραν καὶ φοινικίδας ἀνέσεισαν κατὰ τὸ νόμιμον τὸ παλαιὸν καὶ ἀρχαῖον. If one were to follow LSJ in the interpretation of this phrase, a waving of red flags would accompany this curse. LSJ *s.v.* ἀνασείω cites Lysias 6.51 and glosses "wave," the sense seeming to be "wave flags," since φοίνικις *s.v.* is glossed "'red flag' hung out as the signal for action . . . generally 'red banner.' " But see Clinton 1974: 33–34, who reasons that "red cloaks" is what was meant here rather than "red banners," and Watson 1991: 51, who assumes "red cloaks" without comment.

[35] Taplin 1978: 65 notes some instances. Cf. the kommos, where breast beating, tearing of cheeks, etc. ought to accompany the lament. Cf. Sophocles *Aias* 1175–79, where Teucer utters a curse as he cuts off a lock of his hair.

certain prescribed way one strengthened or completed a curse, the act alone, quite without accompanying words, could express the force of a curse by means of the sort of shorthand communication that gestures effect (as the gesture continues to do in Greece today, although not everyone who shakes his jacket is fully aware of the act's stern antecedents).

CURSES! ARISTOPHANES *LYSISTRATA* 401–2

A comic chorus may refer to movements they are making as they dance.[36] In Aristophanes *Clouds* 275–90 the chorus enter, identify themselves as clouds, and then at lines 287–90 sing, "But let us shake off the rainy mist of our immortal form and contemplate with far-seeing eye the earth." They shake themselves and divest themselves of their cloaks. At the exodos of Aristophanes *Lysistrata*, the chorus can be imagined as jumping (πάλλων, lines 1304, 1310) with their heads shaking out their hair (ταὶ δὲ κόμαι σείονται, line 1312). Earlier in the same play, the chorus shook themselves in an attempt to shake off old age.[37] Another chorus of old men shake torches (Aristophanes *Frogs* 340 with Dover 1993 *ad loc.*), shake their legs vigorously in the dance (γόνυ πάλλεται γερόντων, 345), and shake off the sorrows of old age (346–48).

In view of this practice of self-referencing, consider the old men who make up the chorus of *Lysistrata*. Aristophanes may have been amusing his audience with an implied curse at *Lysistrata* 401–2. The old men have been doused with water, and they complain that among the gross insults they have received from Lysistrata's troops was a soaking, and the result is that they have to shake out their clothes just as though they had pissed themselves.[38] Now senile incontinence was admittedly an element of the humor here,[39] but surely in addition there is a strongly implied stage business. The old men dance about, shaking out their cloaks in the recognized curse gesture, and their anger becomes visible. When a little later they speak again of the soaking (469–70), one can easily imagine them dancing again, and again shaking their cloaks in anger.

CURSES! ARISTOPHANES *ACHARNIANS* 340–46

Another dance scene in which angered old men dance and shake out their cloaks can be envisioned in a play from a decade earlier than the *Lysistrata*, namely Aristophanes *Acharnians* 340–46. There, Dikaiopolis tells the

[36] Cf. Henrichs 1995: 56–111 on such references in tragedy.

[37] πᾶν τὸ σῶμα κἀποσείσασθαι τὸ γῆρας τόδε.

[38] ὥστε θαἰματίδια σείειν πάρεστιν ὥσπερ ἐνεουρηκότας.

[39] See (**A**) Henderson 1987 *ad loc.*

charcoal-burners to empty their cloaks of the stones they had meant to throw at him. They do so and tell him to drop his sword. But Dikaiopolis hesitates. They may have stones still hidden in their cloaks. Now they shake out their cloaks. "It's been shaken out to the ground. Don't you see it being shaken? Come, no excuses please, just lay down your weapon for this is getting shaken as I turn in the dance."[40] Dikaiopolis answers, "So you were all getting ready to shake your shouts at me."[41] The point of this last is obscure, and I will not try to find an explanation for what appears to be a surprise word. It is enough to observe that an element of the fun here can be the dance, which entails shaking out cloaks. The chorus show that their cloaks are empty of stones but at the same time they are cursing Dikaiopolis.

Summary

Demonstrative pronouns without referents, when Aristophanes uses them, point as they do in Homer to communication by signifying motions of head and hands and body. Two instances of another sort of ellipse show that both of them could have been filled by the nod, slight or exaggerated, upward and back used by Greeks in conversation today. Gestures can likewise provide an apodosis, one that could be extravagant in a standard scene such as when a character commits himself, as the Sausage-Seller does, to an oath. In another instance, a modern gesture provides an insight into what the mere words of an ancient text report. A Greek today may shake the front of his or her garment, actually or symbolically, i.e., pluck at but not touch the vicinity of the collarbone, to express abhorrence. From this gesture, we can derive a picture of what Paul was doing in Corinth when he remonstrated with the Jews there. That picture is likewise serviceable when applied to a passage in Lysias, where a formal curse is being uttered. The same picture also helps one to understand or visualize some possible stage business in Aristophanes' *Acharnians* and *Lysistrata*.

[40] ἐκσέσεισται χαμᾶζ'· οὐχ ὁρᾷς σειόμενον; ἀλλὰ μή μοι πρόφασιν, ἀλλὰ κατάθου τὸ βέλος ὡς ὅδε γε σειστὸς ἅμα τῆι στροφῆι γίγνεται.

[41] Ἐμέλλετ' ἆρ' ἅπαντες ἀνασείσειν βοήν. The translation is that of (**A**) Henderson 1998: 101. An alternate reading, ἀνήσειν βοῆς for ἀνασείσειν βοὴν, eliminates one reference to shaking.

SEVEN

ORATORS

Forensic Oratory

NOW TO TURN to oratory, where forensic speeches provide instructive examples. Oratory had a long history in Greece, and Homer attests the power of persuasion long before the art of oratory receives its formal name. By the late fifth century, a highly developed system of popular courts had evolved at Athens. As a result, men who knew how to compose persuasive arguments gained power for themselves by speaking in assemblies and courts. They also wrote speeches for those less gifted friends and clients who found themselves from time to time forced to appear in court, where deficient persuasiveness could end one's life.

These speeches reach modern readers in their edited form, which is to say, a speech as originally composed could have been used in court as an armature on which a speaker could build, or it could have served verbatim as text. But after the trial was over (if in fact a trial took place—some of our speeches may have been composed for trials that never reached court), an author could rewrite extensively if he chose to do so. The speeches therefore in their present form cannot be read as word-for-word accounts of what actually transpired in the court. They can record what the author wrote for himself or for a prosecutor or a defendant who needed help in expressing himself effectively under the constraints of a court trial, but they do not necessarily record exactly what was actually said.

As for what was taken into account in preparation, those who composed speeches included accommodations for nonverbal communication, perhaps without even thinking of it, when they wrote out their texts. The person who performed the text hardly needed to be told to use his body as well as his voice. It is how he conducted himself every day no matter whether he was addressing a court or not.

A word concerning the physical circumstances of a forensic speech: Each party in a court trial had to represent himself. He had to explain, before a judging panel of (often) five hundred citizens, why he was right and why and where his opponent was wrong. But where would an average citizen have learned to speak in court? For those untutored persons, sometimes in court for the first time in their lives, expert help was vital. A man's property, his civic identity, his very life could be at stake. It is this combination of need and expertise that makes texts of forensic speeches a productive source of examples of speech amplified or completed by gesture. Citizens in court needed to look as well as sound as though they were themselves, i.e., private citizens pushed into court through no fault of their own and certainly not through any specially developed skills. In accordance with this need, they moved their hands and heads naturally, as they would at home or in the agora.

Deliberative or Display Oratory

Would deliberative (συμβουλευτική) or display (ἐπιδεικτική) oratory provide comparable examples? I have not undertaken a systematic examination of this question. The orators who regularly addressed a town meeting or who delivered official funeral orations were doing so because they wanted to. That is, they had knowledge and experience and an agenda. The poor soul who found himself in court with only an observer's acquaintance with oratory, needed to appear as just that to the judging panel: a poor, innocent, much abused, ordinary man when defendant, or as a righteously outraged, personally affronted amateur, when prosecutor.

Citizens gathered to hear Pericles speak over the burial of Athenians who had died in battle had a right to expect skillful manipulation of their responses; and when Pericles spoke deliberatively at a meeting of the ekklesia, he likewise employed a highly developed art of persuasion with all requisite attendant gestures. But neither sort of oratory required of its practitioners a delivery that resembled ordinary conversation. For that reason the breaks in conventional syntax which imply gestures cannot be expected in deliberative or display oratory with any great frequency.

Zanker 1995: 45–50, in a discussion of "The Intellectual as Good Citizen," describes a statue of Sophocles that has the poet all wrapped up in his *himation*, his arms obviously not free to gesticulate. He sees Sophocles here as good citizen addressing the assembly. He adduces a well-known exchange between Aeschines and Demosthenes, which started with Aeschines asking a judging panel to remember a statue of Solon located in the agora of the island of Salamis. He reminds the judges that "Solon keeps his arm hidden beneath his mantle" (1.25). Unfortunately he goes on to say that the statue renders Solon as he actually appeared before the Athenian assembly, a bit of imaginative reconstruction that opens him to a thrust from Demosthenes (19.251), who easily disassembles the fantasy statue.[1]

[1] Cf. [Dem.] 25.34; Thomas 1989: 51.

Suppose that for many years speakers addressing the assembly were required not to use their hands as they spoke. It was surely the case that in the fourth century such constraints had less authority. In a lawcourt, where plaintiffs could weep and plead and parade their children, they must have used their hands, and a plaintiff or defendant could express himself with all the resources he had.

Alcidamas

A chapter enitled "Orators" and addressing essential questions of delivery can well begin with a quotation from Alcidamas's essay *On Sophists* 13: "Men who write speeches that are to be delivered in the lawcourts avoid specificities and emulate the expressions of persons who are improvising, and they seem to be writing their best when they provide speeches that are least like written ones."[2]

Alcidamas, writing early in the fourth century, may have had Antiphon in mind for one, whom Thucydides (8.68) describes as especially helpful to people at trial in the courts. And when Alcidamas says "people who are improvising," he can be assumed to mean people who are standing up and telling their story in a natural way, using the same rhythms, intonations, postures, and gestures that they used in day-to-day conversations. But what does it mean to write a speech that is least like a written speech? It ought to mean a speech that resembles normal, everyday talk, which is to say, utterances that are not in tight compliance with the rules of syntax defining formal written prose: it is a medium in which sentences can change subjects in mid-course and where whole clauses can be left to the improvisatory skills of a litigant/performer, to be expressed by gesture, or not.

Antiphon

Antiphon, in writing for such speakers, might be expected to include sentences that asked for improvisation, and it is not surprising to find examples, four of which are noted here: first an "incomplete" conditional sentence of a kind cited throughout this study, one where a protasis is uttered, and then instead of a written apodosis, a contrary protasis is introduced by the phrase "but otherwise" (εἰ δὲ μή) and followed by its

[2] οἱ γὰρ εἰς τὰ δικαστήρια τοὺς λόγους γράφοντες φεύγουσι τὰς ἀκριβείας καὶ μιμοῦνται τὰς τῶν αὐτοσχεδιαζόντων ἑρμηνείας, καὶ τότε κάλλιστα γράφειν δοκοῦσιν ὅταν ἥκιστα γεγραμμένοις ὁμοίους πορίσωνται λόγους.

own apodosis; second, a less common sort of "incomplete" conditional sentence, one introduced by ὅπου; third, a collocation of the particles νῦν δέ . . . γάρ (but as it is, . . . because . . .), which has been noted in Aristophanes (p. 70 above) and is given fuller documentation below (pp. 113–17), where Plato's use of the same collocation is discussed; and fourth, a quotation whose effectiveness would be enhanced by an introductory gesture.

WELL AND GOOD: ANTIPHON 6.23

The speaker is defending himself in the Palladion on a charge of having caused the death of a boy for whom he as choregos was responsible. He recapitulates a challenge he presented to his prosecutor: "I told him to go with all the witnesses he wanted to the people who were present—I named each one—and question and test them, those who were free in a manner befitting free men, who for their own sakes and for the sake of the truth would tell the truth of what happened, and the slaves, if he thought upon questioning them they were telling the truth, <GESTURE = well and good>; otherwise I was ready to give over all of my own for torture and whatever other slaves belonging to others he might order."[3]

THIS IS INCREDIBLE: ANTIPHON 6.19

A second instance shows a less common sort of "incompleteness." The same speaker in reviewing what he represents as the facts lists them in a long subordinate clause that comes to an end without any concluding independent clause. "Where in the first place the prosecutors themselves admit that the boy's death was neither premeditated nor contrived, and where they admit that everything that was done was done in the open and in the presence of many witnesses, both men and boys, free and slave, from whose presence any person who did anything wrong would be wholly visible and whoever charged an innocent person would be wholly exposed. . . . " The sentence ends here without a written independent clause. With the next sentence the speaker begins a new tack, namely a history of the procedure at hand: "It is worthwhile to note both the intent of my opponents and the manner in which they came to this business."

(**A**) Blass 1905 *ad loc.* cites Reiske as thinking an apodosis is lacking at the end of chapter 19 but does not seem wholly convinced ("apodosin deesse putavit R"). (**A**) Gernet 1954 *ad loc.* also is diffident. He asks if

[3] τούτους ἐρωτᾶν καὶ ἐλέγχειν, τοὺς μὲν ἐλευθέρους ὡς χρὴ τοὺς ἐλευθέρους οἳ σφῶν ἕνεκα καὶ τοῦ δικαίου ἔφραζον ἂν τἀληθῆ καὶ τὰ γενόμενα, τοὺς δὲ δούλους, εἰ μὲν αὐτῶι ἐρωτῶντι τἀληθῆ δοκοῖεν λέγειν—εἰ δὲ μή, ἕτοιμος εἴην διδόναι βασανίζειν . . . κτλ.

an apodosis is lacking (deest apodosis?). Suppose, however, that there is an ellipsis? What was the desired sense? And how was it expressed?

If what the speaker wanted to express was amazement at finding himself standing in a courtroom defending himself in view of what he has just related, then a single gesture could have said that vividly. To put it succinctly, the gesture would say: "I shouldn't be here. This is crazy," and if we do not know exactly how an Athenian would have said that with his hands and head, we can be confident that there was a way.

QUOTATION: ANTIPHON 6.4

An actor on the comic stage needed to tell an audience beforehand that he was about to utter a quotation (see pp. 67–70 above). The same is true of a man pleading his case in court. Consider for instance Antiphon 6.4. The speaker is telling the fifty-one *ephetai* who make up the judging body of the Palladion what their duty is. In doing so, he evokes a provision from the Draconian lawcode on homicide by approximating a phrase from that code.[4] "The law has so much force that even if a man kills a person over whom he has full control and even if there is no one to avenge that person, he purifies himself in fear of customary observance and gods."[5] Would that short phrase have the desired force if only pronounced slowly and distinctly, without appropriate gesticulation? Possibly. But in a world where gesticulation was continuous, it is easy to suppose that a speaker moved his hands in a signifying way to alert the audience. The hope was to insinuate into the consciousness of the *ephetai* an intimation of the august source of the precept.

NO: ANTIPHON 1.11

An ellipsis filled by gesture at Antiphon 1.11 is like those in Aristophanes (discussed above, p. 70) and in Plato (discussed below, pp. 113–17). The speaker, who is prosecuting his step-mother for deliberate homicide, lodges a protest before the Court of the Areopagos as follows: "And yet I know very well that if these men had come to me as soon as it was announced to them that I was proceeding against my father's killer, and if they had been willing to hand over the slaves they had and I had been unwilling to accept them, they would have provided this as the strongest sort of evidence that they were not responsible for the killing. But as it is <GESTURE = No, they did not and so there is no use in continuing this line of

[4] (**A**) Gagarin 1997 *ad loc.*

[5] The approximating phrase is καὶ ἄν τις κτείνηι τινά and its model is καὶ ἐὰν μὴ ἐκ προνοίας κτείνηι τίς τινα (*IG* I^3 104.11).

speculation>, because I am the one who is willing to be the examiner,[6] and I am the one who is telling these very people to do the examining instead of me. Surely for me these same things are evidence that <my half-brothers> are responsible for the killing, because if they had been willing to give up their slaves for torture and I had not accepted <the challenge>, it would have been evidence for them. So let the same <reasoning> exist for me, when I am willing to take up an examination of the matter, and they are not willing to give over <their slaves>."

The gesture, for which I have provided a rather wordy equivalent, could have been a simple lift of the chin signifying no.

Andocides

Andocides, aristocrat, sporadically in trouble with the Athenian state, and second in time of the ten canonical Attic orators, was notorious at Athens in 415 as a profaner of the Eleusinian mysteries.

THIS IS INCREDIBLE: ANDOCIDES 1.127

As a later consequence of that profanation, Andocides found himself defending himself in court in 399 B.C.E., against a serious charge: the accusation was that he had exercised certain citizen rights at a time when he had been deprived by law of those rights as a result of his earlier conviction for having profaned the Eleusinian Mysteries.

In the course of his defense, he explains how his accuser, Kallias, might benefit from having Andocides out of the way. But as he makes his explanation, he finds a place for illustrative panels from Kallias's exuberant and self-contradictory domestic life: Kallias married Chrysilla, Ischomachos's daughter, and before a year was out, he had installed Chrysilla's mother in his household, using her as a wife also. He had become, as Andocides puts it with a play on Kallias's family connection with Eleusis, priest to Mother and Maid. Chrysilla in shame tried to hang herself but was kept from doing so and put to bed. She then left the house. Mother had driven out daughter. But then Kallias drove mother out of the house as well, having had his fill of her. But then mother claimed to be pregnant by him. He denied that he was the father. When the mother's relatives appeared at the Apatouria intending to introduce the child as a future citizen, Kallias, as officiating priest of his phratry, asked, "Whose is the child?"

[6] καίτοι εὖ οἶδα γ', εἰ οὗτοι πρὸς ἐμὲ ἐλθόντες, ἐπειδὴ τάχιστα αὐτοῖς ἀπηγγέλθη ὅτι ἐπεξίοιμι τοῦ πατρὸς τὸν φονέα, ἠθέλησαν τὰ ἀνδράποδα ἃ ἦν αὐτοῖς παραδοῦναι, ἐγὼ δὲ μὴ ἠθέλησα παραλαβεῖν, αὐτὰ ἂν ταῦτα μέγιστα τεκμήρια παρείχοντο ὡς οὐκ ἔνοχοί εἰσι τῶι φόνωι. νῦν δ'—ἐγὼ γάρ εἰμι τοῦτο μὲν ὁ θέλων αὐτὸς . . . . κτλ

The response was, "Kallias, son of Hipponikos." Whereupon Kallias answered, "I am he," and the reply was, "The child is yours." In response to this asseveration, Kallias took hold of the altar and swore (λαβόμενος τοῦ βωμοῦ ὤμοσε) that he had never fathered any child except Hipponikos with Glaukon's daughter.

But then at some time later, he fell in love with the adventurous old lady again, i.e., the mother, and installed her once again in his house. Then he took the child, who was big by this time, to the Kerykes to register as his own. He was challenged, and the Kerykes voted that if a father swear that a child is his, they accept the oath and admit the child to their rolls. At this, Kallias took hold of the altar and swore that the child was his own lawful issue, born of Chrysilla. <The child> whom he disowned on oath.[7]

(**A**) MacDowell 1962: 154–55 observes that the aorist ἀπώμοσε (he disowned on oath) makes Kallias's act of disowning either simultaneous with the oath-taking (ὤμοσεν) or subsequent to it, and that neither of these two alternatives gives the required sense. For read literally, the sentence could be, "He took hold of the altar and swore that the child was his own legitimate child, born of Chrysilla, and afterward (or simultaneously) he disowned him on oath." MacDowell, accordingly on the supposition that a πρότερον (previously) has fallen out of the text by haplography, prints ὃν <πρότερον> ἀπώμοσε, which produces the desired sense, viz., "whom he had previously sworn was not his own."

Thiel 1964: 406, note 1, however, in a review offers another way to read the text: "If we consider that Greeks spoke (and speak) with their hands and faces and that Andocides was an extremely lively platform speaker, and if we imagine him being silent for a moment after quoting Kallias's two oaths and then adding—with a grimace and a gesture—those two words, ὃν ἀπώμοσε, we may take it for granted that nobody misunderstood him." That is to say, when a gesture is added, the aorist ἀπώμοσε, which had been contradictory or irrelevant, becomes a comprehensible element of exposition. For consider how the sentence can be translated when the gesture is included: "He took hold of the altar and swore that the child was his own legitimate child, born of Chrysilla. <GESTURE = "imagine my surprise, disgust, dismay at this perjured self-contradiction concerning a child> whom he had disowned on oath."[8]

Thiel's enlightening alternative can be qualified in one respect, for he sees the text as transcript. We follow the words of the manuscript—he assumes—and we can imagine, word by word, the progress of the trial.

[7] Andocides 1.127. The manuscript reads: λαβόμενος τοῦ βωμοῦ ὤμοσεν ἦ μὴν τὸν παῖδα ἑαυτοῦ εἶναι γνήσιον ἐκ Χρυσίλλης γεγονότα. ὃν ἀπώμοσε.

[8] Notice that Andocides, on both of the two occasions (1.126, 127) when he has Kallias swearing an oath, is careful to include the vivid detail that Kallias took hold of the altar. He reveals a necessary or at least strengthening synergy of act and word.

But orators' speeches, no matter to what degree they had been prepared beforehand, could also be edited a little or a lot after they had been used in court, and before being released for general circulation. What we may have, therefore, in the text of Andocides 1.127 is an illustration of how Andocides prepared his speech for himself. He knew beforehand that he would add gesticulation as punctuation here, and so he chose his wording to fit. Or, to imagine a different but equally plausible sequence, in editing his text afterward, he found the spontaneity and naturalness of that mode of expression right, whether or not he said it exactly that way while addressing the judges.[9] And so he made the small change that would enliven that part of his written version.

POINTING: ANDOCIDES 1.133

Andocides turns to an attack on Agyrrhios: "I shall tell you why these men are now showing recognition of these <liturgies I performed>. Agyrrhios here, the perfect gentleman, became the principal in a group that collected the present customs duties."[10] In applying the honorific καλὸς κἀγαθός (literally, "fair and good" but with a sense like "perfect gentleman" in some contexts), Andocides by tone and by gesture evokes the opposite and opprobrious word *vile* or *base* (πονηρός).[11] In fact, to attempt a general rule, whenever a deictic iota appears and it is obvious that the object or person intended is in the vicinity, we should picture for ourselves a pointing finger or hand. In this case, the pointing would in itself underline the phrase ὁ καλὸς κἀγαθός.

Lysias

Lysias came from a monied family, friendly with Socrates and Plato and lacking Athenian citizenship. He suffered under the tyranny of the Thirty (404/3) and he later wrote speeches for Athenians who needed to speak in court, as well as in his own causes. If we cannot be sure which speeches in the body of oratory attributed to him are really his, we can still look there for modes of expression that were contemporary with him.

YOU FILL IN THE REST: LYSIAS 13.37

His oration against Agoratos enlarges on Agoratos's complicity in the terror at Athens in 404/3, and he describes at one point a perversion of

[9] Cf. Dover 1968: 194–95.

[10] Ἀγύρριος γὰρ οὑτοσί, ὁ καλὸς κἀγαθὸς ἀρχώνης ἐγένετο . . .

[11] Cf. Socrates (p. 101 below), Antigone (p. 101 above), Demosthenes (pp. 88–90 below), and Theramenes (p. 101 below).

judicial process. At 13.37 he says: "For the Thirty were sitting on the benches where the *prytaneis* sit now. And two tables were set up in front of the Thirty. And you had to put your ballot not into urns but plain to see on these tables: a ballot to convict on the farther table—so how was anyone going to be acquitted? In a word, all who went into the *bouleutērion* to be judged [in the time of the Thirty] were sentenced to death."[12]

The phrase "a ballot to convict on the farther table"[13] has troubled editors who want in addition a mention of the ballot that acquits. There should be, they assume, a δέ to correspond to that μέν.[14] An Athenian audience, however, would not have had a moment's trouble with the text as Thalheim has given it.

In the first place, in Athenian judicial procedures until sometime early in the fourth century, the order of choices presented to the judges was—outside of this wrongful exception—invariable. A ballot deposited in the nearer urn was that to convict, and a ballot in the farther urn was to acquit. When a change in voting procedure took place, and ballots registered a judicial decision by their configuration rather than by the urn into which they were dropped, the herald first announced the mode of voting to convict, and then that of voting to acquit. At the end of a trial, the herald first announced the number of ballots to convict, and then the number to acquit.[15] And in the single Athenian inscription where a full count of the votes is preserved, the votes to convict are recorded first, and then the votes to acquit.[16]

There was good reason to apply a rule of priority without exception: by keeping the order always the same, Athenians hoped to avoid confusion. Otherwise a judge might unintentionally cast a vote contrary to his decision. The fixed order also made the first decision at the first urn less urgent. Second thoughts are often best, and an arrangement by which a judge first decided whether or not to convict and then whether or not to acquit gave an advantage to the defendant.

[12] οἱ μὲν γὰρ τριάκοντα ἐκάθηντο ἐπὶ τῶν βάθρων οὗ νῦν οἱ πρυτάνεις καθέζονται· δύο δὲ τράπεζαι ἐν τῶι πρόσθεν τῶν τριάκοντα ἐκείσθην· τὴν δὲ ψῆφον οὐκ εἰς καδίσκους ἀλλὰ φανερὰν ἐπὶ τὰς τραπέζας ταύτας ἔδει τίθεσθαι, τὴν μὲν καθαιροῦσαν ἐπὶ τὴν ὑστέραν ὥστε ἐκ τίνος τρόπου ἔμελλέ τις αὐτῶν σωθήσεσθαι; ἑνὶ δὲ λόγωι, ὅσοι εἰς τὸ βουλευτήριον [ἐπὶ τῶν τριάκοντα] εἰσῆλθον κριθησόμενοι, ἁπάντων θάνατος κατεγιγνώσκετο.

[13] τὴν μὲν καθαιροῦσαν ἐπὶ τὴν ὑστέραν

[14] The apparatus criticus in (**A**) Thalheim 1901 attests efforts that began with publication of the Aldine edition and continued until Thalheim's own day to emend what is perceived to be a textual problem. After Thalheim, (**A**) Gernet 1924 *ad loc.* postulated a lacuna; (**A**) Hude 1912 printed the text of the Palatine Codex and noted only C in his apparatus criticus. (**A**) Sauppe 1841 *comm. ad loc.* had previously defended the reading of the Palatine codex, explaining that Lysias had expressed himself a little carelessly.

[15] (**A**) MacDowell 1971: 259; cf. Boegehold 1995: 30, 209–22.

[16] Boegehold 1995: 177, 183–84.

Lysias, it can be seen, describes two perversions of traditional and correct procedure. First, the Thirty have required the voting to be open, not secret, as it had been for almost two generations;[17] and second, they have reversed the traditional order "convict/acquit" and made it "acquit/convict," with psychological if not demonstrably practical ramifications.

To return then to Lysias's presentation: an Athenian, on hearing "the vote to convict on the farther table," did not need to hear "the vote to acquit on the nearer table." He could fill that in for himself. And as Theophrastos advises, it is better to leave something out for the hearer to fill in for himself: that way he feels challenged and fulfilled.[18] But the speaker could have paused briefly after καθαιροῦσαν to let the audience fill in the missing antithesis. At the same time he could have prompted his audience with a gesture, one that said in effect, "You can fill in the rest."

THIS IS INCREDIBLE: LYSIAS 24.2

Lysias 24.2 offers another example of a conditional sentence with a gesture as apodosis. A lame man is speaking in his own defense: he is trying to safeguard a pension he has from the city. He represents his accuser as a professional extortionist or sycophant and asks what sort of lowlife would go after a poor man like him for money: literally, "Because if he is trying by means of a prosecution to extort money from me—"[19] A new sentence then begins, and no syntactical construction (by commonly enunciated rules) concludes the immediately preceding sentence.[20]

But in this developing sentence, a pause, a mere silence, is not an adequate completion. The lame and bedeviled defendant needed to make a gesture to fill out his meaning. He wants to say, "If he is coming after me in hope of getting money, he is obviously misguided." (**A**) Thalheim 1901 *ad loc.* writes, "post συκοφαντεῖ subaudi ἄφρων ἐστί, id quod gestu indicatur," i.e., "After the Greek word συκοφαντεῖ supply 'he is out of his mind,' an expression that is shown by gesture." (**A**) Adams 1905 *ad loc.* comments, "The cripple's look and gesture call out a burst of laughter from the hearers which makes an apodosis quite unnecessary."

The appeal to gesture shows sympathetic reading on the part of Thalheim and Adams, but surely Lysias in composing the version of his speech that

[17] The secret ballot was instituted probably not long after 462. See Boegehold 1995: 20–22.

[18] Demetrios *On Style* 222; cf. Connor 1985: 17.

[19] εἰ μὲν γὰρ ἕνεκα χρημάτων με συκοφαντεῖ—

[20] (**A**) Frohberger 1871: 210 (Anhang) elects to change the text itself and accordingly prints οὐ γὰρ ἕνεκα χρημάτων με συκοφαντεῖ οὐδ' ὡς ἐχθρὸν κτλ (because he is not trying by means of a prosecution to extort money from me and he is not trying to punish me as a personal enemy), while (**A**) Hude 1912 *ad loc.* prints a dash, an editorial convention that shows a break and will usually be taken by readers to signal aposiopesis. (**A**) Edwards and Usher 1985: 264 explain the break as aposiopesis.

he finally published did not break his text off at that point because laughter had drowned out whatever the lame man had wanted to say. The break was a clear sign to his client to improvise with a gesture. The lame man for his part knew what gesture to make, given the condition expressed. If he did not know how to say "This is incredible" with his hands and head, he could be instructed at a rehearsal before the trial.

NO: [LYSIAS] 8.9

In a speech that survives in the body of Lysias's orations but that authorities have agreed is not by Lysias, a single example appears which resembles in structure that of examples noted above in Aristophanes and Antiphon (pp. 70, 82–83) and below in Plato (pp. 113–17) where it receives further discussion. A man is protesting abuse he is receiving from members of a society to which he has belonged. They have been abusing him verbally. How does he know? Someone told him. "Now then, as to the one who told me, don't ask. In the first place, you know already. . . . As a favor to me, he told my family, but you said it to him because you wanted to hurt me. And if I didn't believe this, I would be trying to disprove it. But as it is <GESTURE = No, it is not the case that I do not believe this> because this is consistent with the former, and this is a sufficient sign of that, and that of this."[21]

Demosthenes

Demosthenes, best known of all the Athenian orators to the world in general, is represented in the considerable body of speeches attributed to him by examples of forensic, deliberative, and display oratory. A single example from a forensic speech that may never have been actually delivered, shows what effective use can be made of quotation.

QUOTATION: DEMOSTHENES 21.83

Demosthenes 21.83 introduces the person of Straton. He says of him, "Straton is a person from Phaleron, a poor man and not politically active, but otherwise not 'poneros' and in fact a very good man."[22] He speaks of him again at 21.95: "This man perhaps is poor but he is not '*ponēros.*' "[23]

[21] καὶ ταῦτα εἰ μὲν ἠπίστουν, ἐξελέγχειν ἂν ἐζήτουν· νῦν δέ—ξυμβαίνει γὰρ καὶ ταῦτα τοῖς πρὸ τοῦ καὶ ἐμοὶ σημεῖα ταῦτα μὲν ἐκείνων ἐστίν, ἐκεῖνα δὲ τούτων ἱκανά.

[22] Στρατὼν Φαληρεὺς ἄνθρωπος πένης μέν τις καὶ ἀπράγμων, ἄλλως δ' οὐ πονηρός ἀλλὰ καὶ πάνυ χρηστός.

[23] οὗτος . . . πένης μὲν ἴσως ἐστίν, οὐ πονηρὸς δέ γε.

Jones 1957: 31 says: "Demosthenes is quite apologetic for introducing to the jury a poor hoplite witness—'he is poor maybe, but not a rascal'—a curious remark in a speech devoted to abuse of the rich man Meidias." Jones then goes on, using principally this "curious remark" as a basis, to argue that Athenian judging panels in the popular courts may have consisted more largely of rich men than has usually been supposed. Response to Jones's construction has been measured. Mossé 1962: 283–85 argues that the courts were mainly filled with the poor. Walbank 1963: 317–19, in a review of Mossé, writes, "This [*scil.* question of who filled the courts] is a fundamental matter affecting all questions of Athenian policy . . . and unfortunately the evidence is inconclusive." He concludes that each judging panel may have been unique and that an orator could modulate his appeals according to the nature of the audience.[24] Ober 1989: 210–11 considers Straton's part in the speech and concludes that "Demosthenes was particularly anxious to demonstrate that Strato was attacked because he was poor; this charge is implicit from the first "laborer but no rascal."

In view of the weight Jones has given the passage, further discussion is in order. First, remember that at Athens people who styled themselves ἐπιεικέστεροι (the more reasonable sort), or οἱ ἔχοντες (the haves), or οἱ γνώριμοι (the people one knows), or οἱ καλοὶ κἀγαθοί (the beautiful and good) might designate their less fortunate compatriots as οἱ κακοί (the vile) or οἱ πονηροί (the base). Note, e.g., the phrase πλούσιος καὶ μὴ πονηρός (rich and not base) at Aristophanes *Knights* 265, where the sense is "rich and not <poor, which implies> base." A literal polarity would be "rich and not poor," but the association of πτωχός/πένης (beggared/poor) and πονηρός (base) is taken for granted, and "trash" serves as synonym for "poor." But in whose minds (and mouths) is this an essential association? It is one ordained by upper classes and heard and surely quoted or echoed ironically or bitterly by lower classes.[25]

The poor people of Athens knew that the "better sort" called them κακοί and πονηροί, i.e., "trash." It should as a consequence have been perfectly possible for an orator or a comic playwright to evoke by means of the word πονηρός not only a poor wily Athenian but also a rich Athenian applying that label to a poor Athenian. And so in the case of Straton,

[24] Andocides at 1.146 seems to be talking to judges, all initiates in the Eleusinian Mysteries, who are not in sympathy with radical democracy. Dover 1974: 34, note 1 writes: "It must, however, be noted that since Straton had been charged with misconduct as an arbitrator and disenfranchised, there was a reasonable presumption that he was a very bad man, and also that a man who needed money was more easily corrupted than a man who did not." On pp. 34–35 he suggests that increasingly in the fourth century poor people "will have had a motive . . . for not seeking to be empanelled as jurors." Pay for attending the town meeting (ekklesia) went up but pay for judging in the courts did not (Markle 1985: 265–97; cf. Tod 1990: 146–73).

[25] See, e.g., de Ste Croix 1981: 425–26.

if we imagine Demosthenes making a gesture toward the judges as he pronounced the word πονηρός, the poor among them (supposing for the moment that there were poor) would understand that Demosthenes was saying: "poor but not 'trash' <as you and I know the so-called better sort customarily style a poor man>."

Lycurgus

Lycurgus, a statesman active at Athens in the 40s and 30s of the fourth century B.C.E., is known as an orator principally from the single complete speech of his that has survived. The year is 331. He is acting as prosecutor, and in the course of his speech he quotes extensively from Euripides' *Erechtheus* and other poetry.

QUOTATION: LYCURGUS 1.149

Toward the end of his speech, he tells the judging panel how they must vote. This is standard procedure in forensic speeches, but Lycurgus documents his own version with a quotation. He tells the panel they are to convict Leocrates of treason. He continues, "Each one of you should believe that if you acquit Leocrates you condemn your fatherland to death and slavery, that of the two urns set up here, one stands for betrayal, the other for survival, and that you are casting your ballots in one urn for desolation of your fatherland, in the other for happiness and security in the city."[26]

When he speaks of two urns being set up, each with a separate function, i.e., one for betrayal, the other for survival, he evokes a balloting procedure from a bygone time. In 331 at Athens, a vote to acquit was delivered by means of a bronze ballot, specially designed as a disk with a short, solid axle through its center, and a vote to convict was delivered by an identical bronze ballot, except that the axle was pierced. One or the other was to be deposited in a single amphora. This way of voting had been official procedure for some time, while the procedure Lycurgus evokes is attested in the late fifth century at Athens and not later (except here). An explanation for the seeming anachronism may start with the phrase "the two urns set up here," for the Greek words δυοῖν καδίσκοιν κειμένοιν form two-thirds of an iambic trimeter, the usual metrical scheme in Athenian drama

[26] ὑμῶν δ' ἕκαστον χρῆ νομίζειν τὸν Λεωκράτους ἀποψηφιζόμενον θάνατον τῆς πατρίδος καὶ ἀνδραποδισμὸν καταψηφίζεσθαι καὶ δυοῖν καδίσκοιν κειμένοιν τὸν μὲν προδοσίας τὸν δὲ σωτηρίας εἶναι καὶ τὰς ψήφους φέρεσθαι τὰς μὲν ὑπὲρ ἀναστάσεως τῆς πατρίδος, τὰς δ' ὑπὲρ ἀσφαλείας καὶ τῆς ἐν τῆι πόλει εὐδαιμονίας.

when conversation was being represented. Lycurgus accordingly could be quoting from a fifth-century drama in which a trial was featured or described. To alert his judging panel to the fact that he is quoting, he could make a gesture with his hand or arm, and the judges would recognize that they were being given an allusion, a reference to a scene from the grand days of Athenian tragedy.[27]

The Law Code of Gortyn

It remains now to discuss instances of the "incomplete" conditional sentence where no poet, orator, or historian can be rationally proposed as having anticipated a performance. The Law Code of Gortyn describes a series of laws inscribed on a wall that still stands (as reassembled) in Gortyn in Crete. Its initial publication may have been around the middle of the fifth century B.C.E. (The date is an inference based on language and letter forms.) The wall was taken apart at some unknown time after being inscribed and then reassembled during the reign of Hadrian, the Roman Emperor 117–138 C.E. When that text was inscribed for the first time, how are we to imagine the process? From what sort of text was it inscribed? Answers to these questions, although they can only be conjectural, may serve as guidelines to the resolution of similar questions elsewhere.

WELL AND GOOD: *IC* 4.72.8, LINES 17–20

An "unfinished" conditional sentence is found in the eighth column, in a part of the code that treats marriage and inheritance: *IC* 4.72, col. 8, lines 17–20. καὶ μέν τίς [κ' ὀ]πυίει ἐν ταῖς τριάκοντα ἔ̓ κα ϝείποντι. αἰ δὲ μ<έ>. Willetts 1967: 72 translates, "And if anyone should marry her <it should be> within thirty days from the time they made the proclamation, but if not, she is to be married to another, whomsoever she can. . . . "

The ellipsis, however, of a phrase such as "it should be" is not widely encountered in early Greek writing, while that of "well and good" had a wide currency. It is consequently an easy and natural step to supply here a gesture that signifies "well and good" to fill in the missing apodosis. The translation then would be something like this: "And if anyone marry her within thirty days <GESTURE = well and good>, otherwise . . . etc." But how did the elliptical phrase, characteristic of the language as spoken, find its way into the published version of the Law Code of Gortyn?

[27] Boegehold 1985: 132–35 makes this suggestion with fuller details.

In this case, where the text was inscribed on a wall in large, carefully cut letters, the anticipated readers were local persons with particular concerns, some of whom may have needed a literate reader or interpreter to read the text aloud and explain what it meant. Did such readers or interpreters gesticulate as they read aloud? Possibly they did. But, to look a little further back, was the text of the code first dictated by a speaker who filled in that particular apodosis with a gesture? If that was the case, the scribe who first committed the words to leather or stone or wood wrote down the words without a qualm as he heard them. He knew exactly what was meant, namely "And if anyone marry her within the thirty days in which they made the proclamation <GESTURE signifying "well and good">. Otherwise she . . . etc."

WELL AND GOOD: A COAN CALENDAR

An inscribed calendar from Cos, dated some time after the middle of the fourth century (Sokolowsky 1969: 151A), preserves a remarkable series of four "incomplete" conditional sentences.[28] The translation here is in accord with the text as I have punctuated it in the footnote, not as it is presented in Sokolowsky. "Pamphyli are to drive the three most beautiful oxen <to the selection area>. If one of these is chosen—, if not, Hylleis are to drive three. If one of these is chosen—, if not, Dymanes are to drive the remaining three. If one of these is chosen—, if not, they are to drive the rest into the agora and drive them on under the same conditions. If one of these is chosen—, if not, they are to drive a third under the same conditions. If none of these is chosen, they are to choose an ox from each chiliasty."

Four times in a row, an apodosis that can be assumed to be the equivalent of "well and good" is not written out. Where is the performing reader who supplies a gesture that fills out the conditional sentence? The answer here presupposes a set of circumstances like those in which the Gortynian Law Code was cut. Also, however, note that the calendar is clearly an epitome or abstract of an original, more fully worded text. If an official dictated the text to an amanuensis who wrote down the words he heard, the official could have signed the relevant apodoses by gesture. The amanuensis understood what was meant and so did not fill in the missing words. And then finally the actual inscriber only cut into the stone the words he had before him.

[28] lines 9–16 Π[άμφ]υλοι δὲ ἐπελάντω βοῦ[ς τρεῖς τοὺ]ς καλλίστους. αἰ μ[έγ κα] τούτωγ κριθῆι τις—, αἰ δὲ [μή Ὑλλεῖς τρ]εῖς ἐλάντω. αἰ μέγ [κα το]ύτωγ κριθῆι τις—, αἰ δὲ μ[ή Δυμᾶνες τρ]εῖς τοὺς λοιπούς. αἰ [μέ]γ κα τούτωγ κριθῆι τις—, αἰ [δὲ μή ἁτέρους] ἐλάντω ἐς τὰν ἀγ[ορ]άν καὶ ἐπελάντω κατὰ τα[ὐτά. αἰ μέ]γ κα κριθῆι τ[ις]—, αἰ δὲ μή, τρίτον ἐπελάντω κατὰ τα[ὐτ]ά. αἰ δέ κα τούτωγ κρι[θῆι] μηδείς, ἐπικρινόντων βοῦν ἐκ χι[λιασ]τύος ἑκάστας.

Summary

An Athenian speaking in front of a judging panel consisting of five hundred or more fellow citizens was not expected to be schooled in the techniques of formal oratory. To the contrary, it could work to his disadvantage to appear smooth and polished in that area of civic life. A stock introduction has speakers representing themselves as unaccustomed to public speaking. Since that is the case with the words they speak, the same lack of sophistication should be wanted in their nonverbal communication. They should move and posture and gesticulate very much as they did elsewhere in the city and in the country. And so when we read speeches attributed to Antiphon or Andocides or Lysias or Demosthenes and we find what seem to be ellipses or anomalies in the received text, we might think how a speaker could have expressed the desired sense by means of the silent language of gestures. In this way, we reduce the number of occasions on which we are tempted to alter words in a text or to pronounce the word *aposiopesis* as an explanation.

Similar ellipses in the prose of official documents published on stone can be attributed to the style of the official who dictated the text and the amanuensis who only set down what he heard.

EIGHT

HISTORIANS

IN THE FOREGOING chapters, where examples were drawn from poetry (epic, monody, choral, tragedy, and comedy) and prose (oratory), it was obvious that each author knew that his work was going to be read aloud. In the case of the three major historians, Herodotus, Thucydides, and Xenophon, modern readers do not agree that historians read their histories aloud (or had them read aloud) because the medium in which they worked does not by its nature as conceived in modern times presuppose an oral performance. All three historians present people talking, both formally and informally, and so it is to be expected that the ellipses of spoken Greek might appear from time to time in their writing. And, given what we know about reading in Athens in the late fifth and early fourth centuries, and what we know about the transmission of learning, namely that it was mostly oral, we can imagine a reader gesticulating appropriately when the ellipses appear.

Herodotus and Xenophon do have their characters express themselves in elliptical sentences, and the kind of ellipsis they use suggests that they expected readers to read the text out loud and to perform as they did so. If Thucydides does not, he nevertheless says that his work is directed to a listening audience. Examples drawn from his history here illustrate how gestures could change or enlarge meaning rather than how they can be equivalent to whole clauses.

Herodotus

Herodotus, according to a tradition of uncertain reliability, read some part of his *History* at Olympia, where other writers also read aloud (pp. 6–7 above). Whether that tradition commands perfect trust or not, Herodotus's *History*, like Homer's epic poems, is full of speech, and when Herodotus has a figure in one of his stories speak, he employs characteristics of actual speech in a way that imparts verisimilitude and liveliness to his narrative.

NO: HERODOTUS 1.39.2

Consider first the doomed Atys, who is concocting an interpretation of his father's warning dream, an interpretation that will prove to be persuasive and consequently fatal to himself. Since his father, Croesus, has missed the sense of the dream, he says, it is fair for him, Atys, to point out what the real meaning is. "You say that the dream said that I would die by iron spearpoint, but what sort of hands does a boar have? What kind of iron spear which you fear? Because if the dream had said that I would die by tooth or something else like that, you would have to do what you are doing. But as it is, 'by spear.' So since we do not have battle with men, let me go."[1] Atys's urgency could have been reinforced by a gesture, one that illustrated the rightness of the young man's view and what he conceives to be the fatuousness of his father's. An amplified translation might go as follows: "But as it is, <GESTURE = No> by spear." Atys's backward nod terminates further talk of the danger of a spear.

YES: HERODOTUS 3.80.5

An affirmative nod could have provided a few words, otherwise without proper syntax, with all the construction they needed. Otanes, Megabyxos, and Dareios begin their famous consultation concerning forms of government, in order to determine which one they will give the Persians, who have been recently liberated from the rule of the Magi. Otanes speaks first. In recommending rule by the people, he lists some things that are wrong with rule by a single man. A monarch should be free from feeling envy, he says, because he has all good things, but the opposite turns out to be the case as far as the citizens are concerned. "He envies the best citizens just for living, he rejoices in the bad ones. He is best at entertaining slanders. And the most out of tune thing of all <GESTURE = Yes, I am sure you will agree that this is most out of tune> because if you admire him moderately, he is angry because he isn't being catered to a lot. . . ."[2] The affirmative nod serves to express a demonstrative "this" and to invite agreement.

NO: HERODOTUS 9.60

The phrase νῦν δὲ (but as it is) leads naturally to consideration of a sequence νῦν δὲ . . . γὰϱ (but as it is . . . because), a formulation that often requires a gesture that says no, presumably the nod up and back. This is surely the case with Pausanias at 9.60, where he is remonstrating

[1] εἰ μὲν γὰϱ ὑπὸ ὀδόντος τοι εἶπε τελευτήσειν με ἢ ἄλλου τευ ὅ τι τούτωι οἶκε, χϱῆν δή σε ποιέειν τὰ ποιέεις· νῦν δὲ ὑπὸ αἰχμῆς. ἐπείτε ὦν οὐ πϱὸς ἄνδϱας ἡμῖν γίνεται ἡ μάχη, μέθες με.

[2] . . . διαβολὰς δὲ ἄϱιστος ἐνδέκεσθαι. ἀναϱμαστότατον δὲ πάντων· ἤν τε γὰϱ αὐτὸν μετϱίως θωμάζηις, ἄχθεται. . . .

with the Athenians. He says: "Now if the cavalry had attacked you at the start, we and Tegeans with us, the Tegeans who are not betraying Greece, we would have had to come to your aid. But as it is, <GESTURE = No, this is not the case>. Because the whole force has fallen on us, it is fair for you etc."[3] This example of an ellipsis after "but as it is" (νῦν δέ) differs from those cited and discussed from Aristophanes, Antiphon, and Plato in that the "because" (γὰρ) can be taken to explain what follows. A gesture signifying no, however, could be imagined here.

NO: HERODOTUS 5.20

The same sequence, viz., "But now . . . <GESTURE = No> . . . because . . ." clarified 5.20 as that adventure was being read aloud. Alexander addresses the Persian grandees who have been making free with the Macedonian ladies forced to sit by them. Apparently, however, they have not yet actually bedded them. Alexander (who will replace the women with armed young men) tells the Persians they can certainly do that too, but they ought to let the ladies retire briefly to bathe themselves. He says: "In this matter, give a sign as to what you want. But now <GESTURE = No, please don't signal that you want that right this minute> because it is almost time for bed and I see that you are well fortified with wine, do please let these women bathe . . . etc.[4] Herodotus envisions the Persians making unmistakable signals that they want to enjoy the women fully just as Alexander has invited them to do, and Alexander needs to stop them. He makes an urgent sign that says, "No, please stop" and then adds the reason why he is qualifying his original invitation.

QUOTATION: HERODOTUS 9.48.4

At Plataiai in 479, Pausanias, the Spartan commander, has been shifting his Spartan troops from the right of the line to the left in hope of having them face Boeotians rather than Persians, whose tactics the Spartans did not know. Mardonios has sent a herald who questions the vaunted Spartan valor and issues a challenge: "Why don't we fight equal in number to each other, you for the Greeks, since you have the reputation of being best, and we for the "barbarians."[5]

[3] εἰ μέν νυν ἐς ὑμέας ὅρμησε ἀρχὴν ἡ ἵππος, χρῆν δὴ ἡμέας τε καὶ τοὺς μετ᾽ ἡμέων τὴν Ἑλλάδα οὐ προδιδόντας Τεγεήτας βοηθεῖν ὑμῖν; νῦν δέ—ἐς ἡμέας γὰρ ἅπασα κεχώρηκε, δίκαιοί ἐστε. . . .

[4] νῦν δέ—σχέδον γὰρ ἤδη τῆς κοίτης ὥρη προσέρχεται κτλ.

[5] τί δὴ οὐ πρὸ μὲν τῶν Ἑλλήνων ὑμεῖς, ἐπείτε δεδόξωσθε εἶναι ἄριστοι, πρὸ δὲ τῶν βαρβάρων ἡμεῖς ἴσοι πρὸς ἴσους ἀριθμὸν μαχεσάμεθα;

It is remarkable that a herald calls himself and his people barbarians. Remember the Spartans at Herodotus 8.142 who warned the Athenians against barbarians, in whom there could be neither trust nor truth. Wells (How and Wells 1912: 309) remonstrates: "H. has no more scruple than Aeschylus (*Persae* 187, 337) in making a Persian herald speak of his nation as 'barbarians.' " (**B**) Macan 1895–1908 *ad loc.* sweeps wider: "Herodotus gives himself, his source, his herald, and Mardonios away in this phrase; it is a sheer impossibility. . . . Here the noble Persian commander by the mouth of his herald taunting the premier Greeks writes himself down . . . just at a Greek's evaluation."[6] What Macan says is true, if the text is read flat, as words on a printed page. But if the tone of voice and the accompanying gesture told listeners that "barbarians" was a quotation, a label that Mardonios via his herald was hurling back in the faces of the Greeks, quite a different sense makes itself felt.[7] An elaborate sweep of the arm, ending with fingers on breast, is a gesture that would communicate and reinforce the speaker's ironical use of the word *barbarians.*

QUOTATION: HERODOTUS 7.210.2

These few clues allow one to go further and imagine some sort of gesture alerting readers to a slightly deformed quotation, such as the one at Herodotus 7.210.2: "They made it clear to everyone, and especially to the king himself, that they were a lot of people, but only a few men."[8] The configuration of proverbial sayings like this, stressing some qualitative difference between the many and the few, appears with minor alterations in other Greek prose.[9] A speaker might want to stress it with a gesture.

WELL AND GOOD: HERODOTUS 1.13

There are a few instances where Herodotus may employ the "incomplete" conditional sentence. The first appears not in a representation of direct speech, but in a context where speech is implied, as is the case with Thucydides 3.3.3 (p. 99 below). Gyges has killed Candaules and become king. He has moreover received confirmation from the oracle at Delphi.

[6] (**A**) Broadhead 1960 *comm. ad* Aeschylus *Persae* 187: "This word [scil. βάρβαρος] often has a purely geographical significance. In this play, it is put ten times into the mouths of Persians, an incongruity that reminds us of the Roman dramatist's phrase: Plautus vortit barbare."

[7] Cf. Kratos (p. 54 above), Demosthenes on Straton (pp. 88–90 above), and Alcibiades (pp. 99–100 below).

[8] πολλοὶ μὲν ἄνθρωποι εἶεν, ὀλίγοι δὲ ἄνδρες.

[9] Cf. Zenobios *Centenaria* 5.75 πολλοὶ θριοβόλοι παῦροι δέ τε μάντιες ἄνδρες, with Plato *Phaedo* 69c8, and Demosthenes 19.113. I use the word *deformed* on the assumption that such proverbial sayings were in their original form cast as dactylic hexameters.

His rule is made possible by an agreement between Gyges' partisans and the rest of the Lydians. Herodotus phrases the agreement as the two parties might have pronounced it out loud. The agreement was that "if the oracle pronounced Gyges king of the Lydians, and if he was ruling as king <GESTURE = well and good>; otherwise he was to return the rule to the Heracleidae."

The relevant Greek text is as follows: ἢν μὲν δὴ τὸ χρηστήριον ἀνέλῃ μιν βασιλέα εἶναι Λυδῶν, τὸν δὲ βασιλεύειν—ἢν δὲ μή, ἀποδοῦναι ὀπίσω ἐς Ἡρακλείδας τὴν ἀρχήν. The formulation ἢν μὲν . . . <ἢν> δὲ . . . ἢν δὲ μή . . . is like Athena's in Aeschylus *Eumenides* 885–88 (p. 56 above). Herodotus goes on: "And the oracle did in fact pronounce him king and Gyges did in that way rule as king." Note the sequence: At the beginning of chapter 13, he got the kingship and he got confirmed.[10] That is, he was ruling already when the oracle confirmed him, and in that way he was in conformity with the terms of the agreement, which was (A) if the oracle confirms, and (B) if he is ruling (which the beginning of the chapter tells us he was), then well and good.[11]

WELL AND GOOD: HERODOTUS 8.62.1

Xerxes holds Athens. The Greeks are in disorder. Themistocles at a meeting of ships' captains addresses Eurybiades: "If you stay here and stay brave—. But if you do not, you will overturn Greece."[12] The cast of the translation as I have given it conforms with that of (**B**) Rawlinson 1875 *ad loc*: "If thou wilt stay here, he said, and behave like a man, all will be well—if not, thou wilt bring Greece to ruin." That is, he supplies "all is well" in words.[13] If instead of words, we supply a gesture, the English translation will look like this: "If you stay here and stay brave, <GESTURE = "all will be well>. But if you do not, you will overturn Greece."[14]

[10] ἔσχε δὲ τὴν βασιλήιην καὶ ἐκρατύνθη.

[11] (**A**) Stein 1856: *comm. ad.* 2.149 also compares this passage with 3.36, 4.3, 5.73, and 6.52.

[12] σὺ εἰ μενέεις αὐτοῦ καὶ μένων ἔσεαι ἀνὴρ ἀγαθός. εἰ δὲ μή, ἀνατρέψεις τὴν Ἑλλάδα. 8.62.1.

[13] (**B**) Powell 1939 *ad loc.* takes the same tack. (**B**) Macan 1895–1908: 450, however, presents a different construction: "The expression is hardly in strict grammar, and an *aposiopesis* or a lacuna might be suspected; so Baehr approves of Valckenaer's suggestion to supply mentally σώσεις τὴν Ἑλλάδα. But the excitement of the moment might account for some incoherence. Certainly καὶ μένων is tautologous, and *de trop.* One might try to force a special point in it: 'You, if you are going to remain—yea, in remaining (as you are now) will be a good man and true,' " (**B**) Cary 1908 *ad loc.*, (**B**) Barguet 1964 *ad loc.*, and (**B**) LeGrand 1953 *ad loc.* present similar versions, but as Macan confesses, some force must be applied.

[14] M. H. Chambers suggests in a letter: "The Greek seems to say, 'If you stay here—and in remaining, you will be a good (or brave) man; but if not, you will overturn Greece.' So

Thucydides

Thucydides, with his dense prose style, especially that of the speeches, may seem to concern himself more with content and analysis than with oral presentation, especially in view of his explicit assurances that he is not writing for his listeners' pleasure. But the words of his assurance point to hearers, not silent readers.[15] And if there were hearers, there was someone reading or speaking aloud, someone for whom nonverbal communication was an indispensable element of his delivery.

WELL AND GOOD: THUCYDIDES 3.3

In this connection it is worth noting that Thucydides has at least one conditional sentence without an apodosis. "It was announced to the Athenians that outside the town there was a celebration of Apollo Maloeis in which the whole town of Mytilene took part, and the expectation was that the Athenians, if they hurried, could fall on them suddenly. And if the attempt succeeded,—. Otherwise that they were to tell the Mytilenaians to give up their ships."[16] Here again an apodosis could be expressed by a gesture that said "well and good." Note also that it is a way of implying direct quotation; that is, the "incomplete" conditional sentence is not found where straight descriptive narrative is the mode. From the way Thucydides formed this sentence, one can see that he, like his predecessors, anticipated recitations of his work while he was writing. When he represented speeches, he imagined his orator speaking, and that act of imagination had to involve the orator's postures and gestures.

QUOTATION: THUCYDIDES 6.17.1

An illustration of the possibility of nonverbal communication in a particular speech presents itself where Alcibiades speaks in the ekklesia. He names his "youth" and "folly," neither of which is in accord with the "nature"

I think the GESTURE meaning 'all will be well' has to be assumed as coming after αὐτοῦ, 'here'—not after ἀγαθὸς, 'brave.' "

[15] Thucydides 1.21.4: "And not as prose-writers have composed, with a view to persuasiveness in the hearing rather than the truth" (οὔτε ὡς λογογράφοι ξυνέθεσαν ἐπὶ τὸ προσαγωγότερον τῆι ἀκροάσει ἢ ἀληθέστερον); 1.22.4: "And the lack of storytelling may appear less pleasurable for the hearing" (καὶ ἐς μὲν ἀκρόασιν ἴσως τὸ μὴ μυθῶδες αὐτῶν ἀτερπέστερον φανεῖται); ibid.: "composed as a possession for all time rather than a contest piece for immediate hearing" (κτῆμά τε ἐς αἰεὶ μᾶλλον ἢ ἀγώνισμα ἐς τὸ παραχρῆμα ἀκούειν ξύγκειται). Cf. (**B**) Pritchett 1975 xxviii–xxvix, 65, 67–68, 88–89, 115–16.

[16] Thucydides 3.3.3: καὶ ἢν μὲν ξυμβῆι ἡ πεῖρα· εἰ δὲ μή, Μυτιληναίοις εἰπεῖν.

of a sane and healthy man.[17] Alcibiades is not itemizing his deficits, he is quoting the sort of thing that is being said about him. Now Thucydides knows that a hearer will need a clue if he is to understand immediately that Alcibiades is quoting. He also knows that the person reading his work aloud (originally himself, I suppose) will provide that clue by means of a meaningful motion with his head, hands, or body. That is to say, Thucydides, as he composed, both heard the special ironic emphasis that Alcibiades would have given the quoted words and at the same time saw Alcibiades (and therefore necessarily himself or whoever was going to read the text aloud) speaking.[18]

Alcibiades has identified what is in fact a quotation, that is to say, words others are using when they speak about him. If Thucydides saw him in his mind's eye gesticulating to make sure that people know he is quoting, would Thucydides not also have done so in other situations? There are, for example, occasions when he puts in the mouth of his speakers phrases they have in reality spoken.[19] These phrases were not distinguished in ancient texts by quotation marks or footnote numbers, and yet an author expected them to be recognized. Emphasis could have been supplied by tone, but then again a gesture could have directed listeners' attention to help their focus. Memorable Periclean phrases, such as "The whole earth is a burial place for heroes"[20] and "The city as a whole is Greece's education"[21] might not need such underlining, but absolute necessity is not the issue. As in the case of drama, and in conversation as well, movements of head and hands were there when a writer and performer felt that a movement was in order. Admittedly, in any given instance, a modern reader might think not, but a contemporary of Thucydides quite likely would.

QUOTATION: THUCYDIDES 5.16.1

A gesture might have helped at 5.16.1, where Thucydides assesses reasons for the Peace of 421: Nicias wishes "to cease from toils of war himself and to stop his fellow-citizens from toils."[22] It is not a telling, memorable

[17] Thucydides 6.17.1: ἡ ἐμὴ νεότης καὶ ἄνοια παρὰ φύσιν δοκοῦσα εἶναι. Cf. (**A**) Dover 1970: 249.

[18] This example is like that from the beginning of Aeschylus's *Prometheus Bound* cited above (p. 54), where Kratos deprecates words that others apply to him. Cf. also Demosthenes on Straton (pp. 88–90 above) and the Persian herald (pp. 96–97 above).

[19] This working assumption has the look of an apodictic pronouncement. It is, I recognize, not demonstrable, but I persevere in the belief that it is likely. In support, see Bers 1997: 221–22 and especially note 10.

[20] Thucydides 2.43.3: ἀνδρῶν γὰρ ἐπιφανῶν πᾶσα γῆ τάφος.

[21] Thucydides 2.41.1: τήν τε πᾶσαν τὴν πόλιν τῆς Ἑλλάδος παίδευσιν εἶναι.

[22] Thucydides 5.16: πόνων πεπαῦσθαι καὶ αὐτὸς καὶ τοὺς πολίτας παῦσαι: cf. Aristophanes *Knights* 574–80, Euripides *Suppliants* 950–54, and Boegehold 1982: 147–56.

formulation like the Periclean examples quoted above, but it may contain within it an allusion to a popular catchword of the day: Athenians who wanted to end the war were saying, "Let us cease from the toils of war." If Thucydides wanted his readers to respond to that allusion as it was being made, he or his performing reader alerted the listeners with a gesture. Remember that the popular cry to which Thucydides alludes may have been some years in the past by the time his text was being read aloud at Athens.

THUCYDIDES AND HUMOR

In the four passages from Thucydides that follow, voice modulation and gesture could emphasize certain words, phrases, or constructions to impart a wry or ironic or sardonic color to the narrative. The heading "Humor" may at first glance seem surprising, since Thucydides is usually perceived to be an austere military man whose unpitying analyses and grim sense of reality leave no space for the sort of play popularly identified with humor. An ancient reader did once quote a saying about Thucydides that might seem to imply a humorous view: at 1.126–27 he wrote as scholiast that some people said, "Lion [sc. Thucydides] laughed here" (λέων ἐγέλασε ἐνταῦθα). But he goes on to explain that the readers who said this were admiring the clarity of Thucydides' account of Kylon. Humor therefore did not come into the question.[23]

What I hope to demonstrate is that his wry formulations, while perhaps not playful, can nevertheless be subsumed under the genial rubric "humor." But what shall we call "humor" in an ancient Greek author? With Aristophanes, it is easy: his readers, continents, and millennia remote in space and time, giggle even while reading him in translation. Another sort of humor, however, shows itself, for example, in Sophocles *Antigone* 31, when Antigone speaks of "the good Creon" (ὁ ἀγαθὸς Κρέων), or when Socrates in Plato *Apology* 24b5 speaks of "the good Meletos" (ὁ ἀγαθὸς Μέλητος), or—to take an extreme example—when Theramenes offers a toast "to the fair Critias[24] as he drinks the poison Critias has ordained. The speakers in these circumstances are not praising the named person (who in each case is responsible one way or another for the speaker's death) and so the praise-word comes as a surprise. But such surprises, great and small, are exactly what constitutes humor. It is a sudden and unexpected way of perceiving a set of circumstances, and cruelty, especially in Greek literature, is often an element.

[23] Connor 1985: 36, note 36, cites recent authorities who deny or question the existence of irony in Thucydides. Connor himself notes ironic perspectives throughout the work. Cf. Pritchett 1975: 123: "There are numerous instances of latent irony."

[24] Κριτίαι τοῦτ' ἔστω τῶι καλῶι (Xenophon *Hellenika* 2.3.24).

Humor: Thucydides 1.33.1

Representatives from Corcyra are addressing the Athenian ekklesia: they want to ally themselves with Athens or at least keep Athens from taking action as an ally of Corinth. The ambassadors list three advantages that will accrue to Athens if Athens sides with Corcyra. "First, you will be helping people who are being wrongfully injured and who are not doing harm to others. Next, you will make a deposit for yourselves of imperishable gratitude because you have accepted people who are in danger of losing everything, and as for fleet, we are in possession of one that is apart from yours the biggest."[25]

Why, one might ask, do these ambassadors present to the Athenian people two considerations that do not by any reading of Thucydides constitute adequate grounds for a major policy decision? Thucydides has deliberately chosen to represent the ambassadors as speaking this way. But would any citizen in that gathering have cared deeply about injuries suffered by Corcyraeans? Perhaps in life some did, but the Athenian demos as Thucydides portrays it in his history was not swayed by such considerations. The same questions apply to that "everlasting gratitude."[26] But suppose that in life one or two trusting souls among the Athenians were susceptible to that sort of rhetoric, would their hypothetical presence be enough for Thucydides to include mere postures as relevant and efficacious argumentation? He is systematically clear in his perception of political motives. Can he take this sort of rhetoric seriously? The answer, I think, is no. Those humane considerations are put forth as a kind of throat-clearing, as items in a short series at whose end the true operative reason is revealed, the one that in fact decided the outcome of the vote.

Note the clinching consideration: it is tacked on economically with a modest connective particle, viz. τε, (oh, yes, and by the way . . .). The rhetorical tactics[27] are those of Thucydides, and he could possibly have smiled a thin smile as he added the third of the Corcyraean points. Would the orator he had in mind have drawn attention to that last clause with a gesture? Or would he simply have thrown it away? The former seems the more likely: a gesture at "fleet" could emphasize that potent word in its potent position, and another gesture would emphasize "biggest," which was also pronounced in a telling position, last in the sentence.

[25] πρῶτον μὲν ὅτι ἀδικουμένοις καὶ οὐχ ἑτέρους βλάπτουσι τὴν ἐπικουρίαν ποιήσεσθε, ἔπειτα περὶ μεγίστων κινδυνεύοντας δεξάμενοι ὡς ἂν μάλιστα μετ' αἰειμνήστου μαρτυρίου τὴν χάριν καταθήσεσθε· ναυτικόν τε κεκτήμεθα πλὴν τοῦ παρ' ὑμῖν πλεῖστον.

[26] M. H. Chambers suggests in a letter that "imperishable gratitude" might be diplomatic language for some assurance such as "we will provide military assistance to you when you come to need it."

[27] Cf., e.g., Thucydides 2.65.9 and 2.65.12; also Denniston 1966: 499–500.

Humor: Thucydides 4.28.5

The year is 425. An unknown number of Spartans are besieged on the island Sphacteria, just off the southwestern coast of the Peloponnese. The Athenians, who have them trapped there, are not moving toward any aggressive strategy, and so Cleon, back in Athens, announces to an assembly that he will either bring the Spartans back from Sphacteria alive or kill them on the spot. "His empty bragging made the Athenians laugh, but at the same time the prudent among them (σώφροσι) were glad, because they figured they would get one of two good things: either they would get rid of Cleon, which they hoped for the more, or they would have been mistaken and they would have beaten the Spartans."[28]

This analysis presents a surprise.[29] Does Thucydides really mean that the σώφρονες are sensible or prudent? Could prudent men hope for defeat? Or be glad in expecting a defeat? Would they in fact accept a victory as second best? The answer to both these questions, if we use the normal expectations of humanity as guidelines, should be no. But is it beyond belief that there existed in Athens an identifiable group of like-minded folk who styled themselves (or were styled ironically by others) as "prudent?" They would be men who could be depended upon to look first to their own interests, and second to the concerns of Athens, the ones who profited from the war to the detriment of the city (Thucydides 2.65.7). Such profiteers might very well describe themselves as "only prudent" or "only sensible." If that were the case, Thucydides was using the word as Socrates used ἀγαθός of Meletos in the Platonic *Apology*, when he spoke of "the good Meletos."[30] A hand gesture could underline the term *prudent*, opening it up to ironic interpretation. And irony in some of its contexts is an aspect of humor.

Humor: Thucydides 5.11.1

In 422 the Athenians have lost a battle at Amphipolis, their sometime colony. Cleon, the Athenian general, is dead, as is Brasidas, the victorious Spartan general. For the people of Amphipolis, the Athenian Hagnon had been their founding hero, but now they make Brasidas their founding

[28] τοῖς δὲ Ἀθηναίοις ἐνέπεσε μέν τι καὶ γέλωτος τῆι κουφολογίαι αὐτοῦ, ἀσμένοις δ' ὅμως ἐγίγνετο τοῖς σώφροσι τῶν ἀνθρώπων, λογιζομένοις δυοῖν ἀγαθοῖν τοῦ ἑτέρου τεύξεσθαι, ἢ Κλέωνος ἀπαλλαγήσεσθαι, ὃ μᾶλλον ἤλπιζον, ἢ σφαλεῖσι γνώμης Λακεδαιμονίους σφίσι χειρώσεσθαι.

[29] Cf. Connor 1985: 113–18.

[30] Cf. Antigone, Theramenes, Andocides, and Demosthenes, pp. 85, 88–90, 101), and also Alcibiades' greeting to Eryximachos at Plato *Symposium* 214b3–4, where βέλτιστε βελτίστου πατρὸς καὶ σωφρονεστάτου cannot be considered wholly complimentary.

hero. All structures and memorials of Hagnon's heroic status accordingly have to be destroyed. "This was in the belief that Brasidas had saved them. At the same time they now were tending their alliance with Sparta in fear of the Athenians. Also they thought that Hagnon, in view of their state of war with Athens, would not be similarly useful for them, and he would not enjoy having the honors anyhow."[31] The series of reasons advanced to explain the Amphipolitans' cool change of identity has an affinity with the Corcyraean ambassador's speech at 1.33.1. In both explanations Thucydides first proposes a humane consideration. Next he offers an operative reason. First, the Amphipolitans are grateful to Brasidas because he has saved them. Second, alliance with Sparta has become expedient. And third, Hagnon is no longer useful; besides, he would not enjoy having the honors. Is this last Thucydides' own inference, or did he hear it from someone who was there? We cannot know certainly, but it has the look of a wry summary, the sort of rationalization Amphipolitans might contrive. Thucydides, in reading the sentence aloud, could with a telling gesture emphasize the practical reasoning that terminated the historical existence of a founding hero and replaced him with another. The added thought, delivered deadpan, seems in its unexpectedness close to humor.

If, however, as the Greek makes possible, we translate the final words, "They, i.e., the people of Amphipolis, would not enjoy his having the honors," the descent from considerations of expedience to a surmise as to what might be pleasurable, could also convey an ironic commentary.

Humor: Thucydides 8.73.2

Thucydides reports that in 411, when the Four Hundred were getting organized, thanks to them something like the following happened on Samos: "The Samians who at that time had revolted against the establishment and were being turned around again, as a "*dēmos*" will, convinced by Peisander, when he came, and by the Athenian conspirators on Samos, made up a conspiracy numbering three hundred and they were going to attack the other Samians for being '*dēmos*.' "[32]

Thucydides plays here with the colors and meanings of the word *dēmos* which in varying contexts takes on different meanings. First, he says that

[31] νομίσαντες τὸν μὲν Βρασίδαν σωτῆρά τε σφῶν γεγενῆσθαι καὶ ἐν τῶι παρόντι ἅμα τὴν τῶν Λακεδαιμονίων ξυμμαχίαν φόβωι τῶν Ἀθηναίων θεραπεύοντες, τὸν δὲ Ἅγνωνα κατὰ τὸ πολέμιον τῶν Ἀθηναίων οὐκ ἂν ὁμοίως σφίσι ξυμφόρως, οὐδ' ἂν ἡδέως τὰς τιμὰς ἔχειν.

[32] οἱ γὰρ τότε τῶν Σαμίων ἐπαναστάντες τοῖς δυνατοῖς καὶ ὄντες δῆμος μεταβαλλόμενοι αὖθις καὶ πεισθέντες ὑπό τε τοῦ Πεισάνδρου, ὅτε ἦλθε, καὶ τῶν ἐν τῆι Σάμωι ξυνεστώτων Ἀθηναίων ἐγένοντό τε ἐς τριακοσίους ξυνωμόται καὶ ἔμελλον τοῖς ἄλλοις ὡς δήμωι ὄντι ἐπιθήσεσθαι.

the conspirators, who in opposing themselves to the establishment declare themselves *dēmos*, i.e., "the people," were turned around because of what a "*dēmos*" is. That is, a *dēmos* is a volatile thing, one whose inherent instability brings on constant turnabouts. Next he shows the same word denominating what the conspirators, "*dēmos*" themselves a breath previously, see as "people" *qua* enemy or opposition. And so, to sum up briefly, "the people" revolt against the establishment, and because they are "the people" and therefore have no essential identity, they are easily converted into conspirators who will attack the rest of the Samians because they are "the people."

It is hard to believe that Thucydides did not smile a little as he wrote this. And anyone who read this passage aloud, one can imagine, might very well have stressed the participial phrases containing the word *dēmos* by making a gesture of some kind with head or hand.[33]

Xenophon

Xenophon, notable for his adventures as a soldier, his friendship with Socrates, and his spare prose style, does not at a glance appear a likely composer of elliptical dialogue. And yet in his reminiscences of conversations with Socrates and in his romance, the *Cyropaideia,* he has his characters speaking with the same kinds of ellipsis that we have seen in his predecessors.

XENOPHON *HELLENIKA* 1.1

Xenophon therefore reveals occasional opportunities for a speaker to enlarge or interpret the text with a gesture. In fact, once one has firmly in mind a picture of the performing reader, the opening words of Xenophon's *Hellenika* take on another look. He starts his history with three simple words, namely μετὰ δὲ ταῦτα, which say in English, "After this." "After what"? a reader reasonably asks, and the generally agreed upon answer is, "After the events recorded at the close of Thucydides' unfinished history of the Peloponnesian War." But if we can imagine a reading at which the last few chapters of Thucydides were read aloud, to be followed by Xenophon himself or by a performing reader, Xenophon's laconic beginning becomes an easy and natural continuation, rather than an unusual literary gesture of recognition. The reader who pronounced the words "after this" makes a motion with his hand, thereby drawing attention to the reader who has

[33] (A) Dover 1970: 257, 455 notes the antithesis but does not raise the possibility of irony or humor here.

just finished reading from the eighth book of Thucydides. Or the gesture conjures up a sense of past time.

GESTURE FOR APODOSIS

Now it is possible to argue that in English, where most talk goes on without significant reliance on gesticulation, one can say, “Do this or else,” and the sentence is in effect an incomplete conditional sentence. You are saying, “If you do not do this, something bad will happen to you,” but you are not telling what will happen. And you do not need to indicate by gesture what will happen. Tone and context supply all the information that is needed: “Do this or something bad will happen to you.” But this example is relevant for English-speaking people, not for Greeks of any observable era. A Greek, who would in any case have been gesticulating as he uttered the protasis (e.g., “if you do not do this”), would naturally provide or emphasize an apodosis by means of a gesture. The conditional sentences analyzed below show further use of gestures as apodosis. Usually the gesture is one that signifies “all is well.”

This is not to say that such sentences would not have been comprehensible without a gesture. The inscribers of the Gortynian Law Code and the Coan calendar did not need to foresee a gesturing performer (pp. 91–92 above). But at the same time, that does not mean that the person reading Xenophon aloud did not gesticulate while reading.

Speak Up: Xenophon *Anabasis* 7.7.15

At *Anabasis* 7.7.15, the Spartan Charminos, at Xenophon’s request, addresses Medosades. His first words are forthright: “If you, Medosades, have something to say to us—, otherwise, we have something to say to you.”[34] Here again is the familiar “incomplete” conditional sentence: the gesture to be supplied this time is one that says, “Speak up.”

Well and Good: Xenophon *Memorabilia* 3.1.9

Socrates is finding out what a young man has learned as a student of generalship, and it turns out to be principally where to station the best and the worst troops. Now Socrates wants to know if the young man has been taught to distinguish and identify “best” and “worst” troops: “If he taught you therefore to distinguish the good troops from the bad <GESTURE = well and good>, but if he did not, what is the good to you of what you have learned?”[35]

[34] εἰ μὲν σύ τι ἔχεις, ὦ Μηδόσαδες, πρὸς ἡμᾶς λέγειν—εἰ δὲ μή, ἡμεῖς πρὸς σὲ ἔχομεν.

[35] εἰ μὲν τοίνυν ἔφη καὶ διαγιγνώσκειν σε τοὺς ἀγαθοὺς καὶ τοὺς κακοὺς ἐδίδαξεν—εἰ δὲ μή, τί σοι ὄφελος ὧν ἔμαθες;

Absit Omen: Xenophon *Cyropaideia* 2.3.2

"Gentlemen, the contest is near. The enemy approach." In this way, Xenophon represents Cyrus addressing his assembled troops. He says: "The prizes of victory, if we win—we must always say this and do this—it is obvious that the enemy and all the enemies' good things will be ours. But if we lose—that way too all the possessions of the losers are on each occasion prizes for the winners."[36] Cyrus concludes with a conditional sentence which, although it does not lack an apodosis, changes in direction, and in doing so shows reluctance to say the words that might naturally have followed such a beginning. He does not say, for instance, "But if we lose, we and all we own will belong to them." But even what he does say is dangerous. To say it might make it happen. And so Xenophon may have imagined a reader—any Greek reader—making a gesture to guard against any such unwelcome outcome. Some readers might have spit almost automatically.[37]

Well and Good . . . Too Bad: Xenophon *Cyropaideia* 4.10.5

Cyaxares has been abandoned by his troops, and he wants them back. He orders that the following message be sent: "Now if Cyrus likes it, <GESTURE = well and good>; if he does not <GESTURE = too bad>. You be here as quickly as you can."[38]

Well and Good: Xenophon *Cyropaideia* 7.5.54

Artabazus is rebuking Cyrus for not giving his best old friends as much of himself as they deserve. He says: "So now if it is going to be that we who deserve the most share the most of you <GESTURE = well and good>, otherwise I am willing to announce on your authority that everyone is to depart from you except for those of us who were your friends from the start."[39]

The End: Xenophon *Cyropaideia* 8.7.24

Cyrus recognizes that he is dying and so presents his sons with a few last lessons. Toward the end of his homily, he says: "Now if I am giving you

[36] τὰ δ' ἆθλα τῆς νίκης ἢν μὲν ἡμεῖς νικῶμεν (τοῦτο γὰρ ἀεὶ καὶ λέγειν καὶ ποιεῖν δεῖ) δῆλον ὅτι οἵ τε πολέμιοι ἡμέτεροι καὶ τὰ τῶν πολεμίων ἀγαθὰ πάντα. ἢν δὲ ἡμεῖς νικώμεθα—καὶ οὕτω τὰ τῶν νικωμένων πάντα τοῖς νικῶσιν ἀεὶ ἆθλα πρόκειται.

[37] On spitting, see pp. 27–28 above.

[38] καὶ νῦν ἂν μὲν Κῦρος βούληται—εἰ δὲ μή, ὑμεῖς γε τὴν ταχίστην πάρεστε.

[39] νῦν οὖν εἰ μὲν ἔσται πηι ὅπως οἱ πλεῖστοι ἄξιοι γεγενημένοι πλεῖστόν σου μέρος μεθέξομεν—εἰ δὲ μή, πάλιν αὖ ἐγὼ ἐθέλω παρὰ σοῦ ἐξαγγέλλειν ἀπιέναι πάντας ἀπὸ σοῦ πλὴν ἡμῶν τῶν ἐξ ἀρχῆς φίλων.

sufficent instruction as to how you must be with each other,—otherwise, learn from past events, for this is the best kind of instruction."[40] What sort of gesture will a reader have made here? "All is well" does not seem sufficient. The dying king might be expected in the imagination of a performing reader to have made a gesture signifying, "Go forth and act on these precepts." Or the reader could have represented him as being near death and accordingly made a gesture that signed a limp dismissal. "I have said what I am going to say. I am finished." In either case, the essential sense would be, "This interview is now over."

WELL AND GOOD: XENOPHON *MEMORABILIA* 3.9.11

A long sentence includes an "incomplete" condition toward its end. It comes with a slight anacolouthon, as one might expect in such a sentence. Socrates explains what it means to be in charge (ἄρχειν): "Because whenever anyone would admit that it is the function of the person in charge to order what needs to be done, and that of the person in his charge to obey, he would show that onboard ship the man who knows is in charge, and the captain and everybody else onboard obey the man who knows; likewise in farming, the owners of fields obey the man who knows, and in the case of sickness, the sick obey the man who knows, and in bodily training the men being trained obey the man who knows, and everyone else who has something that needs responsible oversight, if they think they themselves know how to effect that supervision <GESTURE = well and good, they just do it>, otherwise they not only obey the men who know when those men are present, they even send for them when they are away so that they can by obeying them do what they have to do."[41]

Summary

The three early major historians provide examples in their histories where a reader's gestures supply needed information and draw attention to special effects. Not surprisingly, signals of nonverbal communication appear where characters are represented as talking.

Herodotus as a result can be appreciated for his evocations of actual, vivid, ungrammatical speech, and quotations, which include an ironic

[40] εἰ μὲν οὖν ἐγὼ ὑμᾶς ἱκανῶς διδάσκω οἵους χρὴ πρὸς ἀλλήλους εἶναι—εἰ δὲ μή, καὶ παρὰ τῶν προγεγενημένων μανθάνετε· αὕτη γὰρ ἀρίστη διδασκαλία.

[41] ὁπότε γάρ τις ὁμολογήσειε τοῦ μὲν ἄρχοντος εἶναι τὸ προστάττειν ὅ τι χρὴ ποιεῖν, τοῦ δὲ ἀρχομένου τὸ πείθεσθαι, ἐπεδείκνυεν ἔν τε νηὶ τὸν μὲν ἐπιστάμενον ἄρχοντα, τὸν δὲ ναύκληρον καὶ τοὺς ἄλλους τοὺς ἐν τῆι νηὶ πάντας πειθομένους τῶι ἐπισταμένωι, καὶ ἐν γεωργίαι τοὺς κεκτημένους ἀγρούς, καὶ ἐν νόσωι τοὺς νοσοῦντας καὶ ἐν σωμασκίαι

quotation of a disparaging label, namely "barbarian." Thucydides likewise forms a mental picture of his characters as they speak. He sees them using heads and hands to expand the sense of what they are saying. When he speaks in his own voice as wry commentator, he achieves a humorous, ironic effect. A reader could have conveyed this by tone of voice, but it would have been natural for performing readers to gesture as well. Xenophon also has his speakers express themselves elliptically in the interest of representing real speech, and real speech was accompanied by gestures.

τοὺς σωμασκοῦντας, καὶ τοὺς ἄλλους πάντας οἷς ὑπάρχει τι ἐπιμελείας δεόμενον, ἂν μὲν αὐτοί ἡγῶνται ἐπίστασθαι ἐπιμελεῖσθαι—, εἰ δὲ μή, τοῖς ἐπισταμένοις οὐ μόνον παροῦσι πειθομένους, ἀλλὰ καὶ ἀπόντας μεταπεμπομένους, ὅπως ἐκείνοις πειθόμενοι τὰ δέοντα πράττωσιν.

NINE

PLATO

Plato's Characters in Action

PLATO SHOWS in some dialogues with what detail he saw his characters, men and boys, as they took part in the discussions he unfolded, and with this detail he would provide an adumbration of the physical scene of the action, and the action itself. Think how clearly readers today see the middle-aged men who are sitting on a bench in Taureos's palaestra. The beautiful Charmides enters, and the men almost as a reflex begin to wiggle, each hoping to make a place for Charmides next to himself. And the comic effect: two of them as a result are pushed right off the bench (Plato *Charmides* 155b9–c4). Again, think of Socrates' description of Protagoras and his students: we are given what amounts to a choreography as they pass to and fro in the stoa (Plato *Protagoras* 314e3–315b8), and of course Alcibiades, drunk and eloquent, requiring a wine-cooler full of wine (Plato *Symposium* 213e10–214a5) as a challenge to Socrates.

Plato's contemporaries in actual life, it seems natural to suppose, postured, gestured, rolled their eyes, coughed, shuffled, did in short all sorts of things to amplify or transmit the sense of what they felt or meant to say, and that is how Plato saw them as he reconstructed or invented their conversations. Whenever a character in conversation affirms or dissents either with a simple yes or no or with an equivalent, Plato saw that person making the appropriate motion with his head. Likewise, when Plato's Socrates says to Ion, "just as I recognize that these are five fingers," Plato in his mind saw Socrates raise his hand and spread his fingers (Plato *Ion* 537e5–6). But no matter how often or how densely Plato employed special tactics to enhance an impression of actuality, he always worked within the constraints that distinguish art from the apparent scatteredness of everyday life. There was more ellipse and gesticulation in an actual conversation in the Agora, or in a private house, than appears in any of his dialogues. As composer, he implies actual conversation: he does not transcribe.

COMPLEMENT: PLATO *APOLOGY* 19E4–20A2

One special tactic is that of inconsequence. Plato's speakers speak ungrammatically sometimes. They start a sentence with one construction and end with another, and this deliberate inconsequence, *anacolouthon*, is one way of intimating the informality of live conversation. Socrates, for instance, at Plato *Apology* 19e4 breaks up a sentence just the way a person might in conversation. He says: "Because every one of them, gentlemen, can go to every city, and the young men—the young men can associate with any of their own citizens they want to without paying—they persuade those young men to abandon their associations with those <fellow citizens> and to associate with them, while paying money and being grateful in addition."[1]

A relative clause qualifies the young men, but then after that clause, the original, singular subject of the sentence becomes a plural, and a demonstrative pronoun reintroduces the young men. The inconsequence is slight but effective: a hearer can almost have a sense of participating in the formulation of the thought. Plato on reading the sentence aloud could acknowledge the inconsequence with a slight motion of hand or head.

COMPLEMENT: PLATO *APOLOGY* 30B2–4

Always, of course, the meaning of any sequence of words could vary with the way one spoke: *Apology* 30b2–4 shows the necessity of proper reading aloud. Socrates says: οὐκ ἐκ χρημάτων ἀρετὴ γίγνεται, ἀλλ' ἐξ ἀρετῆς χρήματα καὶ τὰ ἄλλα ἀγαθὰ τοῖς ἀνθρώποις ἅπαντα καὶ ἰδίαι καὶ δημοσίαι. Now the mere words on a printed page can be construed to say that excellence does not come come into existence from money, but humankind gets money and all other good things both public and private from excellence.[2] But Plato's Socrates cannot really have said such a thing. At least from all we can tell by reading Plato's (and others') representation of him, he would not say that seriously. His own spare circumstances would in themselves belie the assertion. It may be that Plato here has contrived a deliberately opaque precept. One first sees paradox but then on reflection recomposes the emphases to reach a sense that is more in accord with the actuality of the Platonic Socrates. The hiatus at τὰ ἄλλα

[1] τούτων γὰρ ἕκαστος, ὦ ἄνδρες, οἷός τ' ἐστιν ἰὼν εἰς ἑκάστην τῶν πόλεων τοὺς νέους—οἷς ἔξεστι τῶν ἑαυτῶν πολιτῶν προῖκα συνεῖναι ὧι ἂν βούλωνται—τούτους πείθουσι τὰς ἐκείνων συνουσίας ἀπολιπόντας σφίσιν συνεῖναι χρήματα διδόντας καὶ χάριν προσειδέναι.

[2] So, e.g., (**B**) Jowett 1892: "I tell you that virtue is not given by money but that from virtue comes money and every other good of man. . ." Cf. (**B**) Grube 1975: 33: "Wealth does not bring about excellence, but excellence brings about wealth and all other public and private blessings for men." Also (**B**) Tredennick 1969: 62 *et alibi*. (**A**) Slings 1994: 138 offers, "Not from money does the value (of man) come, but from this value money and every other good thing (will come) to men both in private and in public life." He describes (**A**) Burnet's (1924) interpretation as "desperate . . . from the stylistic point of view" (note 39), adding a subjective rationale on p. 334. For Burnet's interpretation, see note 3 below.

ἀγαθὰ may have provided the micro-second of silence that established the correct meaning—that and other expected modulations such as changes of timing and stress. But a gesture as well could help. And so the sense was not in doubt: one understood that "from excellence do money and all else become good for mankind."[3]

PLATO *MENO* 82C–85C

Another way to represent people as actually talking appears in early and middle dialogues, such as *Euthyphro, Gorgias, Meno, Apology, Republic,* and *Symposium.* Later dialogues such as *Politicus, Sophist, Philebus,* and *Laws* do not show the same interest in dramatic representation. When verisimilitude is the end, characters speak of things they see as "this" or "that" without needing to stipulate exactly what "this" or "that" was. Plato's *Meno* provides a good example of this sort of exposition.

Socrates, in a demonstration to Meno, Anytos, and others, undertakes to draw from Meno's household slave a recollection of the geometric theorem, the square of the two sides of a right angle triangle equals the square of the hypotenuse. Socrates' aim is to show that the slave's soul acquired that particular understanding (along with all else) in some state other than his present life. The whole demonstration, which Socrates insists cannot be defined as "teaching," implies by its language continuous supplementary activity beside the inquiry being carried on in words. Plato does not say that Socrates is scratching lines and figures in the sand with a stick, but unless we imagine him doing that, or something like that, we will have difficulty in following his demonstration.

The beginning of Socrates' lesson shows that Plato conceived the scene as one in which a performer points to things outside the written text. Consider the following exchange:

> *Socrates:* Tell me now, boy, you know that a square figure is like *this*?
> *Boy:* Yes, I do.
> *Socrates:* So a square figure is one that has all *these* straight lines equal?
> *Boy:* Yes, indeed.
> *Socrates:* And it is one that also has *these* lines through the middle equal, isn't it?
> *Boy:* Yes.
> *Socrates:* And there could be both bigger and smaller figures *like this*, couldn't there?[4]

[3] (**A**) Burnet 1924 *comm. ad loc.* provides the correct interpretation: "The subject is χρήματα καὶ τὰ ἄλλα ἅπαντα and ἀγαθὰ τοῖς ἀνθρώποις is predicate." (**A**) Slings 1994: 138, note 39 compromises his assertion that Burnet's interpretation is "generally" ignored by citing responsible authorities who have in fact accepted it.

[4] Plato *Meno.* Translation of (**B**) Day 1994: 48–49. Added italics emphasize the demonstrative pronouns. Cf. Plato *Republic* 509d6–511e5. Socrates says, "as though you were to take

A similar effect is found where Homer and Aristophanes and Andocides use demonstrative pronouns requiring an object to complete their meaning and accordingly gesticulate to locate the object (pp. 36–37, 71, 85 above).

I AM LEAVING: PLATO *EUTHYPHRO* 15E3–6

A pattern of exposition by which body language—or in the case of οἴμοι, a cry of pain—is noted and labeled with a word immediately after its expression and thereby emphasized, has been introduced above (pp. 58–59) in the context of Sophocles' exchange between Oedipus and Teiresias. Plato uses the same pattern at the close of *Euthyphro* 15e3–6, where Euthyphro says, "Another time, Socrates, because now I am in a hurry to go somewhere, and it is time for me to leave." Socrates answers: "What you are doing, my friend, you are leaving, and you are casting me down from the great hope I had, hope that . . . etc."[5] The phrase, "You are leaving" (ἀπέρχηι), although not necessary to the sense of Socrates' disappointment, evokes for a second time a picture of Euthyphro turning around and walking away.

NO, THAT IS NOT AN OPTION

The richness and variety of modal particles in the ancient Greek language has been noted above (p. 53). Centuries of rigorous and inspired contemplation have opened up some of their intricacies and nuances, but the discipline and tight focus required for such study has in a way cast a veil over possible combinations of particle and gesture. One such combination may be the sequence, νῦν δέ. . . γάρ. . . . Examples taken from Aristophanes, Antiphon, [Lysias], and Herodotus have appeared above (pp. 70, 82–83, 88, 96) but without elaboration that includes assessment of earlier interpretations and comment. In Plato, however, previous attempts at explanation can usefully be cited to show the inadequacy of appeals to strict grammar as it is universally prescribed today, i.e., without reference to nonverbal communication. (**A**) Riddell 1877: 184 explains the force of this sequence as follows: "This combination is always preceded by a hypothesis of something contrary to facts, and is parallel to the Protasis of that sentence which it contradicts. The δέ and the γάρ exercise a simultaneous force; δέ represents that the condition stands differently in fact from what it is in the supposed case, and γάρ further represents that

a divided line . . ." (ὥσπερ τοίνυν γραμμὴν τετμημένην λαβὼν . . .), and it is easy to imagine some supplementary activity such as the actual sketching of the hypothetical line proposed.

[5] ΕΥΘ. εἰς αὖθις τοίνυν, ὦ Σώκρατες, νῦν γὰρ σπεύδω ποι, καί μοι ὥρα ἀπιέναι. ΣΩ. οἷα ποιεῖς, ὦ ἑταῖρε. ἀπ' ἐλπίδος με καταβαλὼν μεγάλης ἀπέρχηι ἣν εἶχον. . . .

the inference must be different. . . . There is of course no Ellipse to be supplied; that is, we are not to look on to a sentence beyond to supply a clause to the νῦν δέ." Denniston 1966: 70, in a discussion of anticipatory γάρ, says: "In Plato, the γάρ clause, as modern punctuation implies, often tends to acquire independence, by anacolouthon. This is clearly illustrated in *Apology*, 38b, where τοσούτου οὖν τιμῶμαι refers to the afterthought εἰ μὴ . . . ἀργυρίου, not to οὐ γάρ ἔστιν."

Since an aim of the present study, expressed throughout, is to locate ellipses in syntax that a gesture could fill, it should not be necessary here to present a catalogue of detailed reasons for taking issue with two such authoritative figures.[6] Instead I list all of the examples cited by Riddell, as well as a few more, and try to show in each case that there is in fact an ellipse. What is lacking every time is the sense, "No, that is not an option," and a speaker could have expressed that negation by means of a single motion of hand or head. Once the gesture is accepted as reality, assumptions of an anticipatory γάρ become irrelevant for this particular combination of particles, since the γάρ explains a foregoing statement that has been made silently by means of head, hand, or torso.

NO: PLATO *APOLOGY* 38B1–4

Socrates has just uttered his resonant prescription, "The unexamined life is unliveable for humankind," and now to a panel of judges who moments before have found him guilty he must propose for himself a money fine or other punishment as alternative to the death penalty proposed by his accusers. This was standard procedure. For certain charges, once the defendant has been found guilty, prosecutor and defendant in formal presentations recommend what the defendant must pay or suffer. The moment in the *Apology* is critical. Socrates—most Athenians would suppose—should propose a penalty for himself that would keep him alive but at the same time satisfy the punitive impulse of the judging panel. He thinks it over: "If I had money, I might have proposed as much as I would be in a position to pay, because it wouldn't have done me any harm. But as it is—because I don't have any money, unless you want me to fine myself as much as I might be able to pay."[7]

The sense required by context seems to be, "But as it is, <that is not an option> for I don't have any money." A slight pause here would be in itself a gesture, one that says in effect, "Pay attention." But in a world

[6] Cf. also Sicking and van Ophuijsen 1993: 24: "Those who consider that γάρ by itself introduces a reason or cause are regularly faced with the need to supply (in thought) from the context the statement which is supposed to call for such a causal explanation." Sicking then recommends that the reader supply in thought a hypothetical question.

[7] . . . οὐδὲν γὰρ ἂν ἐβλάβην· νῦν δὲ—οὐ γὰρ ἔστιν, εἰ μὴ ἄρα ὅσον ἂν ἐγὼ δυναίμην ἐκτεῖσαι, τοσούτου βούλεσθέ μοι τιμῆσαι.

where everyone talked constantly with head and hands, the expected sense is easily supplied by a generally recognized movement of head or hand, one signifying futility, or simply negation. One editor of the *Apology* has Socrates shrug his shoulders here. Greek readers, he supposes, understood that Plato meant them to supply, either physically or mentally, an appropriate gesture.[8] This supposition is a step in the right direction, although the specific recommendation, namely that Socrates shrugged his shoulders, may be an anachronism.[9] Still, if he did not shrug his shoulders, he did somehow convey by means of body language the qualification "That is not an option."

NO: PLATO *EUTHYPHRO* 11C AND 14C

Socrates teases Euthyphro at 11c1–5: "And if I were saying them, you might be laughing at me. But as it is <GESTURE = No, that is not an option> because the notions are yours. You need some other way to mock me."[10] He continues at 14c2–4: "If you had answered that, I would have learned sufficiently from you by now what "piety" is. But as it is <GESTURE = No, that is not an option> because the necessity is that lover follow beloved wherever he leads."[11]

NO: PLATO *PROTAGORAS* 347A

Socrates is interpreting Simonides, and at the close of his hermeneutic he paraphrases: "And so I wouldn't ever blame you, Pittakos, if you were saying things that were even halfway reasonable and true. But as it is <GESTURE = No, that supposition is not an option> because while you appear to tell the truth you are lying altogether about the most important things. This is why I am blaming you."[12]

[8] (**A**) Dyer 1885 *et alibi*.

[9] Sittl 1890: 113 does not find mention of the gesture until Roman Imperial times. Quintilian 11.3.83 disapproves and in doing so testifies that the gesture was popular enough to merit comment: "The raising and pulling in of the shoulders is rarely fitting, for it shortens the neck and produces a lowly and servile gesture and makes it in a way fraudulent when people fashion themselves in postures of adulation, wonder, and fear." ("Humerorum raro decens adlevatio atque contractio est; breviatur enim cervix et gestum quendam humilem atque servilem et quasi fraudulentum facit cum se in habitum adulationis admirationis metus fingunt." Argyle 1988: 53, in speaking of "very common, or universal" gestures, gives the shrug as an example.

[10] καὶ εἰ μὲν αὐτὰ ἐγὼ ἔλεγον . . . ἴσως ἄν με ἐπέσκωπτες . . . νῦν δέ—σαὶ γὰρ αἱ ὑποθέσεις εἰσίν. ἄλλου δή τινος δεῖ σκώμματος.

[11] εἰ ἀπεκρίνω, ἱκανῶς ἂν ἤδη παρὰ σοῦ τὴν ὁσιότητα ἐμεμαθήκη. νῦν δέ—ἀνάγκη γὰρ τὸν ἐρῶντα τῶι ἐρομένωι ἀκολουθεῖν ὅπηι ἂν ἐκεῖνος ὑπάγηι.

[12] σὲ οὖν, καὶ εἰ μέσως ἔλεγες ἐπιεικῆ καὶ ἀληθῆ, ὦ Πίττακε, οὐκ ἄν ποτε ἔψεγον· νῦν δὲ—σφόδρα γὰρ καὶ περὶ τῶν μεγίστων ψευδόμενος δοκεῖς ἀληθῆ λέγειν, διὰ ταῦτά σε ἐγὼ ψέγω.

NO: PLATO *CHARMIDES* 175A–B

Socrates and Critias have been exploring the sense of *sophrosynē*, and it now turns out that that virtue seems to have no real use. Socrates says that it is as he feared, and he blames himself, because "I don't suppose that that which is the fairest of all things would have revealed itself as useless, if there were any use in me as a proper investigator, but as it is <GESTURE = No, to suppose that there is any use in me is not an option> because we are being worsted everywhere."[13]

NO: PLATO *LACHES* 184D1–4

Nicias and Laches have just assessed the art of fighting in armor as exhibition, and they come to opposite conclusions. Lysimachos turns to Socrates and asks him to act as additional judge in the matter. "Because if these two were in agreement, there would be no need of such a judge. But as it is <GESTURE = No, they are not agreed> because Laches, as you see, registered a judgment opposite to that of Nicias. It is a good thing to hear from you with which of the two men's judgment yours concurs."[14]

NO: PLATO *LACHES* 200E

Lysimachos asks Socrates if he would be willing to contribute to the education of his (Lysimachos's) and Melias's sons, this after an inquiry into the nature of courage. Socrates replies: "Now if in the conversations we just had it had become manifest that I knew and that these two did not, it would be fair for you to invite me especially to perform this task. But as it is <GESTURE = No, that is not the case> because we have all alike ended up in a quandary. Why then would a person pick any one of us over the others?"[15]

NO: PLATO *SYMPOSIUM* 180C3–D1

Guests at a drinking party recline on couches at Agathon's house. They have chosen "Love" as a theme for praise that evening. It is Pausanias's

[13] οὐ γὰρ ἄν που ὅ γε κάλλιστον πάντων ὁμολογεῖται εἶναι, τοῦτο ἡμῖν ἀνωφελὲς ἐφάνη, εἴ τι ἐμοῦ ὄφελος ἦν πρὸς τὸ καλῶς ζητεῖν. νῦν δέ—πανταχῆι γὰρ ἡττώμεθα.

[14] εἰ μὲν γὰρ συνεφερέσθην τώδε, ἧττον ἂν τοῦ τοιούτου ἔδει· νῦν δέ—τὴν ἐναντίαν γάρ, ὡς ὁρᾶις, Λάχης Νικίαι ἔθετο· εὖ δὴ ἔχει ἀκοῦσαι καὶ σοῦ ποτέρωι τοῖν ἀνδροῖν σύμψηφος εἶ.

[15] εἰ μὲν οὖν ἐν τοῖς διαλόγοις τοῖς ἄρτι ἐγὼ μὲν ἐφάνην εἰδώς, τώδε δὲ μὴ εἰδότε, δίκαιον ἂν ἦν ἐμὲ μάλιστα ἐπὶ τοῦτο τὸ ἔργον παρακαλεῖν. νῦν δέ—ὁμοίως γὰρ πάντες ἐν ἀπορίαι ἐγενόμεθα. τί οὖν ἄν τις ἡμῶν τινα προαιροῖτο;

turn to praise love, but before he can begin he needs to define the object of his discourse. He is troubled by the way the discussion has proceeded, “because if Love were one that would be fine, but as it is <GESTURE = No, that is not the case> because Love is not one. Since Love is not one, it is more correct to say beforehand what sort of Love one should praise.”[16]

NO: PLATO *LAWS* 875C3–D3

The Athenian stranger offers some prescriptions for good government: the common good is most important; after that, private good. Alas! even humans who grasp this concept are not able to put it into practice. “If ever by divine dispensation some mortal came into being who could apprehend this, he would not need laws to govern him. . . . But as it is <GESTURE = No, speculation along these lines is vain> because he does not exist anywhere in any way, except partially.”[17]

In each of the preceding nine passages, a protasis is expressed vocally and then dismissed with a gesture.[18] As a consequence, an utterance that appears in print to be elliptical becomes, with the addition of nonverbal communication, an unremarkable syntactical unit. The gestured dismissal can be simple, a slight backward tilt of the head (ἀνανεύειν), expressing nothing more complex than negation. When it is put in place, a following explanation, introduced by “because” (γάϱ), continues: “This is why we cannot consider it as a possibility.” An English-speaking person today might shrug or throw up both hands, palms up, to chest level.

QUOTATION: PLATO *GORGIAS* 447B1

The *Gorgias* is rich in possibilities for nonverbal communication. At the beginning of the dialogue, there is some play between Socrates and Chairephon (447a1–b1). Socrates blames Chairephon for making them late, and Chairephon responds with an allusion to the story of Telephos: “For I shall also be the cure” (ἐγὼ γὰϱ καὶ ἰάσομαι). (**A**) Dodds 1959: 189–90 cites the oracle that told Telephus, “Who has wounded will also heal”

[16] εἰ μὲν γὰϱ εἷς ἦν ὁ Ἐϱώς, καλῶς ἂν εἶχε· νῦν δέ—οὐ γάϱ ἐστιν εἷς· μὴ ὄντος δὲ ἑνὸς ὀϱθότεϱόν ἐστι πϱότεϱον πϱοϱϱηθῆναι ὁποῖον δεῖ ἐπαινεῖν. (**A**) Hug 1909 *ad loc.* equates νῦν δὲ . . . γὰϱ with ἀλλὰ γὰϱ and cites Kühner 1966: 2.725. Bury 1932: 30 says, “We may assume the ellipse of οὐ καλῶς ἔχει after νῦν δὲ” and compares Plato *Theatetus* 143e *et al.* (**A**) Dover 1980: 96 explains: “This γὰϱ is related to D1 οὖν: but as it is—for he is not one . . . I then will try; cf. *Laches* 200 e. . . .”

[17] ἐπεὶ ταῦτα εἴ ποτέ τις ἀνθϱώπων φύσει ἱκανὸς θείαι μοίϱαι γεννηθεὶς παϱαλαβεῖν δυνατὸς εἴη, νόμων οὐδὲν ἂν δέοιτο τῶν ἀϱξόντων ἑαυτοῦ . . . νῦν δὲ—οὐ γάϱ ἐστιν οὐδαμοῦ οὐδαμῶς, ἀλλ᾽ ἢ κατὰ βϱαχύ.

[18] Cf. also Plato *Theaetetus* 143d1–6.

(ὁ τρώσας καὶ ἰάσεται) and evokes a world in which such allusions were a staple of graceful conversation. One might go a step further and imagine Plato imagining a gesture as he wrote. Chairephon could assume a stagey posture or merely extend his right hand with index and middle fingers spread and extended, as he said, "I shall also be the cure."[19]

WELCOME! PLATO *GORGIAS* 447B7–8

Soon after, Kallikles invites Socrates to come to his house, if Socrates would like sometime to talk to Gorgias. The form of the invitation, when read as words unaccompanied by body language, lacks an apodosis. "Whenever you want to come to me at my house—because Gorgias is staying with me, and he will give you a demonstration.[20] The lack has occasioned efforts to rearrange the text, which are neatly summed up in (**A**) Dodds's (1959) footnote *ad loc.*: "There is no need to manufacture an apodosis by treating ἥκειν as imperatival (Ast) or the καὶ before ἐπιδείξεται as merely responsive (Schleiermacher, Reinhard); still less to delete the καὶ (Schanz), or alter ἥκειν to ἥκετ' (Cobet) or ὅταν βούλησθε to ὦ τᾶν, βούλεσθε (Hemsterhuis). Some MSS restore normal syntax at the cost of sense by omitting γὰρ." Dodds himself makes sense of the text as it is but does not avail himself of an apodosis that a welcoming gesture could supply. He writes, "The omission of the apodosis (ἥκετε or the like) is natural in colloquial Greek as in colloquial English, since the invitation is already sufficiently implied in the ὅταν clause." But if Plato envisioned Kallikles in action, the sentence might be presented as follows: "Whenever you want to come to me at my house <GESTURE = Welcome!!> because Gorgias is staying with me . . . etc."

WELCOME! PLATO *REPUBLIC* 328C5

To turn briefly from the *Gorgias* to the *Republic*, Socrates has come to Kephalos's house in the Peiraeus, and he finds the old man seated in a courtyard, finishing his sacrifices. Kephalos greets Socrates warmly; an embrace and a kiss would be in order. Then his first words are: "And you don't come down to us in Peiraeus very much."[21] But why does he say

[19] On this gesture, see pp. 25–26 above.

[20] οὐκοῦν ὅταν βούλησθε παρ' ἐμὲ ἥκειν οἴκαδε· παρ' ἐμοὶ γὰρ Γοργίας καταλύει καὶ ἐπιδείξεται ὑμῖν.

[21] ἠσπάζετό τε καὶ εἶπε· Ὦ Σώκρατες οὐδὲ θαμίζεις ἡμῖν καταβαίνων εἰς τὸν Πειραιᾶ. (**A**) Adam 1969 *ad loc.* says, "A negative must be supplied" to account for οὐδὲ, which means "also not." He then reviews and rejects a number of solutions proposed by previous editors. Kephalos also avails himself of a Homeric formula: cf. Homer *Iliad* 18.385, *Odyssey* 5.88.

"and" (οὐδέ) when these are the first words Plato gives him? Where is the question or assertion to which his remonstrance is added? The assertion could be in the welcoming embrace, and his words when they come follow that implicit statement as a continuation.[22] An amplified translation therefore might run somewhat as follows: "<HUG = Welcome! We've missed you> and yet you don't come down to us here in Peiraeus very much."

YES: PLATO *GORGIAS* 449B4–8

Returning to the *Gorgias*, Socrates at 449b4–8 seems to refer to a promise that Gorgias is making, but Gorgias has not said "yes" or "I promise." Socrates says, "Would you like to continue, Gorgias, just as we are talking now? Asking and answering questions but putting off to another time the extended kind of speech that Polos began? But don't go back on what you are promising. Be willing to answer briefly what is asked." What has seemed to be a problem here is that there is not in the text a single word that shows Gorgias making any kind of promise. If, however, we imagine the two speakers as Plato might have seen them, the problem disapppears, because in that case when Socrates says "putting off to another time . . . etc.," Plato saw Gorgias nodding yes.[23] And so Socrates could respond just as though he had received the assent in words.

YES/NO: PLATO *GORGIAS* 460C 1–2 *ET AL.*

A little later, Socrates and Gorgias are talking. The text of the dialogue here has seemed to editors excessively full from 460b8 to 460c6, and various emendations have been proposed.[24] There is one point, however, where a nod saying yes might help. Socrates asks, "Doesn't a man trained in rhetoric have to be honest? And doesn't an honest man have to do what is honest?"[25] Given the staccato tempo of the dialogue here, one

[22] At Plato *Charmides* 153b1 ἠσπάζοντο obviously does not mean "embraced," because the welcomers are at a distance. Cf., however, Homer *Odyssey* 19.415, χερσίν τ' ἠσπάζοντο ἔπεσσί τε μειλιχίοισι ("They greeted him with embraces and gentle words").

[23] (**A**) Dodds 1959 comments *ad loc.*: "Editors have found a difficulty here, since Gorgias has so far given no undertaking to answer briefly . . . one or two late MSS provide the promise by inserting ναί after ἀποθέσθαι. This is a possibility, as is Morstadt's ὅπερ [ἂν] ὑπισχνῇ (generic subjunctive with future reference). But it is perhaps sufficient to suppose that S. has in mind Gorgias' general undertaking to answer questions, on the strength of which he now hopes to pin him down to a strict 'dialectical procedure.' "

[24] See (**A**) Dodds 1959: 219–20.

[25] οὐκοῦν ἀνάγκη τὸν ῥητορικὸν δίκαιον εἶναι; τὸν δὲ δίκαιον βούλεσθαι δίκαια πράττειν; *Gorgias* 460c1–2.

could have expected a yes after εἶναι and a nod could have supplied that concession.[26]

At 461b2 we learn of Gorgias's real discomfiture through the intervention and solicitude of Polos. At 465a7 Polos can be understood to signal either yes or no, but in either case he allows Socrates to proceed. Socrates, however, forces an explicit answer from Polos at 468c7–8 because it is dramatically useful to have Polos recognize and confess the difficulty of his position. At 468d6, where Socrates asks, "Why aren't you answering?" his question is a stage direction. Plato adumbrates disinclination to answer a potentially troubling question in a similar way at 474c8, 475d6, 478a1, 515b2, 515c2–4; at 489a1ff. Dodds compares 482c–e, 487b.

YES: PLATO *EUTHYDEMOS* 286E2–7

An exchange at Plato *Euthydemos* 286e2–7 is comparable: Socrates asks, "Is this possible by your account to refute, if no one tells lies?" And Euthydemos answers that it is not possible. Then Socrates asks, "Dionysodoros therefore was not telling me just now to refute him?" And Euthydemos answers, "Because how could a person tell you to do something that does not exist?"[27] Plato has Euthydemos move his head down and to the side in order to signify assent or up and back to reinforce the no. We can accordingly picture to ourselves, if we like, whoever it was who read the dialogue aloud, moving his head appropriately as he pronounced the words of Euthydemos's answer.[28]

SO BE IT: PLATO *GORGIAS* 521B2–3

Another apodosis could be supplied by another gesture when Socrates asks Kallikles whether he, Socrates, ought to serve the city as healer, battling to make everyone as good as they can be, or as attendant, talking to please. "Attendant," says Kallikles, and Socrates says he really means "brown-nose (κολακεύσαντα)." Kallikles, offended at the bluntness, says, "If you prefer to name the Mysian, Socrates. So unless you do do

[26] See (**A**) Dodds 1959: 220 *ad loc.*: "But there are other cases where S. adds a second question without waiting for an answer to his first (F. Levy, *Phil. Wochenschrift* 41, 1921, p. 115)." Cf. (**A**) Dodds 1959: 184. (**B**) Helmbold 1952: 20 imposes a causal sense that is not in the Greek when he translates, "Then it follows that the rhetorician will be just, inasmuch as a just man will wish to act justly."

[27] τὸ γὰρ μὴ ὂν πῶς ἄν τις κελεύσαι;

[28] See (**A**) Hawtrey 1981: 112 on the text. (**A**) Wilamowitz 1920: 370 *comm. ad* Plato *Euthydemos* 286e1, to account for the explanatory γάρ writes: "vor dem γάρ des Euthydem ergänzt sich leicht wie so oft in Dramen der Gestus der Zustimmung die damit als selbsverständlich erscheint."

this. . . ."[29] The gesture that provides an apodosis here might have been one that expressed a response, such as "So be it" or, as Dodds suggests, "So much the worse for you."

THIS IS INCREDIBLE: PLATO *LYSIS* 204C3–D5

Socrates has just entered a newly built palaestra and finds himself in company with a merry band of young men. Socrates wants to know who is the current darling among the younger lads, and Ktesippos not only names the boy, Lysis, but also takes the opportunity to make fun of Hippothales, who makes his friends impatient with his praises of Lysis and family. In the course of his representation of Hippothales, Ktesippos says: "And what he gives us in detail in conversation—yes, they are awful, but they are not really awful. But when he tries to soak us in his poems and prose <GESTURE = it is not to be believed!>. And what is more awful than these is what he sings to the object of his affection in a weird voice."[30] It would be pleasant to be able to recreate that original gesture.

AT YOUR SERVICE: PLATO *REPUBLIC* 337A8

To continue with the phenomenon just noted in Plato's *Euthydemos*, some additional instances in the *Republic* deserve mention, not only because they are nice illustrations of the explanatory particle γάϱ signaling a preceding gesture, but also because they can be thought to suggest in some way a speaker's characteristic responses. Socrates' response to Thrasymachos may be an example. Thrasymachos with a sardonic laugh accuses Socrates of using irony and being unwilling to answer questions, and Socrates answers, "Because you are smart" (σοφὸς γὰϱ εἶ). Why the explanatory particle? Possibly because Plato sees Socrates making a gesture, one that signs (ironic) admiration: he is acknowledging Thrasymachos's keen perception.[31]

AT YOUR SERVICE: PLATO *REPUBLIC* 337D1–7

Thrasymachos asks Socrates what punishment Socrates should suffer if he, Thrasymachos, provides a better answer concerning justice (τί ἀξιοῖς

[29] ". . . to name the Mysian," Dodds glosses "to call a spade a spade" (εἴ σοι Μυσόν γε ἥδιον καλεῖν, ὦ Σώκρατες· ὡς εἰ μὴ ταῦτά γε ποιήσεις—).

[30] καὶ ἃ μὲν καταλογάδην διηγεῖται δεινὰ ὄντα, οὐ πάνυ τι δεινά ἐστιν, ἀλλ' ἐπειδὰν τὰ ποιήματα ἡμῶν ἐπιχειϱήσηι καταντλεῖν καὶ συγγϱάμματα. καὶ ὅ ἐστιν τούτων δεινότεϱον, ὅτι καὶ αἴδει εἰς τὰ παιδικὰ φωνῆι θαυμασίαι

[31] Denniston 1966: 75 sees γάϱ in a sentence like this as providing "a motive for the language used, or the tone adopted by the previous speaker. 'You say this (or talk like this) because.' " He cites as examples Plato *Republic* 337d, 338d, and 340d.

παθεῖν·). With these words he alludes to a formulaic expression, found in quotations of Athenian laws, which authorizes the Heliaia to determine what a convicted person should suffer or pay.[32] Socrates in return plays with a famous Aeschylean formulation that presents increased wisdom as an exponent of having (bad) things happen to you (πάθει μάθος, Aeschylus *Agamemnon* 176). He says: "I should only suffer what a person who does not know should suffer. That person should, I suppose, learn from the person who does know. And so I deserve to suffer this." Thrasymachos acknowledges Socrates' reference, saying, "Because you are a pleasure" (ἡδὺς γὰρ εἶ), and then adds (and includes at the same time the alternate element found in the legal formula), "but in addition to learning, you are to pay money" (ἀπότεισον ἀργύριον).[33]

The question again presents itself, Why does Thrasymachos say "Because"? An economical answer once again is that his "because" explains his gesture of recognition or approval at the same time.

PTUI! PLATO *REPUBLIC* 338D3

Thrasymachos at Plato *Republic* 338d2 says to Socrates, "Because you are disgusting" (βδελυρὸς γὰρ εἶ). It is plain why Thrasymachos is annoyed: He has just triumphantly produced what he thought was a succinct and surprising definition of justice, and Socrates has characteristically given it an odd turn. But nothing in Socrates' words calls for a "because" from Thrasymachos. Thrasymachos, we may suppose, says "because" since he is annotating his own nonverbal expression of disgust. He himself, if asked why he said "because," might not be able to say, because gesture and explanatory sound were almost inseparable. Or rather Plato has him say "because" since Plato, composer of dialogue, knows that Thrasymachos (and others like him at Athens, or indeed singularly Thrasymachos) would accompany or precede such a statement with a hand or head motion, perhaps even a hint at spitting. For that reason, when Plato has Thrasymachos say, "You are disgusting," he includes the "because" that was an integral component of that declaration.

PTUI! PLATO *REPUBLIC* 340D1

Again Thrasymachos protests when Socrates seems to be pointing out an inconsistency. He says, "Because you are an extortionist in arguments" (συκοφάντης γὰρ εἶ). The explanatory γάρ, when it follows an abusive

[32] τί ἂν δοκεῖ ἄξιος εἶναι παθεῖν ἢ ἀποτεῖσαι;

[33] Cf. (**A**) Adams 1969: 27.

word, may look to some nonverbal expression of anger or impatience, such as spitting.

YES: PLATO *REPUBLIC* 353E9

Thrasymachos again at 353e9 says, "Because we agreed" (συνεχωρήσαμεν γάρ) because he has nodded agreement. There is no need to find a word for that explanatory particle in translation or paraphrase: it is enough to have in mind that Thrasymachos shows assent by gesture.[34]

I AM STAYING: PLATO *REPUBLIC* 344E4

Thrasymachos, Socrates tells us, has wanted to leave. From this we can imagine Thrasymachos standing up, adjusting his *himation,* perhaps even taking a step or two toward the door. Socrates detains him, asking if Thrasymachos thinks it is a small thing to try to determine what is the best way for a person to live his life. Thrasymachos responds, "Because do I think otherwise?"[35] The explanatory particle here may tell us what Thrasymachos has done. He has given up his attempt to leave. He sits down again, ready to resume the argument.[36]

WELL AND GOOD: PLATO *PROTAGORAS* 311D1–4

Finally, consider four passages where an apodosis is supplied by a gesture that says "well and good." At *Protagoras* 311d1–4, Socrates is quizzing his young friend, Hippokrates: "You and I have come to Protagoras now, and we are going to be ready to pay him money in your behalf, if our money is enough and if we can persuade him with it, but otherwise, spending our friends' money in addition."[37] The addition of a signifying gesture will produce a paraphrase somewhat as follows: ". . . if our money is enough and if we can persuade him with it, <GESTURE = 'well and good'> otherwise, spending our friends' money in addition."

[34] Ibid.: 60 refers γάρ to earlier agreements in the dialogue.

[35] ἐγὼ γὰρ οἶμαι . . . τουτὶ ἄλλως ἔχειν;

[36] Denniston 1966: 78–79 writes: "Sometimes a γάρ question, forming the answer to a preceding question, conveys a surprised recognition of the grounds which occasioned that question." In the instances Denniston cites, including this one, each γάρ could well be justifying some gesture.

[37] παρὰ δὲ δὴ Πρωταγόραν νῦν ἀφικόμενοι ἐγώ τε καὶ σὺ ἀργύριον ἐκείνωι μισθὸν ἕτοιμοι ἐσόμεθα τελεῖν ὑπὲρ σοῦ, ἂν μὲν ἐξικνῆται τὰ ἡμέτερα χρήματα καὶ τούτοις πείθωμεν αὐτόν—εἰ δὲ μή, καὶ τὰ τῶν φίλων προσαναλίσκοντες.

WELL AND GOOD: PLATO *PROTAGORAS* 325D5–7

At *Protagoras* 325d5–7, Protagoras is telling Socrates that *aretē* can be taught, and he adduces the education of a child as example: everyone tells the child what to do in an effort to make the child be as good as he can be. "And if the child is willing to be persuaded . . . otherwise, they straighten him with threats and blows just as though he were a bent and twisted stick."[38] When a gesture is added, the condition looks like this: "And if the child is willing to be persuaded, <GESTURE = 'well and good'> otherwise they straighten him . . . etc."

WELL AND GOOD: PLATO *REPUBLIC* 575D3–7

Adeimantus and Socrates are talking, and Socrates has been describing the genesis of a tyrant: he is only one from a number of petty animals, but he is the one with the most intractable dictates in his own mind. As for the rest: "There's no problem if they're happy to defer to him, but if the community refuses to submit, then if he can, it'll be his fatherland's turn for the same punishment he inflicted on his mother and father before."[39] The translation is that of (**B**) Waterfield 1993. A literal translation <amplified> might go as follows: "And so if they willingly give in, <GESTURE = well and good>, but if the city does not permit, then just as he punished his mother and father that other time, just so again he will have his fatherland punished, if he can."

WELL AND GOOD: PLATO *SYMPOSIUM* 185D6

When it is Aristophanes' turn to speak, he has the hiccoughs, and so he asks Eryximachos, who knows about medicine, either to speak in his place or to cure him of his hiccoughs. Eryximachos says he will do both. "I'll talk in your place and you talk in mine after you've stopped. But while I'm talking, if the hiccoughs stop as you hold your breath for a long time. Otherwise, gargle with water."[40]

[38] καὶ ἐὰν μὲν ἑκὼν πείθηται—εἰ δὲ μή, ὥσπερ ξύλον διαστρεφόμενον καὶ καμπτόμενον εὐθύνουσιν ἀπειλαῖς καὶ πληγαῖς.

[39] οὐκοῦν ἐὰν μὲν ἑκόντες ὑπείκωσιν—ἐὰν δὲ μὴ ἐπιτρέπηι ἡ πόλις, ὥσπερ τότε μητέρα καὶ πατέρα ἐκόλαζεν, οὕτω πάλιν καὶ τὴν πατρίδα, ἐὰν οἷός τ' ἦι.

[40] ἐν ὧι δ' ἂν ἐγὼ λέγω, ἐὰν μέν σοι ἐθέληι ἀπνευστὶ ἔχοντι πολὺν χρόνον παύεσθαι ἡ λύγξ—εἰ δὲ μή, ὕδατι ἀνακογχυλίασον. (**A**) Bury 1932 *ad loc.* writes: "We have here a case of 'aposiopesis' or suppressed apodosis. Cf. *Prot.* 311d etc." (**A**) Rose 1981 *ad loc.* follows (**A**) Bury. (**A**) Dover 1980 *comm. ad loc.* writes, "In sentences of the form 'if μὲν . . . , but if not, . . . ,' the first 'if ' can be translated 'perhaps' or 'possibly.' " Students who are reading Plato's Greek for the first time will be grateful for this advice, although they may still want an explanation.

The protasis "if the hiccoughs stop" has no written apodosis. "Otherwise" begins a new sentence. Here as in other dialogues but perhaps especially in the *Symposium,* Plato intimates the speech he heard around him. He gives to each symposiast a way of speaking that differs from the others, with the result that Agathon, Phaedros, Pausanias, Eryximachos, and Aristophanes all use words, formulations, and rhythms that a contemporary acquaintance might have recognized as close to their own actual ways of speaking. Even modern readers, equipped only with a written text, can perceive distinctions Plato has made. And yet a speaking style defines itself as much by characteristic ellipses as by use of abstract nouns, balanced clauses, impersonal constructions, density or choice of particles, or rhythm generally. In the present case, Eryximachos would want to say: "If the hiccoughs stop for you as you hold your breath for a long time, well and good! A quick and happy cure professionally effected." He could express the sentiment of all of that part after ". . . long time," with an exuberant wave of the hand, or, given the somewhat dry and inhibited character of Eryximachos (as Plato represents him), with a single tight little outward turn of the open palm.[41]

Summary

Plato in composing his dialogues saw and heard his characters speaking. This use of imagination is especially evident in the so-called dramatic parts of some early and middle dialogues. These are the sections in which speakers are moving themselves to places or becoming acquainted or setting the tone of the ensuing discussion.

[41] Assuming that Eryximachos as an orderly person expresses himself less expansively than lesser folk. Cf. Plato *Laws* 816.

CONCLUSION

A BASIC OBSERVATION that sustains the principal theme of this study is not new. It is that for a hundred years and more, certain Hellenists have been intuiting nonverbal communication sporadically as they read their Archaic and Classical Greek texts. The names Wilamowitz, Beazley, Dodds, Dover, Thiel, Fraenkel, Thalheim, Lloyd-Jones, Adams, Taplin, Henderson, Lateiner, Arnott, Biehl, Mastronarde, Ameis, and Hentze, are representative of this company. They—and others, to be sure—saw characters as diverse as Agamemnon, Clytaemnestra, Oedipus, Nicias, and Andocides supplying yeses and noes, emphasis, color, and meaning with head, hand, and torso. But for all the authority and wide-ranging influence of these interpreters, many readers to this day demur when asked to imagine a single gesture sufficing where a whole clause seems to be needed. One reason for this recalcitrance may be respect for the Greek system of modal particles. The density and variety of these small words that modulate most ancient Greek utterances in literature, give the impression that the particles by themselves provide as much extra as any speaker could want. As a consequence, to imagine a whole different set of signals, none of them written and most of them seemingly redundant, is a stretching exercise that readers do not think to take, once they have absorbed and put the particles to use.

Another obstruction in the way of recognizing nonverbal communication in ellipses of syntax is the particularity of scholarly commentary. When an editor or commentator at one specific point in a text suggests that someone has nodded, a silent reader assimilates the supplementary information and reads on. But such tightly focused explanations lack staying power. The supposition of a gesture works there at that point, but then it stops, unless later, perhaps hundreds of lines or several books later, another egregious example emerges. The single quick act of imagining does not spread and enlarge itself and encourage a reader to envision other, different motions made by other different characters.

Why not? Possibly because readers associate that one motion with the interior life of one particular character in the text, or one syntactical question, and not with the continuing voice and gestures of a performer, who can have been the poet or prose-writer himself or someone necessarily associated with the creation of the text. It is an index to the genius of Homer, Pindar, Lysias, Plato, and the rest that their latter-day readers submerge themselves in the story that is being told and do not hear or see who is telling the story.

And so it has been expedient in this study to treat brief passages from poets, historians, philosophers, and orators, for all these composers read their own work aloud. They were performing their work, and as they told their stories, they supplied the gestures that filled in or amplified meaning. And once these performers appear in a modern, silent reader's mind, seeming ellipses in meaning turn out to be not blank places but actual signals. For they show where a performer could improvise: where he asked a question, or issued a command, or expressed a hope or denial by means of nonverbal communication.

The "incomplete" conditional sentence is one example: it is found in authors as various as Homer, Pindar, Aeschylus, Sophocles, Euripides, Aristophanes, Thucydides, Herodotus, Andocides, Lysias, Xenophon, and Plato. A protasis in most examples is written out in words, but no written apodosis precedes or follows. A few times it is the protasis that is not written out. Editors in commenting on such seeming anomalies may blunt further inquiry by summoning as explanation a rhetorical tactic called "aposiopesis." This term, which means "falling silent," alerts modern readers to the writer's intention. They learn that the ellipsis is deliberate, and not a fault in the transmission of the text. This is helpful information for readers who must depend on the transmitted learning of editors and transcribers, but it is not always the case that a momentary silence produces all of the intended rhetorical effect.

Furthermore ancient authorities do not define aposiopesis merely as a falling silent. A speaker was to fall silent when silence was in itself a gesture. The unexpected silence came as a surprise. The aim was to elicit from the audience their own formulation, one for which they had been skillfully prepared. The way it worked was this: if at a key point, a place where the word or phrase that needed to be filled in was shocking or ugly, or where the speaker would somehow compromise himself by saying it, the speaker would pause and not pronounce the expected words. Clear-cut instances of this sort of aposiopesis are quoted in our standard grammars (pp. 38–39 above), and it is easy to suppose that a posture or gesture of some sort helped an audience appreciate the timing and the effect of the silence. But there are at the same time other breaks or sudden silences that do not allow themselves to be explained the same way. Where these are found, readers search in vain for hints of rhetorical effectiveness. And these are the cases where nonverbal communication can have filled out what additionally needed to be said.

A recommendation, therefore, is respectfully tendered here: it is that editors and commentators pause before they gloss a break in sense as aposiopesis or anacolouthon and then pass on to the next item. It might be the case that a nod or motion with the hand originally said what needed to be supplied.

Greeks used gestures widely in antiquity, and students of ancient art have produced study after study analyzing and explaining particular postures in sculpture and painting. The explanations, however, are seldom fully satisfying because a gesture in life has movement while a gesture in a sculpture or painting does not. As a result, any motion of head or body that started out as a signifying gesture in an artist's conception becomes a posture in the sculpture or painting. It is a shorthand reference, a reminder to those who know the language that something is being said. One sees only a single stroboscopic flash.

To recreate the whole of what an ancient gesture might have been, a modern student might look to body language as it can be observed in the intercourse of Greek speakers today. Some elements of nonverbal communication seem to be almost universal, and interpreters of Greek literature and art have been using such accessible data for years. There is no need for one to pause, for instance, when asked to interpret an image of a person or deity pointing with the index finger, or biting the lip, or shading the eyes to give a sense of searching, or putting the hand under the chin while thinking something through. Such postures and gesticulations are reliable keys to the whole motion of analogous ancient gestures.

The same, however, is true of some gestures that appear to be peculiarly Greek, or at least Mediterranean, and the utility of this approach has not been seriously tested. Too many nations, races, and tribes have passed through Greece in the past millennia. Nothing that was originally Greek can have survived intact. So at least runs a surprisingly unchallenged *communis opinio*. But in answer, one need do no more than point to the continuity of the Greek language. If a vocabulary of words endured, why should one of gestures not likewise endure, especially in view of the priority of body language in the development of a newly born child's means of communication? Let us therefore use as keys the head motions that say yes and no, the shaking of the front of a garment in obsecration, spitting three times into the bosom to avoid the evil eye. These gestures attest some continuities and encourage us to seek others.

Once circumstantial references in literature along with the evidence of images and continuities have been introduced as sources for the study of nonverbal communication in literature, observations concerning a few Attic red-figure vase paintings are offered. What the observations have of novelty comes from a heightened recognition of the degree to which nonverbal communication played a part in the Archaic and Classical Greek world. In this world in motion, Athena becomes an umpire when overseeing the Vote on the Arms of Achilles, and "Law and Order" beckons to "Good Fame" to come and stand by her side.

Following the introduction of these means and measures, lively pictures of rhapsodes and poets, actors and chorus in tragedy and comedy manifest themselves, as well as new approaches to questions of syntax and interpretation. There is also the audience. What can they have been expected to have in their heads? Could a comic playwright be sure that a majority of his audience would appreciate effects as slight and delicate as a line of tragedy with one word replaced? An actor could certainly emphasize words, phrases, or lines by means of voice alone, but in a society where nonverbal communication always accompanied speech, an actor would not fail to use head, hands, and arms throughout the piece. And it is this unceasing communication by means of gesture that helps us to see how single words and phrases, although not marked or emphasized by particles or by position in a sentence, would have been recognized and appreciated in an epic recitation, in a comedy, in a forensic speech, or the reading of a history, or in a philosophical dialogue.

In oratory, especially forensic oratory, body language is important. In deliberative and display oratory, nonverbal communication must meet exacting standards of decorum. By means of a nod or wave of the hand, an orator can fill in a variety of seeming ellipses; he can also give special emphasis to single words or phrases in a way that makes an audience recognize a special application of the word. The desired effect might be in the service of irony, pathos, humor, whatever in short an orator wanted. The technique enabled Demosthenes, for instance, to turn a potentially abusive word like *ponēros* into a reproach to the people who used the word abusively, and Lycurgus could evoke a heroic past by quoting part of a line from an earlier drama. Ordinary folk speaking in court had much greater freedom. They could express themselves with all the motions of head, hand, and body that might be thought to improve their case.

A sense of body language gives added life to the historians. Elliptical utterances in Herodotus, irony and quoted words and phrases in Thucydides, and lively conversational exchanges in Xenophon come to light. The same is true, and to a much higher degree, in many Platonic dialogues. Plato obviously saw his characters expressing themselves with their hands, heads, and torsos as he steered them in and out of marketplace, palaestras, symposia, and opulent residences.

The foregoing chapters have not been the outcome of a systematic scrutiny of any single author. They represent, rather, observations made in the course of reading over the past ten years or so—since the time, that is, when I first became conscious of the need for some other approach to explain certain ellipses in Classical and Archaic Greek literary texts. I believe that intensive study of any of the authors whose work is touched upon here will reveal more opportunities for the informed reader to see the speakers in action.

BIBLIOGRAPHY

(A) EDITIONS

Aeschylus

Broadhead, H. D. 1960. *Aeschylus. "The Persae."* Cambridge.

Denniston, J. D., and D. L. Page. 1989. Aeschylus. "*Agamemnon.*"

Fraenkel, Edouard. 1950. *Aeschylus, "Agamemnon."* 3 vols. Oxford.

Garvie, A. F. 1986. *Aeschylus. "Choephoroi."* Oxford.

Griffith, Mark. 1983. *Aeschylus. "Prometheus Bound."* Cambridge.

Johansen, H. F., and E. W. Whittle. 1980. *Aeschylus. "The Suppliants."* 3 vols. Denmark.

Radt, Stefan. 1985. *Tragicorum Graecorum Fragmenta.* Vol. 5. Göttingen.

Rose, Herbert J. 1957–58. *A Commentary on the Surviving Plays of Aeschylus.* 2 vols. Amsterdam.

Schütz, C. G. 1780. *Commentationem in Aesch. "Agam."* I. Jena.

Alcidamas

Radermacher, L. 1951. *Artium Scriptores.* Oesterreichische Akademie der Wissenschaften, Philosophisch-historisch Klasse. Sitzungsbericht 227, Abhandlung 3, 135–41.

Andocides

MacDowell, Douglas. 1962. *Andocides. "On the Mysteries."* Oxford.

Antiphon

Blass, Friederich. 1905. *Antiphontis Orationes et Fragmenta.* Leipzig.

Edwards, M., and S. Usher. 1985. *Greek Orators. Antiphon and Lysias.* Warminster.

Gagarin, Michael. 1997. *Antiphon.* Cambridge.

Gernet, Louis. 1954. *Antiphon.* Paris.

Archilochus

West, M. L. 1981. *Iambi et Elegi Graeci.* 2 vols. Oxford.

Aristophanes

Dover, Kenneth. 1993. *Aristophanes "Frogs."* Oxford.

Dunbar, Nan. 1995. *Aristophanes. "Birds."* Oxford.

Fritzsche, Franz Volkmar. 1838. *Aristophanes. "Thesmophoriazusae."* Leipzig.

Henderson, Jeffrey. 1987. *Aristophanes. "Lysistrata."* Oxford.

———. 1998. *Aristophanes. "Acharnians," "Knights."* Cambridge, MA, London.

Kassel, R., and C. Austin. 1984. *Poetae Comici Graeci.* III, 2. Leipzig.

MacDowell, Douglas. 1971. *Aristophanes. "Wasps."* Oxford.

Neil, Robert A. 1901. *The "Knights" of Aristophanes.* Cambridge.

Radermacher, Ludwig. 1954. *Aristophanes' "Frösche."* Vienna.

van Leeuwen, Jan. 1909. *Aristophanis Comoediae. "Equites."* Leiden.

ARISTOPHANES, SCHOLIA

Holwerda, D. 1991. *Scholia in "Vespas," "Pacem," "Aves," et "Lysistratam."* Fasc. 3. Groningen.

Jones, D. Mervyn, and Nigel G. Wilson. 1969. *Scholia vetera in Aristophanis "Equites."* Fasc. 2. Groningen.

Wilson, Nigel G. 1975. *Prolegomena de Comoedia. Scholia in "Acharnenses," "Equites," "Nubes."* Fasc. 1 B. Groningen.

Aristotle

Lucas, D. W. 1968. *Aristotle. "Poetics."* Oxford.

[Cicero]

Caplan, H. 1954. *Ad C. Herrennium.* Cambridge, MA, London.

Demosthenes

MacDowell, Douglas. 1990. *Demosthenes. "Against Meidias."* Oxford.

Euripides

Austin, C. 1968. *Nova Fragmenta Euripidea in Papyris Reperta.* Berlin.

Barrett, W. S. 1964. *Euripides. "Hippolytus."* Oxford.

Biehl, Werner. 1986. *Euripides "Kyklops."* Heidelberg.

Bond, G. W. 1988. *Euripides. "Heracles."* Oxford.

Diggle, J. 1986. *Euripidis Fabulae.* Oxford.

Nauck, A. 1966. *Tragicorum Graecorum Fragmenta.* Supplement by B. Snell. Hildesheim.

Seaford, Richard. 1984. *Euripides. "Cyclops."* Oxford.

Stevens, P. T. 1971. *Euripides. "Andromache."* Oxford.

Eustathios

van der Valk, M.H.A.L.H. 1971–87. *Commentarii ad Homeri "Iliadem."* Leiden.

Herodotus

How, W. W., and J. Wells. 1912. *A Commentary on Herodotus.* Oxford.

Stein, Heinrich. 1856. *Herodotos I–II.* Berlin.

Homer

Ameis, Karl F., and Karl Hentze. 1965. *Homers "Ilias."* 5th ed. Leipzig, Berlin.

Kirk, Geoffrey, *et al.* 1985–93. *The "Iliad," a Commentary.* 6 vols. Cambridge.

Leaf, Walter. 1895. *The Iliad.* London.

Monro, D. B. 1906. *"Iliad," Books I–XII.* Oxford.

Stanford, W. B. 1967. *The "Odyssey" of Homer.* 2 vols. New York.

HOMER, SCHOLIA

Erbse, Hartmut. 1971–83. *Scholia Graeca in Homeri "Iliadem."* Berlin.

Lysias

Adams, C. D. 1905. *Lysias. Selected Speeches.* New York, Cincinnati, Chicago.

Frohberger, H. 1871. *Ausgewählte Reden des Lysias.* III. Leipzig.

Gernet, L., and M. Bizot. 1924. *Lysias.* Paris.
Hude, Carl. 1912. *Lysiae Orationes.* Oxford.
Sauppe, H. 1841. "Epistola Critica." *Philologus* 15.
Thalheim, T. 1901. *Lysiae Orationes.* Editio maior. Leipzig.

Menander

Körte, A. 1957–59. *Menandri quae supersunt.* Leipzig.

Pindar

Farnell, L. R. 1932. *The Works of Pindar. Critical Commentary.* Vol. 2. London.
Gildersleeve, Basil L. 1885. *Pindar. The Olympian and Pythian Odes.* New York, Cincinnati, Chicago.
Kirkwood, Gordon. 1982. *Selections from Pindar. Edited with an Introduction and Commentary.* Chico.
Maehler, H. 1987. *Pindarus, Pars I. "Epinicia."* Leipzig.
Willcock, M. M. 1995. *Pindar. Victory Odes.* Cambridge.

Plato

Adam, James. 1969. *The "Republic" of Plato.* 2 vols. Cambridge.
Burnet, J. 1924. *"Euthyphro," "Apology of Socrates" and "Crito."* Oxford.
Bury, R. G. 1932. *The "Symposium" of Plato.* 2nd ed. Cambridge.
Dodds, E. R. 1959. *Gorgias.* Oxford.
Dover, Kenneth. 1980. *Symposium.* Cambridge.
Dyer, Louis. 1885. *Plato. "Apology of Socrates" and "Crito."* Revised by Thomas Day Seymour. Boston, New York.
Hawtrey, R. S. 1981. *Commentary on Plato's "Euthydemos."* Philadelphia.
Hug, Arnold. [1884] 1909. *Platons "Symposion."* Leipzig.
Nicoll, W.S.M., *et al.* 1995. *Platonis Opera* I. Oxford.
Riddell, James. 1877. *The "Apology" of Plato with a Revised Text and a Digest of Platonic Idioms.* Oxford.
Rose, Gilbert. 1981. *Plato's "Symposium."* Bryn Mawr.
Slings, S. R., and E. de Strycker. 1994. *Plato's "Apology of Socrates."* Leiden, New York, Cologne.
Wilamowitz-Moellendorff, Ulrich von. 1920. *Platon II.* Berlin.

Rhetores

Spengel, Leonard. 1856. *Rhetores Graeci.* Leipzig.

Sophocles

Dain, Alphonse, and Paul Mazon. 1960–65. *Sophocle.* I–III. Paris.
Jebb, Richard. 1893. *The Oedipus Tyrannus.* Cambridge.
———. 1903. *The Oedipus Coloneus.* Cambridge.
———. 1906. *The Antigone.* Cambridge.
Kamerbeek, J. C. 1967. *The Plays of Sophocles. Commentaries* Part 4. *The "Oedipus Tyrannus."* Leiden.
Lloyd-Jones, Hugh, and N. G. Wilson. 1990a. *Sophoclea. Studies on the Text of Sophocles.* Oxford.

———. 1990b. *Sophoclis Fabulae*. Oxford.
Radt, Stefan, 1977. *Tragicorum Graecorum Fragmenta*. Vol. 4. Göttingen.

Theocritus

Gow, A.S.F. 1950. *Theocritus*. 2 vols. Cambridge.

Theophrastus

Rusten, J. 1993. *Theophrastus. "Characters."* Cambridge, MA, London.

Thucydides

Gomme, A. W., A. Andrewes, and K. Dover. 1970. *A Historical Commentary on Thucydides* 4. Oxford. [= Dover 1970]

(B) TRANSLATIONS

Aristophanes

Rogers, B. B. 1967. *Aristophanes*. Cambridge.

Aristotle

Halliwell, Stephen. 1987. *The "Poetics" of Aristotle. Translation and Commentary*. Chapel Hill.

Dionysius of Halicarnassus

Pritchett, W. K. 1975. *Dionysius of Halicarnassus: "On Thucydides."* Berkeley, Los Angeles, London.

Herodotus

Barguet, A. 1964. *Historiens grecs* I. *Hérodote. Thucydide*. Bruges.
Cary, Henry. 1908. *Herodotus*. London.
Legrand, Philippe-Ernest. 1940–60. *Hérodote "Histoires."* Paris.
Macan, R. W. 1895–1908. *Herodotus*. London.
Powell, J. Enoch. 1939. *The "History" of Herodotus*. Cambridge.
Rawlinson, George. 1875. *The "History" of Herodotus*. New York.

Homer

Fagles, Robert. 1990. *Homer, "The Iliad."* New York.
Fitzgerald, Robert. 1974. *Homer, "The Iliad."* New York.
Lattimore, Richmond. 1951. *Homer, "The Iliad."* Chicago.

Plato

Day, Jane M. 1994. *Plato's "Meno" in Focus*. London and New York.
Grube, G.M.A. 1975. *Plato. The Trial and Death of Socrates*. Indianapolis.
Jowett, Benjamin. 1892. *The Dialogues of Plato*. II. Oxford.
Helmbold, W. C. 1952. *Plato. "Gorgias."* New York.
Saunders, Trevor. 1984. *Plato. The "Laws."* London.

Tredennick, H. 1969. *Plato. The Last Days of Socrates.* London.
Waterfield, Robin. 1993. *Plato. "Republic."* Oxford.

Sophocles

Grene, D., and R. Lattimore. 1959. *The Complete Greek Tragedies.* II. *Sophocles.* Chicago.
Lloyd-Jones, Hugh. 1994. *Sophocles* II. Cambridge, London.
Watling, E. F. 1947. *The Theban Plays: "King Oedipus," "Oedipus at Colonus," and "Antigone."* New York.
Wykoff, E. 1954. *Antigone.* In Grene and Lattimore 1959.

SECONDARY LITERATURE

Argyle, Michael. 1988. *Bodily Communication.* 2nd ed. Madison.
Andreotis, N. 1974. *Lexikon der Archaismen in neugriechischen Dialekten.* Vienna.
Arnott, Peter. 1991. *Public Performance in the Greek Theatre.* London and New York.
Austin, Gilbert. 1806. *Chironomia, or a Treatise on Rhetorical Delivery.* London.
Axtell, Roger. 1997. *Gestures. The Does and Taboos of Body Language around the World.* New York.
Bain, David. 1977. *Actors and Audience: A Study of Asides and Related Conventions in Greek Drama.* Oxford.
Barasch, Moshe. 1976. *Gestures of Despair in Medieval and Early Renaissance Art.* New York.
Beazley, J. D. 1952. "The New York Phlyax-Vase." *AJA* 56: 193–95.
———. 1956. *Attic Black Figure Vase Painters.* Oxford.
———. 1971. *Paralipomena: Additions to Attic Black-Figure Vase-Painters and to Red-Figure Vase-Painters.* Oxford.
———. 1982. *Attic Red Figure Vase Painters.* 2nd ed. Oxford.
———. 1986. *The Development of Attic Black-Figure.* Ed. Dietrich von Bothmer and Mary B. Moore. Berkeley, Los Angeles, London.
Bérard, Victor. 1918. "Le Geste de l'Aède et le Texte Homérique." *REG* 31: 1–38.
Bers, Victor. 1997. *Speech in Speech. Studies in Incorporated Oratio Recta in Attic Drama and Oratory.* Lanham, Boulder, New York, London.
Bieber, Margarete. 1961. *The History of Greek and Roman Theater.* Princeton.
Birdwhistell, R. 1952. *Introduction to Kinesics.* Washington, D.C.
Boegehold, Alan. 1982. "A Dissent at Athens: Ca. 424–421 B.C." *GRBS* 23: 147–56.
———. 1985. "Lycurgus 1.149." *CP* 132–35.
———. 1989. "A Signifying Gesture: Euripides, *Iphigeneia Taurica* 965–966." *AJA* 93: 81–83.
———. 1995. *Agora* XXVIII. *Law Courts at Athens.* Princeton.
———. 1997. "Some Modern Gestures in Ancient Greek Literature." *Acta. First Panhellenic and International Conference on Ancient Greek Literature* (23–26 May 1944), 419–29. Athens.

———. 1999. "Antigone Nodding Unbowed." In Titchener, F., and R. Moorton Jr. *The Eye Expanded: Life and the Arts in Greco-Roman Antiquity.* Berkeley, Los Angeles.

Bogen, K. 1969. *Gesten in Begrüssungsszenen auf attischen Vasen.* Diss. Giessen.

Bogucka, Maria. 1991. "Gesture, Ritual, and Social Order in Sixteenth to Eighteenth Century Poland." In Bremmer 1991: 190–209.

Brandt, Elfriede. 1965. *Grüss und Gebet.* Bayern.

Bremmer, Jan, and Herman Roodenburg. 1991. *A Cultural History of Gesture.* Ithaca, NY.

Brilliant, Richard. 1963. *Gesture and Rank in Roman Art.* New Haven.

Browning, Robert. 1969. *Mediaeval and Modern Greek.* London.

Bulwer, John. [1644] 1974. *Cheirologia, or the Natural Language of the Hand and Cheironomia, or the Art of Manual Rhetoric.* Ed. James W. Cleary. Rpt. Carbondale and Edwardsville, IL.

Burkert, W. 1983. *Homo Necans.* Berkeley, Los Angeles, and London.

Burn, L. 1987. *The Meidias Painter.* Oxford.

Burnett, Anne P. 1983. *Three Archaic Poets. Archilochus, Alcaeus, Sappho.* Cambridge, MA.

Cadbury, Henry J. 1933. "Note XXIV. Dust and Garments." In F. J. Foakes-Jackson and Kirsopp Lake, *The Beginnings of Christianity*, Part I: *The Acts of the Apostles.* Vol. 5, *Additional Notes to the Commentary*, ed. Kirsopp Lake and H. J. Cadbury. London.

Caskey, L. D., and John D. Beazley. 1934–63. *Attic Vase Painting in the Museum of Fine Arts.* 3 vols. Boston.

Chantraine, Pierre. 1953. *Grammaire Homérique II. Syntaxe.* Paris.

Clinton, Kevin. 1974. "The Sacred Officials at the Eleusinian Mysteries," *Transactions of the American Philosophical Society* n.s. 64: 3.

Cohen, Beth. 1978. *Attic Bilingual Vases and Their Painters.* New York and London.

Coldstream, J. N. 1977. *Geometric Greece.* New York.

Connor, W. R. 1985. *Thucydides.* Princeton.

Cook, A. B. 1907. "ΣΥΚΟΦΑΝΤΗΣ." *CR* 21: 133–36.

De La Coste Messelière, Pierre. 1943. *Delphes.* Paris.

Denniston, J. D. 1930. "Notes on the Greek Particles." *CR* 44: 213–15.

———. 1966. *The Greek Particles.* 2nd ed. with corrections. Oxford.

de Ste. Croix, G.E.M. 1981. *The Class Struggle in the Ancient World.* Ithaca, NY.

Dover, Kenneth. 1968. *Lysias and the "Corpus Lysiacum."* Berkeley and Los Angeles.

———. 1974. *Greek Popular Morality in the Time of Plato.* Oxford.

———. 1978. *Greek Homosexuality.* London.

Efron, D. 1972. *Gesture, Race and Culture.* The Hague.

Eibl-Eibesfeldt, I. 1972. "Similarities and Differences between Cultures in Expressive Movements." In *Non-Verbal Communication,* ed. R. Hinde. Cambridge, 297–311.

Eitrem, Samson. 1983. "Die Gestensprache—Abwehr oder Kontakt." In *Geras Antoniou Keramopoullou.* Athens, 598–608.

Fantham, Elaine. 1982. "Quintilian on Performance: Traditional and Personal Elements in *Institutio* 11.3." *Phoenix* 36: 243–63.

Ferrari, Gloria. 1990. "Figures of Speech: The Picture of Aidos." *Metis* 5: 185–203.

———. 1995. "The End of Aponia." *MMJ* 30:17–18.

Firth, R. 1972. "Verbal and Bodily Rituals of Greeting and Parting." In A. I. Richards, *The Interpretation of Ritual. Essays,* ed. J. S. La Fontaine. London, 1–38.

Flory, S. 1978. "Medea's Right Hand: Promises and Revenge." *TAPA* 108: 69–74.

Fortenbaugh, William. 1985. "Theophrastus on Delivery." In *Theophrastus of Eresos. On His Life and Work,* ed. William Fortenbaugh with P. Hanby and A. A. Long. Rutgers University Studies in Classical Humanities. New Brunswick, Oxford, 2.

Ghali-Kahil, Lilly B. 1955. *Les Enlèvements et le retour d' Hélène dans les textes et les documents figurés.* Paris.

Goffman, Erving, ed. 1967. *Interaction Ritual.* New York.

Goodwin, William W. 1900. *Syntax of the Moods and Tenses of the Greek Verb.* Boston.

Gould, J. 1973. "Hiketeia." *JHS* 93: 74–103.

Grajev, F. 1934. *Untersuchung zur Bedeutung der Gebärdensprache in der griechischen Epik.* Diss. Freiburg.

Gross, K. 1969. "Finger." *RAC* 7 cols. 909–46.

Gross, W. H. 1967. "Gebärden." *Der Kleine Pauly* 2, 707–8.

Haigh, A. E. 1889. *The Attic Theatre: A Description of the Stage and Theatre.* Oxford.

Haspels, C.H.E. 1936. *Attic Black-Figured Lekythoi.* Amsterdam.

Henrichs, Albert. 1995. "Why Should I Dance?: Choral Self-Referentiality in Greek Tragedy." *Arion,* 3rd series, 1: 56–111.

Herman, G. 1987. *Ritualized Friendship and the Greek City.* Cambridge.

Hildburgh, W. L. 1946. "Apotropaism in Greek Vase-Painting." *Folk-lore* 62: 154–78.

Hopfkes-Brukker, Charline. 1935. *Frühgriechische Gruppenbildung.* Leiden.

Hoppin, J. C. 1919. *A Handbook of Attic Red-Figured Vases.* 2 vols. Harvard.

Hummel, Pascal. 1993. *La Syntaxe de Pindare.* Louvain, Paris.

Jackson, John. 1955. *Marginalia Scaenica.* Oxford.

Jacoby, F. 1913. "Herodotus 7." In *RE* Supplementband 2: 205–520.

Jenkins, Ian. 1983. "Is There Life after Marriage? A Study of the Abduction Motif in Vase Paintings of the Athenian Wedding Ceremony." *BICS* 30: 137–45, Plate 18.

Johnston, S. I., and T. J. McNiven. 1996. "Dionysus in the Underworld in Toledo." *Museum Helveticum* 53: 25–36.

Jones, A.H.M. 1957. *Athenian Democracy.* Oxford.

Jones, L. W., and C. R. Morey. 1931. *The Miniatures of the Manuscripts of Terence prior to the 13th Century.* 2 vols. Princeton, London, Leipzig.

Jousse, Marcel. 1969. *Anthropologie du geste.* Paris.

Jucker, Ines. 1956. *Der Gestus des Aposkopein. Ein Beitrag zur Gebärdensprache in der antiken Kunst.* Zurich.

Kaimio, Maarit. 1988. *Physical Contact in Greek Tragedy.* Helsinki.

Kapsalis, P. T. 1946. "Gesture in Greek Art and Literature." Diss. Johns Hopkins University.

Katsouris, Andreas. 1990. ΡΗΤΟΡΙΚΗ ΥΠΟΚΡΙΣΗ. Iannina.
Keramopoullos, A. 1923. Ὁ ΑΠΟΤΥΜΠΑΝΙΣΜΟΣ. Athens.
Keuls, Eva. 1983. "Attic Vase Painting and the Home Textile Industry." In *Ancient Greek Art and Iconography*, ed. Warren G. Moon. London.
Knox, Bernard M. W. 1968. "Silent Reading in Antiquity." *GRBS* 9: 421–35.
———. 1993. *Oldest Dead White European Males and Other Reflections.* New York.
Kötting, Bernhard. 1978. "Geste und Gebärde." *RAC* 10 cols. 895–902.
Kühner, Raphael, and Bernhard Gerth. [1904] 1966. *Ausführliche Grammatik der griechischen Sprache.* Hannover and Leipzig. Rpt. Darmstadt.
Langlotz, Ernst. 1965. *Ancient Greek Sculpture of South Italy and Sicily.* New York.
Lateiner, Donald. 1988. Review of Stephen Portch, *Literature's Silent Language: Nonverbal Communication. Style* 22.4: 664–70.
———. 1989. "Teeth in Homer." *Liverpool Classical Monthly* 14.2–3: 18–23.
———. 1992. "Heroic Proxemics." *TAPA* 122: 133–63.
———. 1995. *Sardonic Smile.* Ann Arbor.
Lefkowitz, Mary. 1995. "The First Person in Pindar Reconsidered—Again." *BICS* 39: 117–39.
Lesky, A. 1969. "Abwehr und Verachtung in der Gebärdensprache." *AWien* 106: 149–57.
Lloyd-Jones, H. 1990. *Greek Epic Lyric and Tragedy. The Academic Papers of Sir Hugh Lloyd-Jones.* Oxford.
Mackridge, Peter. 1985. *The Modern Greek Language.* Oxford.
Markle, M. M. III. 1985. "Jury Pay and Assembly Pay at Athens." In *Crux: Essays in Greek History Presented to G.E.M. de Ste. Croix*, ed. P. A. Cartledge and F. D. Harvey. London, 265–97.
Mastronarde, Donald. 1979. *Contact and Discontinuity: Some Conventions of Speech and Actions on the Greek Tragic Stage.* Berkeley and Los Angeles.
McLeish, Kenneth. 1980. *The Theatre of Aristophanes.* Bath.
McNiven, Timothy John. 1982. *Gestures in Attic Vase Painting: Use and Meaning 550–40 B.C.* Ann Arbor.
Méautis, George. 1932. *L' Âme hellénique d'après des vases grecs.* Paris.
Monro, D. B. [1891] 1978. *A Grammar of the Homeric Dialect.* 2nd ed. Oxford. Rpt. New York.
Morris, Desmond, et al. 1979. *Gestures: Their Origins and Distribution.* New York
Morris, Sarah. 1986. Review of R. Garland, *The Greek Way of Death. Phoenix* 40: 469–71.
Mossé, Claude. 1962. *La Fin de la démocratie athénienne.* Paris.
Muecke, Frances. 1984. "Turning Away and Looking Down: Some Gestures in the Aeneid." *BICS* 31: 105–12.
Murray, Alexander. 1991. "Making a Gesture." *Times Literary Supplement*, April 26: 3–4 (review of Schmitt 1991).
Nadeau, R. 1964. "Delivery in Ancient Times: Homer to Quintilian." *The Quarterly Speech Journal* 50: 53–60.
Neumann, Gerhard. 1965. *Gesten und Gebärden in der griechischen Kunst.* Berlin.
Oakley, John, and Rebecca Sinos. 1995. *The Wedding in Ancient Athens.* Madison.

Ober, Josiah. 1989. *Mass and Elite in Democratic Athens.* Princeton.

Ohms, Th. 1948. *Die Gebetsgebärden der Völkern.* Leiden.

Pfuhl, E. 1923. *Malerei und Zeichnung der Griechen.* Munich.

Pickard-Cambridge, A. W. 1953. *The Dramatic Festivals of Athens.* 2nd ed. rev. by D. M. Lewis and J.P.A. Gould. Oxford.

Pinney, Gloria F. 1986. "Money-Bags?" *AJA* 90: 218.

Portch, S. R. 1985. *Literature's Silent Language: Nonverbal Communication.* New York.

Rau, Peter. 1967. *Paratragodia.* Zetemata 45. Munich.

Ricottilli, Licinia. 1992. " 'Tum breviter Dido voltum demissa profatur' (*Aen.* 1.561): Individuazione di un 'cogitantis gestus' e delle sue funzioni e modalità di rappresentazione nell' Eneide." *Materiali e Discussioni per l'analisi dei testi classici* 28: 179–225.

Rossi, Luigi Enrico. 1989. "Livelli di Lingua, Gestualità, Rapporti di Spazio e Situazione Drammatica sulla Scena Attica." *Scena e Spettacolo nell' Antichità,* Atti del Convegno Internazionale di Studio, Trent, 28–30 March 1988, 63–78.

Ruesch, J., and W. Kees. 1956. *Nonverbal Communication.* Berkeley and Los Angeles.

Schefold, K. 1937. "Statuen auf Vasenbildern." *Jahrbuch des deutschen archäologischen Instituts* 52: 30–75.

Schmitt, Jean-Claude. 1991. *La Raison des gestes dans l'occident mediéval.* Paris.

Schwyzer, E. 1966. *Griechische Grammatik.* II. Munich.

Shapiro, H. A. 1984. "Ponos and Aponia." *GRBS* 25: 107–10.

———. 1991. "The Iconography of Mourning in Athenian Art." *AJA* 95: 629–56.

———. 1993. *Personifications in Greek Art. The Representation of Abstract Concepts 600–400 B.C.* Zurich.

Shisler, E. L. 1945. "The Use of Stage Business to Portray Emotion in Greek Tragedy." *AJP* 66: 377–97.

Sicking, C.M.J., and J. M. Van Ophuijsen. 1993. *Two Studies in Attic Particle Usage. Lysias and Plato.* Leiden, New York, Cologne.

Sittl, Carl. 1890. *Die Gebärden der Griechen und Römer.* Leipzig.

Smyth, H. W. 1956. *Greek Grammar.* Cambridge.

Sokolowsky, F. 1969. *Lois Sacrées des cités grecques.* Paris.

Sonkowsky, R. 1959. "An Aspect of Delivery in Ancient Rhetorical Theory." *TAPA* 90: 256–74.

Speyer, W. 1969. "Fluch." *RAC* 7 cols. 909–46.

Stephanopoulos, T. K. 1983. "ΣΥΜΒΟΛΟΝ ΤΟΥ ΝΕΝΙΚΗΣΘΑΙ." Ἀριάδνη 1: 58–60.

Sullivan, F. A. 1967. "Tendere Manus: Gestures in the *Aeneid.*" *CJ* 63: 358–62.

Taladoire, B. A. 1951. *Commentaire sur la mimique et l'expression corporelle de la comédie romaine.* Montpellier.

Taplin, Oliver. 1978. *Greek Tragedy in Action.* Berkeley and Los Angeles.

———. 1993. *Comic Angels and Other Approaches to Greek Drama through Vase-Paintings.* Oxford.

Thiel, J. H. 1964. Review of MacDowell 1962, *Mnemosyne* 17, series 4: 406.

Thomas, Rosalind. 1989. *Oral Tradition and Written Record in Classical Athens.* Cambridge.

Tod, S. 1990. "*Lady Chatterley's Lover* and the Attic Orators: The Social Composition of the Athenian Jury." *JHS* 110: 146–73.

Trendall, A. D. 1967. *The Red Figured Vases of Lucania, Campania, and Sicily.* Oxford.

Trendall, A. D., and T.B.L. Webster. 1971. *Illustrations of Greek Drama.* London.

Vermeule, Emily. 1979. *Aspects of Death in Early Greek Art and Poetry.* Berkeley and London.

von Bothmer, Dietrich. 1982. "Notes on Makron." In *The Eye of Greece. Studies in the Art of Athens*, ed. Donna Kurtz and Brian Sparkes. Cambridge, London, New York, New Rochelle, Melbourne, Sydney.

Wakker, Gerry. 1994. *Conditions and Conditionals. An Investigation of Ancient Greek.* Amsterdam Studies in Classical Philology, Amsterdam.

Walbank, F. W. 1963. Review of Mossé 1962, *CR* n.s. 13: 317–19.

Watson, L. 1991. *Arae. The Curse Poetry of Antiquity.* Leeds.

Webster, T.B.L. 1958. Review of Jucker 1956, *JHS* 78: 174–75.

———. 1962. *Monuments Illustrating Tragedy and Satyr Play. BICS* Supplement 14. London.

Wilamowitz-Moellendorff, Ulrich von. 1922. *Pindaros.* Berlin.

Wiles, David. 1991. *The Masks of Menander.* Cambridge.

Willetts, R. F. 1967. *The Law Code of Gortyn.* Berlin.

Zanker, Paul. 1995. *The Mask of Socrates. The Image of the Intellectual in Antiquity.* Trans. Alan Shapiro. Berkeley, Los Angeles, Oxford.

Zucchelli, Bruno. 1962. Ὑποκρίτης*—origine e storia del termine.* Genoa.

Zschietzschmann, W. 1924. *Untersuchungen zur Gebärdensprache der alten griechischen Kunst.* Jena (an extract of his dissertation).

ART INDEX

INDEX LOCORUM

Note: Boldfaced numbers to the left of the colon represent primary-source loci; those on the right identify relevant pages within this book.

GENERAL INDEX

Note: **Boldface** used within a rubric is equivalent to "see also" (the visual equivalent of an on-line "button"); it signals that anything within a rubric so marked is also the subject of a separate rubric; it is used at beginnings as a visual aid and also to enhance all end-of-rubric cross-references.